Britain and America

AN INTERPRETATION OF
THEIR CULTURE
1945–1975

Britain and America

AN INTERPRETATION OF
THEIR CULTURE 1945–1975

Daniel Snowman

HARPER TORCHBOOKS
HARPER & ROW, PUBLISHERS
NEW YORK, HAGERSTOWN, SAN FRANCISCO, LONDON

This book was originally
published in Great Britain in 1977
by Maurice Temple Smith Ltd.

BRITAIN AND AMERICA: AN INTERPRETATION
OF THEIR CULTURE, 1945–1975. Copyright © 1977
by Daniel Snowman. All rights reserved. No part of this
book may be used or reproduced in any manner without
written permission except in the case of brief quotations embodied in critical articles and reviews. For information address Harper & Row, Publishers, Inc., 10 East 53rd Street,
New York, N.Y. 10022.

First HARPER TORCHBOOK edition published 1977

Library of Congress Catalog Card Number: 76–48858

International Standard Book Number: 0–06–131922–8

Contents

Introduction

This book is about the two societies that I know best. During most of my first twenty years I lived in suburban north-west London. During the next fifteen I became something of a transatlantic commuter (spending an aggregate of nearly four years in the USA), changed my job every so often and my place of residence rather more frequently and, in general, developed a fairly mobile, though clearly structured, style of life. The mobility gave me constantly refreshed perspectives for there is nothing like a new job or a new home for seeing the old one in a new light; the structure helped me to maintain such insights as I obtained over time and to begin to relate them.

From adolescence on I developed the habit of making a note of anything that struck me as interesting or odd or typical, with no conscious intention of ever doing anything with it. An incurable collector, not only of books but also of printed ephemera, I accumulated more and more 'material' about British and American society for no other reason than that it interested me.

At the same time, I was becoming familiar with the pictures of American and British society drawn by thoughtful commentators of the past—Bagehot's description of the British and their unwritten constitution, Tocqueville and Turner on the characteristics of the Americans. There were more recent interpretations, too. In the USA, David Riesman explained that his compatriots were increasingly 'other-directed' while, to David Potter, the essential characteristics of Americans lay in their response to material abundance. In Britain, Richard Hoggart painted a word-picture of the working-class society that he had grown up in, while Anthony Sampson described the anatomy of Britain's 'top' institutions and 'top' people. British writers like Geoffrey Gorer and Denis Brogan wrote perceptively about the Americans, while sharp American observers like Samuel Beer or Richard Rose began to devote their attention to the British.

Gradually, my experience, my collection of 'material',

and my serious reading converged to suggest that the two cultures of which I was a product, those of Britain and America, were developing—separately and also in relationship to each other—according to certain patterns. It became important to me to know something about the nature of those patterns.

Thus, the inner incentive behind the writing of this book was a desire to achieve some intellectual mastery over the societies that had nurtured me, and to be able to answer the question: if you lived in those two societies, what sort of person were you likely to become, and why? I wanted to understand the changing values and attitudes of the British and the Americans during the generation or so following the end of the second world war and the relationship between those values and attitudes and wider social patterns. Also, there was the question of the connection between American and British cultures; was there any truth in the old cliché that what happened in the USA was bound to happen in the UK five years later?

In order to tackle these questions, it was necessary to keep in mind a number of factors: an Anglo-American comparison, an awareness of the flow of historical change, and some understanding of the relationship between a society and the individual psyche—all three of which play an important part in the argument of this book. But despite the intellectual juggling that this involved, it would be foolish to deny that the book is also in part a testimony to the belief that the experiences of an author can enhance—and should certainly not be programmed out of—his thoughts about his own society.

In writing the book, I have had primarily in mind the island of Great Britain, and continental USA. Much of what is written will of course, be largely true of Northern Ireland and of Hawaii and Alaska too, and indeed, of Canada—and may be less true of, say, blacks in the Old South or of the cultural elite in the British or American cities of Cambridge. However, the advantages of concentrating on continental USA and the island of Great Britain include an intellectual tidiness that was hard to resist.

This tidiness cannot easily be extended to the names of the two societies in question, both of which lack clarity. When

the 'United States of America' first became independent, it
was a nation (the 'first new nation' in Lipset's useful phrase)
that contained only the weakest forms of central control. It
was important that the new nation's title should imply unity
and diversity. The 'United States of America', in other words,
like the 'Union of Soviet Socialist Republics' or the 'Federal
Republic of Germany', was a name designed to remind
people of a series of political points that they might be easily
inclined to forget, and was not merely a title. For nearly a
century after independence, the inhabitants of the United
States of America continued to think of the name of their
country as a plural word and of themselves primarily as
Virginians or New Yorkers or whatever and only secondarily
as Americans. In the twentieth century, however, the nation
and its inhabitants have commonly become 'America' and
'Americans' — the susceptibilities of Canadians and other
New World residents notwithstanding.[1]

A similar lack of clarity has characterized 'Britain' and
the 'British'. There is no single word for the United Kingdom of Great Britain and Northern Ireland (or for the main
island of Great Britain) or for its inhabitants. In the British
case as in the American, cumbersome and inadequate official
terminology is a reflection of various geographical and
historical uncertainties and divisions.

On balance, it seemed wise to adopt a looseness of language that, while no doubt technically incorrect, does correspond to popular perceptions and usages. This book,
therefore, is about the society and the values of the 'Americans' and the 'British'.

The Americans and the British share many assumptions
about society. In both societies most babies are born to mono-
gamously married parents; personal privacy is considered
important; much commercialized lip-service — and some real
spiritual attention — are paid to Christmas; hands are shaken
— especially between males (though cheeks tend not to be
kissed — especially between males); children are taught that
school is good and that it prepares them for a career, and so
on. The public rhetoric of both countries emphasizes that all
people should be treated equally before the law and that they
should be considered by the law as individuals even though,

in their social relationships, they might also be considered as representatives of groups. In both countries, political power is supposed to lie with elected representatives of all the people. In any global study of civilizations and cultures, the British and the Americans would look very much alike.

To each other, however, they can in some ways look very unalike. To a considerable extent it depends on who is doing the observing.

The similarities and differences that an observer might see between cultures depend on at least three types of perspective. The first is geographical. Americans and Brazilians probably look pretty similar to Hottentots whereas Paraguayans and Uruguayans seem dissimilar to each other. In this book the British and the Americans are discussed within the context and from the perspective of each other.

The view of the observer varies not only with place but also with time. The aim in the pages that follow is to maintain a double historical perspective. The essential argument will be applied to a comparative study of British and American societies in the thirty years or so following the second world war. It will, however, be premised on an awareness of the previous several centuries of history.

A third factor is the position of the observer in the society that he or she describes and, as I have made clear, my own social and psychological experience has played a part in filtering the material and building up the arguments of this book.

The attempt to write comparatively about two or more cultures or nations is uncommon except perhaps at the microlevel. It is a relatively straightforward task to do controlled fieldwork on the kinship structure or courtship rituals of two primitive tribes, or the portrayal of love or heroism in the stage plays or novels produced by two societies in one and the same year. But to develop hypotheses about the comparative development of two vast and complex cultures over a period of thirty years or so is a task whose pitfalls are of a considerably greater magnitude. In particular, the level of generalization must be far higher than would normally be acceptable in a careful academic argument (unless, that is, one were prepared to extend almost every sentence with qualifications and disclaimers of the 'but-less-so-among-working-class-mothers-in-the-South' variety).

There are particular problems arising out of the cultures chosen for this study. The historiographical tradition of the British is among the world's finest but it has been largely devoted to the writing of national history. The most celebrated British historians usually wrote of England and Englishmen, or on occasion, of other nations·and their heroes. Except in the case of someone like Gibbon, whose emphasis was on an utterly different civilization, or as an occasional offshoot of military or diplomatic history, they were rarely inclined to see the British in a social context of international dimensions. In addition to this tendency towards Anglocentrism, the British have also been inclined to write of the past as primarily the unfolding story of British or English institutions — the monarchy, the cabinet, the 'gentry', the English working class — whose existence evolved and developed in a manner characteristic of these isles. Intellectual traditions such as these (which were not, of course, unique to the British) enabled much outstanding work to be produced but also make it hard to incorporate British material into studies of a comparative nature.

American historiography, too, tended to be largely national in orientation. But American historians were generally more prepared than their British counterparts to consider the part played in their nation's past by psychological factors and by ideas; emphasis would sometimes be given to such intangibles as the 'American mind' or the 'mind of the South'[2] — concepts that, while loose in themselves, suggested a line of inquiry free from the relative thraldom to social and political institutions that had sometimes restricted the British field of vision.

There is, however, a special difficulty in trying to write comparatively about American cultural history. Many influential observers of US society have proclaimed the uniqueness of the American experiment and implied that because it is *sui generis* it is also incomparable. This tradition can be

traced to earliest times, perhaps to the day in 1630 when John
Winthrop, still on board the *Arbella*, told his fellow passengers that 'We shall be as a City upon a Hill, the eyes of all people
are upon us; so that if we shall deal falsely with our God . . .
and so cause Him to withdraw His present help from us, we
shall be made a story and a by-word through the world.' The
picture of America as an example to other societies was taken
up by generation after generation of historians, many of
whom, in celebrating the success of the American experiment,
would also emphasize what they considered to be the ideo-
logically continuous and uninterrupted nature of American
history. In recent times, a leading historian like Daniel J.
Boorstin[3] could write of 'the amazing, the unique, continuity
of American history and, in sharp contrast, the *dis*continuity
of European history', while Richard Hofstadter[4] emphasized 'the need for a reinterpretation of our political traditions which emphasizes the common climate of American
opinion'. The tradition that proclaimed the uniqueness,
the incomparability, and the ideological continuity of
American history was probably at its zenith in the heady
years following the second world war.

But as the years went by and the USA became wracked
by the social tensions of the 1960s, there developed new ways
of looking at the past, and the 'consensus' historians were
subjected to severe criticism. For one thing, said the sceptics,
if American history were really all that unique, it would
presumably also have been uniquely difficult to analyse or
assess for there would have been virtually no standards of
comparison or contrast. Second, the view that American
history (unlike that of Europe) was free of divisive ideologies, was exposed by younger 'revisionist' historians as in
itself an ideological stand, one built on a form of *status quo*-
ism. Third, as many Americans became increasingly worried
by the rifts within their society, the maldistribution of the
nation's wealth, the injustices to minority groups, the gaps
between the generations, and above all the sharp divisions
of opinion over the Vietnam war, some began to reassess
the analogous rifts of the past and thus to question the authen-
ticity of the judgements of those who had emphasized the
role of 'consensus' in earlier American history. Finally,

stimulated in part by their country's new global role, the revisionists began to interpret the history of American foreign policy as an attempt by successive US power elites to impose their own eschewal-of-ideologies ideology upon other parts of the world—an approach that just happened to coincide with America's trading interests.[5]

As a result of these reinterpretations, many younger American historians began to see new links between the history of the United States and that of other parts of the world, a perspective in sharp contrast to the view of American experience as having been unique. There were those who saw American history as having been one example, albeit the first, of the sort of history likely to develop in any newly-independent nation. Others considered the story of America as having been above all a part of the history of modern technological Western (and perhaps white) society, so that the American and British (and continental European) experiences were similar and could usefully be considered as lying along the same section of a continuum of historical comparability.

Thus, the attempt to write comparatively about historical continuity and change in British and American social values flies in the face of aspects of the intellectual tradition of both cultures. But the attempt has more than mere academic interest. For, as time and distance separate nations and continents less and less, it becomes not merely convenient but essential to understand the life of the other societies with which we come increasingly into contact. Everybody knows the importance to our own survival as a species of our capacity to make internationally controlled and rational use of our huge but limited natural resources. International perspectives are vital too, in the economic, political and military spheres of this shrinking world of ours. But these must be complemented by similarly out-going social and psychological viewpoints.

For similar reasons this study is not only cross-cultural but also interdisciplinary in its approach. In particular, it represents an attempt to cross-fertilize the outlook of the social scientist with the perspective of the historian. Like many other academic empires, history and the social sciences have tended to keep themselves in separate intellectual compartments. Only by opening the doors between them can real insights be gained into the nature of post-war American and British culture.

In such fields as anthropology and sociology, some of the best-known work has attempted to produce detailed descriptions of certain aspects of life in specific communities — sexual roles in north-west Melanesia or among the mountain-dwelling Arapesh, for example, or nearer home, an enclave of elderly people in London's East End, social class in a New England town, divorced people, youth gangs, and so on. The anthropologists have tended to concentrate on myth and symbol in simple and often primitive communities, and the sociologists on aspects of social structure; there has been some methodological and conceptual overlap. Geographically, however, the two have carved up the world between them by means of a largely unbroken rule that anthropology is about people like 'them', while sociology is about people like 'us'.

Psychologists have generally looked not at the community so much as at the individual. Occasionally, an imaginative writer such as Robert J. Lifton or Kenneth Keniston will examine the psychological characteristics of an individual or a small number of individuals and then, in an appropriately tentative fashion, try to infer from the results a few general truths about the wider society.[6]

The problem of relating the limited psychological truths that one's researches reveal to equally limited social truths represents one of the most intriguing frontiers of theory and practice in the social sciences today: the attempt to liberate anthropology and sociology from their thrall to the analysis of the structures and functions of social institutions, and to liberate psychology from its equally powerful thrall to the analysis of the individual subconscious. A variety of shaky marriages have been effected between these youthful social sciences in the form of social psychology and social and cultural anthropology. These new amalgamations are full of promise but their theoretical structure is often weak and their hard data fragmentary. As a result, ambitious cross-disciplinary projects in the social sciences have, as yet, been somewhat scarce.

Particularly lacking are studies conducted over a period of time. In addition to the difficulties of working longitudinally with relatively new and largely untried amalgamations of social science disciplines, there are the further problems of the time, money and bother of doing a continuing study with subjects who all have their own lives to lead and, as likely as not, will eventually be dispersed geographically.

A third reason why longitudinal studies are few on the ground is related to the common assumption that any society or individual psyche is in some ways like a human body: composed of elements each of which would normally function in such a way as to maintain the health of the whole. If any element was not contributing to the health of the whole it was said to be 'dysfunctional'. Since a healthy society or psyche was normally characterized by stability and controlled change, any element within it that was conducive to *in*-stability or *uncontrolled* change was by definition dysfunctional. Social studies, in other words, would often take on the character of pathology; you examined what was wrong, deviant, dysfunctional, maladjusted—and, by implication, had a clear image of what was right, normal, functional and adjusted.[7] Once you knew what the 'norm' was you could devote your intellectual energies to the relationship between your case study and that norm. Implicit in this type of approach was the assumption that these social and psychological norms were unlikely to vary substantially from one period to the next within any given culture. The idea of normality therefore involved the idea of continuity. Hence, for what one might almost call ideological reasons, there was a paucity of social or psychological studies (and *a fortiori* studies on the relationship between the social and the psychological) that incorporated a time dimension.

The one discipline above all that *does* involve a time dimension is history. 'History' is not what happened in the past but what we believe or think or remember or, most often, read about what happened in the past. The 'past' is always there. It is what happened. And even if nobody ever wrote about it—or even knew anything about it—the past would still be there. But history is another thing altogether. History is not what happened; it is what is subsequently said or written about what happened. And every age, it has been rightly pointed out, has to write its own history. As the present slips away and becomes the past, it is the responsibility of the person who writes history to know as much as he or she can about the 'past', to capture it, to recreate it, to evoke it to people in the new 'present'.

'History' has its own present and past, and its own past — the history that was itself written in the past — is full of the stories of kings and queens and generals and presidents, and of the more visible and spectacular effects that the doings and misdoings of those leaders had on the led. The great majority of the people were usually data largely to the extent that they were acted upon. The emphasis, furthermore, was on discontinuity: the discrete and memorable events, the crises and catastrophes, the battles and famines, the identifiable personalities and dates. The great continuities of life that form the basis of most people's day-to-day experience would generally be much less adequately chronicled. Finally, many historians have believed part of their professional duty to consist of the identification of causes and effects and consequently have been reluctant to chronicle and explain situations that had not yet run their course. 'Contemporary history' is still, to many purists, a contradiction in terms.

Thus, the self-imposed limitations of both the social sciences and traditional history were considerable, and neither would have provided adequate equipment for the study here undertaken. However, it seemed possible that one could make a virtue out of the imaginative cross-fertilization between both. This book is an attempt to evoke and examine some of the continuities as well as the discontinuities in the experience of ordinary people in modern America and Britain; I hope that it has been enriched by both the chronological perspective of the historian and the type of observation provided by the social scientist.

Finally, the thorny question of the selection of data: what do you put in and what do you leave out? Future historians may choose to portray, say, Britain in the 1960s as a society torn by self-doubt (no longer an Empire, not yet part of Europe) or the USA as preoccupied with social protest and the agonizing over Vietnam. Most people most of the time were not, however, primarily concerned with the great public issues of the day, but would spend their waking hours doing and thinking about relatively mundane things: eating, working, travelling to and from work, watching television, visiting friends and relatives, going out to sports events and cinemas, washing the car, cooking, chatting. I take it that, except at times of extreme drama, things were not markedly different in the past. Thus, if one is trying to examine popular attitudes and values in the 1960s, what people felt about the Common Market or Vietnam may not necessarily be more enlightening than what they felt about their social superiors and inferiors, or about opportunities for work and play, or about food, drink, and clothes.

When dealing in Part I with the more distant past and with what I have called 'traditional' values, it was necessary to rely on data that might also be thought to be of a more traditional type. The chief reason for this is the relative lack of data on 'popular' culture. But there is a further argument. The traditional social values of many people, particularly in a fairly deferential culture like that of Britain, tended to filter down by a combination of imitation, reaction, and osmosis from the lead given by various social and cultural elites. In recent years, it is true, a number of distinguished historians[8] have emphasized material that suggests the existence of a vibrant working-class culture in pre-industrial and industrial Britain, while our knowledge of the American past has long been enriched by songs, jokes, stories, broadsheets and other products of popular culture. However, this type of material has not infrequently constituted either a direct response to the cultural elites of the day or an expression of what people would like to have believed rather than of what they really did believe. Either way, elite values were, in one form or another, rarely absent.[9]

One of the ways in which elites might attempt to maintain the ascendancy of their own preferred values is by building those values into the myths of history. For this reason, much of Part I consists of an attempt to infer from the 'official' mythologizing of American and British history the traditional social values of those two societies.

In Part II, however, which examines the 'new' values of the post-war decades, these considerations do not apply with such force. For one thing, of course, there is no scarcity of material. Furthermore, it is arguable that modern popular culture is less obviously a direct response to elite values than in earlier times, or, at least, that the line of causality between the two is less marked. In addition, the 1950s and 1960s have not yet had time to slip into a mould of more or less fixed mythologization; the myths of the post-war years are still being made. Consequently, in Part II, every popular phrase or slogan, novel or TV series or comic character is a candidate for serious attention; so are styles of dress or home cooking; so are children's songs and games and the listings in the Yellow Pages; and so, indeed, are people's unspoken and often unconscious dreams and nightmares, hopes and fears. Every artefact in a society can be turned round again and again, examined from different perspectives, and thought of as a product of the cultural processes of that society. Every experience, indeed, is indicative of some quality or qualities of the society in which it occurs. And, unless the experience is a totally non-social one, it is likely to be to some degree a pointer to—and maybe a carrier or communicator of—some aspect of the values fundamental to the society in which it occurs.

The problem that presented itself in the writing of Part II, therefore, was this: how, from all the plethora of material, could one try to isolate those social values that were in the ascendant? One way of trying to identify what people believe is to ask them. Opinion pollsters have been doing this for forty years now and some of their results have been utilized. However, I have tended to use survey material sparingly. There are two main reasons for this. In the first place, while people's opinions on specific issues at one particular time are relatively easy to discover from polls, it is by no means clear that their continuing attitudes and values[10] can be inferred from them. Few pollsters have made attempts to assess the stability or otherwise of attitudes and values over a

period of time. Second, while the Americans have a long
history of trying to understand themselves, the British have
not.[11] One irritating by-product of this disparity is that,
while there are polls on all manner of topics in the USA,
opinion surveys in Britain (other than on questions of immediate political or economic significance) have been relatively rare. So, even to the extent that polls can provide useful
data, their comparative use is strictly curtailed by the inadequacy of British material.

Most people do not, in any case, subscribe to a single set
of beliefs but carry around in their heads a variety of not
always consistent attitudes and values. A person at work in a
factory, waiting at table, attending a church service, or helping children across a road will in many ways become a different person once sitting idly on a train or bus, wandering
through a supermarket, relaxing in the bowling or bingo
club, or at home watching television. The sense of personal
responsibility and self-control will be less intense, while
that of legitimate self-indulgence will increase. When involuntary external pressures are on, we accept, or pay lip-
service to, all manner of values that, maybe later that same
day, no longer have much hold on us.[12] A person's real or
'dominant' values are those espoused when the pressures
are self-imposed or absent and such values are best identified
by observing not only what a person has to do but above all
what he chooses to do. Such values, furthermore, are more
likely to be displayed and embodied in what a person con-
sumes than in what he produces. Thus, the data of most
importance in Part II are primarily derived from what one
might call the leisure and luxury enclaves of life.

Some people have more access to leisure and luxury than
others and are, therefore, likely to be in the van of various
cultural trends. Middle-class people in the 1950s and 1960s
were more likely than working-class people to have economic access to the most representative of the newer luxuries,
while younger people and women would generally have
more leisure time than men of working age. The world of
middle-class women and children, therefore, was one to
which it seemed important to devote considerable attention.
Hence, for example, the frequent use of popular advertise-

ments for consumer luxuries as an indication of the ascendant
social values of the day.[13]

These values were not, of course, entirely self-generating.
Indeed, the 'leisure/luxury' values were often deliberately
provoked or fanned and sometimes almost instigated by
manufacturers whose own primary values—economic growth
and competitiveness, deferred rewards for hard work—corresponded more closely to the 'traditional' ones. Nevertheless, the appeals of advertisers would hardly have been
successful if they had not to some extent corresponded to
the value predispositions of those towards whom they were
directed. It is for this reason that in the search for the social
values of modern America and Britain, 'indirect' evidence—
such as advertisements—was generally preferred to such
'direct' evidence as public opinion polls.

PART I

1 The eye of the beholder

EACH TO THE OTHER

The Americans and the British are fond of making generalizations about each other, but what validity do these hold?

British people in the post-war decades were apt, when
asked, to make facile and often contradictory generalizations
about 'Americans', based on hopelessly inadequate criteria.
Those who remembered friendly and often bountiful US
troops during the days of wartime solidarity were predis-
posed to think of Americans as generous; those relying on
chance encounters with the noisier American tourists (largely pre-selected from the richer strata of US society) were
more inclined to think of them as brash or conceited. In a
survey of Londoners in the 1960s, three-quarters of the respondents endorsed the view that Americans were 'boastful'
and 'over-patriotic', and about the same proportion voted
them 'friendly' and 'courteous'. The British student whose
chief contacts were with American Fulbright Fellows might
have thought of Americans as dedicated and industrious —
or as long-haired and radical; those with strong political
views might have seen Americans as 'saviours of the Free
World' or, alternatively, as 'imperialistic and aggressive'.
Richard Hoggart, in *The Uses of Literacy*, wrote that '. . . the
most striking feature in working-class attitudes to America
is . . . a large readiness to accept. This arises mainly from the
conviction that in most things the Americans can "show us
a thing or two" about being up to date.' Few people from
Britain ever got the chance of visiting the States and, even
if they did, they would rarely get outside the big cities or the
social circles dominated by the white middle class.

British perceptions of 'America' and 'Americans' would
often not allow for the immense size and variety that characterize the society and the geography of the USA. It was one
thing to know that the USA is 3000 miles across and 1500
miles from north to south, that it contained 145 million
people at the end of the war and 220 million people three

23

decades later, or that Texas is five times the size of England but has only one-fifth the population; facts such as these were reasonably familiar in Britain if hard to digest. But British people would none the less tend to picture US society as a fairly homogeneous unit composed of eighty-something per cent of white Anglo-Saxon Protestants plus a few peripheral non-WASP 'out' groups. In fact, as Tables 1 and 2 demonstrate, no single national or religious group constituted anything approaching a majority.

Geographical variation doubtless played its part in maintaining the diversity of life-styles and beliefs to be found in the USA. In parts of Nevada there are about 8-10 inches of rain every year while in Mobile, Alabama, the average is about 68 inches. Temperatures vary from -44° F (recorded in Bismarck, North Dakota) to 118° F (Phoenix, Arizona). In West Virginia and Kentucky there were destitute coal-miners, in Texas fabulously wealthy cattle and oil tycoons; there were great automobile factories in Michigan and vast aeronautical works in California. Nebraska lived off its wheat, Florida off its fruit and its tourists. It was not easy for people in Britain to appreciate that the differences between the life-styles of, say, a student at Columbia University, a banker in small-town Iowa, or a Chicano grape-picker in California were as great as those between the life-styles of a student at Bristol or Nanterre, a jeweller in Zürich, and a peasant in Calabria.

If the British sometimes made the mistake of assuming the USA to be one big white Anglo-Saxon Protestant community of friendly but boastful patriots (with, of course, a few exceptional minority groups thrown in), many Americans—particularly those amiable old Virginians and effusive pop-loving moppets who suffered from chronic Anglophilia—were apt to make the reverse mistake and assume that Britain was all (in the case of the Virginians) Stratford and Oxford and the Queen and rose gardens, and (in the case of the screaming kids) the Mersey Sound and Carnaby Street. In fact, the fifty-odd million people living in the long, thin, densely populated little island off the north-west coast of Europe were differentiated in a number of ways. The

Table 1   National origins of American society

Americans primarily of	millions
British descent	52
German	21
African	16
Irish	14
Italian	7
Scandinavian	6
Polish	5
Others	30
Total (1950)	151

(Adapted from Theodore H. White, *The Making of the President 1960,* Pocket Books Inc., New York, 1961, pp. 270-71)

Table 2   Religious affiliations in American society:
         Groups with more than one million adherents

	millions
Roman Catholic	48
Baptist (17 different branches)	28
United Methodist Church	10 ½
Jewish	6
Lutheran Church in America	3
Lutheran Church, Missouri Synod	3
United Presbyterian Church	3
Episcopal Church	3
American Lutheran Church	2 ½
Churches of Christ	2 ½
Church of Jesus Christ of Latter-Day Saints	2
Greek Orthodox	2
United Church of Christ	2
Christian Church (Disciples of Christ)	1 ½
Orthodox Church of America	1
Christian Churches and Churches of Christ	1
Assemblies of God	1

(Adapted from the *Statistical Abstract of the US,* 1973)

class system, although splitting at some of its seams, never-theless had a firm hold, and the Scotland of Sir Alec Douglas-Home and that of the unemployed Clydeside shipworker, both authentic British experiences, were totally different. The Cumberland depicted in the novels of Melvyn Bragg, the working-class Leeds of Richard Hoggart's *The Uses of Literacy*, the educated elderly seaside Tories of Susan Hill's early stories, the pudding eaters of the north-east and the fruit eaters of the south-west, the 'shabby genteel' of a thous-and outwardly neat but inwardly chilly and slightly un-hygienic guest houses—all were as characteristic of modern Britain as Mick Jagger or Paul McCartney or Lord Snowdon.

The social and cultural contrasts in Britain were different in kind from those in the more obviously varied United States. In America, there was a population largely compos-ed of the descendants of fairly recent immigrants who went (or were pushed) to the North American continent to avoid one type of life and to live some other type of life. One would expect many variations to exist and evolve in a society with such a basis. But in little Britain, uninvaded for nine hun-dred years, traditionally wary of foreigners and never dis-posed to let them immigrate except in small numbers and for special reasons; in Britain with her stable social and politi-cal system, her monarchy, her class system—all this tended to make for a small number of fairly consistent British life-styles, different from each other but not easily changed or augmented.

The clarity and relative immutability of these cultural variations within Britain are the more remarkable when one recognizes a number of apparently standardizing forces at work in the society. Take, for instance, the traditional in-clination of the British to be rather more deferential than the Americans towards their supposed superiors. Deference can easily take the form of cultural imitation and can tend to create a fairly tight and homogeneous culture. However, deference in Britain would often involve, not imitation, so much as an awareness of how to keep one's appropriate and clearly delineated distance. Thus, one of the by-products of deference in Britain was probably that the culture tended to form around a few relatively fixed centres of gravity.

A further factor that might well have helped to standard-
ize British culture was the early development of broadcasting. For the first thirty years of its life, from the early 1920s
until the early 1950s, the BBC had a total monopoly over
the public air-waves in Britain and people would often turn
to their 'wireless' as the one unimpeachable source of honest
and accurate information. After the war, however, the BBC
lost its monopoly (first of television and later of radio) and,
like the commercial companies, introduced regional and
local variations in programming. These post-war developments were, in part, a recognition of the cultural variations
that continued to exist in Britain.

Again, Britain was the first country to industrialize in
the nineteenth century and was the most thoroughly industrialized by the beginning of the twentieth. Massive industrialization brought in its train the mass production (and
almost universal availability) of inexpensive and standardized personal and household goods. Wherever you lived in
Britain you could buy the same type of chair, motor-car,
television set, or sweater. And since the nationalization of
the health services, the power industries, and the railways
in the later 1940s, there was also considerable standardization of many of the social services that were provided. Yet
personal tastes continued obstinately to vary by class, by
region, and by whim.

No amount of industrialization or nationalization would,
for instance, alter the fact that the accent with which the
language was spoken in Britain, and even the vocabulary
with which it was larded could often vary more over small
geographical areas than in America. The Birmingham accent
was different from the Manchester accent, and both were different, sometimes to the point of incomprehensibility, from
the flat cockney of the working-class suburbs of London, the
lilting sing-song of the hillier parts of Wales, or the guttural
Glaswegian. These variations occurred within an area that
would fit snugly between the midwestern cities of Minneapolis and St Louis or Lincoln (Nebraska) and Abilene (Texas).

Thus the varieties of cultural experience in Britain were
fewer, but more sharply differentiated, than in the country
where variety was almost an article of religious faith, the

United States of America. And in both cultures, despite
frequent facile generalizations suggesting the contrary, the
wide range of experience was more characteristic than any
other single quality.

STABILITY

One quality which was often attributed to Britain but which
characterized America as well, was stability. The USA and
the UK in the post-war decades were among the world's most
stable societies.

In the first place, they were societies in which things
usually felt comfortably predictable. This is not to suggest
that change did not occur; on the contrary, anybody who
had died in Britain or America in 1945 and was resurrected
a generation later would have been amazed at the speed and
scope of air travel, or the omnipresence of the television set,
or the high rate of certain types of urban crime. But these
changes were the product of gradual and comprehensible
tendencies, linear or quantitative changes, by and large,
rather than unforeseen or qualitative ones. Throughout the
post-war years people continued—despite occasional delays
and disruptions—to send letters in the strong expectation
that they would be delivered; they continued—despite the
occasional crash or hijack—to fly in aeroplanes, confident that
they would take off and land where planned, and continued
to expect the same type of guaranteed efficiency from their
radios and televisions and telephones and their police, fire
and medical services. Indeed, they made increasing use of
these facilities as the years went by.

The point is all the more striking if one contrasts Britain
and America politically with other countries in the 1970s.
About eighty of the world's 130-odd national societies did
not exist as such thirty years before. Some that came into
being during the earlier years of our period were dismem-
bered later on. And even among those national societies that
existed throughout the period, there were often instances of
sharp political disruption. The USA and UK remain two of
the small band of national societies that throughout the
thirty years or so on which this study concentrates (and

indeed for far longer than that), continued to enjoy a form of government that was almost universally accepted and even taken for granted.

Closely related to predictability as characteristic of a stable society is a second, namely that the society should appear to those within it to be more or less cohesive. A cohesive society is (a) one regarding which people have a reasonably clear idea as to who is within and who is without, and (b) one in which there is a more or less agreed set of social values guiding the behaviour of members. Post-war America and Britain were among the most cohesive of national societies, but the cohesiveness was not absolute. Let us look first at Britain.

It is probably true, as Richard Rose has written,[1] that 'Englishmen have an unusually well-defined sense of identity, developed through centuries of island life.' Despite the growing number of people in Scotland and Wales who felt that their countries ought to have increased political and social autonomy, and despite the disruptive and sometimes violent repercussions that the Northern Ireland conflict had within mainland Britain, at no time was there widespread questioning by those who had lived all their lives within the bounds of Great Britain that they and others like them were members of something that they all thought of loosely as 'British' society.

However, there were two respects in which the concept of British society as a cohesive unity was challenged, and these arose out of Britain's imperial legacy. During the 1950s, small numbers of immigrants from the non-white Commonwealth began to enter Britain. Commonwealth citizens were permitted to do this in an unrestricted way. In the early 1960s, immigration rose sharply in conjunction with the decision by the British government that the time had come for the flow of immigration to be controlled. For the rest of the 1960s, debate raged about the rights and wrongs of non-white Commonwealth immigration, and successive governments passed further measures of immigration restriction, often followed by bills supposedly giving protection to non-whites already in Britain.

Until this period, people living in Britain had usually had a fairly clear image of themselves. For the most part, they considered themselves Protestants (of a rather watery kind), English-speaking (with a range of more or less acceptable accents), tolerant in a slightly stand-offish way, patriotic in an implicit rather than a jingoistic fashion, Anglo-Saxon in origin—and white. But the debate over immigration called into question this national self-definition. Could you be a more or less patriotic, half-hearted Protestant *black* and still be British? Could you be a Hindu or a Sikh—and not even speak English—and still be British? If 'they' could claim to be 'us', then who are 'we'?[2]

There was an additional threat to the cohesiveness of British society in those years. In 1945, most people in Britain had probably felt, in a vague and subdued way, that they, along with the Americans, had won the war and that a basis existed for a continuing 'special relationship' between the UK and the USA. Such a special relationship had clearly existed between the two war-time leaders, Roosevelt and Churchill, though, in the later 1940s, with Roosevelt dead and Churchill out of office, the relationship no longer seemed so special. Britain's identity, for many people, was now primarily as the centre of a multi-racial global system of trade and friendship once called the Empire and now, increasingly, the Commonwealth.

By the late 1950s, however, it was clear that the imperial—or Commonwealth—tie was no longer capable of providing the core of Britain's identity. This was partly a result of the acquisition by the countries of the former Empire of political independence; to some extent it arose out of the fact that these new nations, unlike Britain herself, were almost all non-white; and it was in part due to the erosion of the old trading patterns whereby tiny industrialized Britain had been able to import at preferential rates food and raw materials from a grateful Empire.

As Britain's imperial identity evaporated, the special relationship with the USA was reinvoked. The early 1960s saw the heyday of this idea and a series of high-level meetings and pronouncements emphasized the idea of Anglo-American entente. Meanwhile, the British government—

strongly backed by its friends in Washington—applied to join the European Economic Community, the Common Market. For a while, in 1961-2, it looked as though Britain might be able to operate effectively in both an American and a European orbit. The widespread resentment in Britain at Dean Acheson's remark that 'Great Britain has lost an Empire and has not yet found a role' suggested that the Empire-Commonwealth orbit too still provided an important frame of reference for many British people. In 1962, far from having no role or identity, Britain had no less than three— the slackening but still potent tie with the Commonwealth, the resurgence of the special relationship with America, and a new and positive interest in the progress of her neighbours in Western Europe.

Dean Acheson's harsh judgement proved prophetic. At the end of 1962, a series of dramatic events arising out of the Cuba crisis proved with cruel clarity that American policy makers thought of the British not as equal partners but as poor relations who had merely to be informed of what was being done in their joint name. The British Prime Minister, Harold Macmillan, met President Kennedy at Nassau and tried to work out a defence agreement that would appear to salvage something of Britain's self-image as an 'equal' and 'special' partner. And, for his pains, Macmillan found President de Gaulle vetoing Britain's application to join the EEC in January 1963 on the grounds that the British (a possible Trojan Horse full of American interests) were not yet sufficiently European-minded. As for Britain's self-image as the heart of a happy and productive Common-wealth, this too, suffered severe setbacks. By the mid-1960s, two Commonwealth countries (India and Pakistan) were at war, as another, Southern Rhodesia, prepared itself for a unilateral declaration of independence from Britain and in time, self imposed republican status.

These developments did not directly affect the cohesive-ness of British society. But the cohesiveness of a society, like that of an individual psyche, is partly a product of its self-image or identity. Self-images are a product of computing likenesses and unlikenesses, comparisons and contrasts, the result of asking questions such as 'Whom are we like and

whom are we unlike?' To the extent that Britain's self-image
was fractured and went through a number of kaleidoscopic
turns during the 1950s and 1960s, her cohesiveness as a society
was, if not seriously shaken, at least tested.

The cohesiveness of American society was subjected to
somewhat greater strains. During much of the history of
modern America, there were people who emphasized the
internal tensions of US society and at times—particularly
during the more turbulent years of the 1960s—some even
talked of American society as about to 'break down' or 'disintegrate'.

In particular, it sometimes looked as though America,
like the England that Disraeli wrote about in *Sybil* more than
a century before, could polarize into two nations, the haves
(most of whom in modern America happened to be white)
and the have-nots (a disproportionately high number of
whom were black).[3] This nagging relationship between
white and non-white Americans induced some people, particularly among the militant black leadership, to question the
cohesiveness of US society. Malcolm X, for instance, would
suggest that white America owed it to non-whites to enable
them to live in one politically and economically separate part
of the United States, while other black leaders argued, like
Marcus Garvey before them, that American blacks should
return to Africa whence their ancestors had originally come.

The alienation of militant blacks from the mainstream of
American culture probably constituted the greatest single
threat to the cohesiveness of US society. But once they had
given vent to powerful negative feelings against whites,
even the most alienated often seemed to want, above all else,
a fair slice of 'the American pie'. Malcolm X and Stokely
Carmichael recommended that black Americans own and
operate their own businesses; the Watts rioter soon turned
looter and wanted nothing so much as a sparkling new car or
a colour television set; the Black Panthers appealed for their
rights under the United States Constitution. The plea, ultimately, was for the black man and woman to be able to share
the advantages—material goods and legal rights—that
whites were thought to enjoy. Most blacks did not want to be
separate; what they wanted was to share, to join in.

This was true of other groups that appeared, at times, to question their own membership of American society. Lewis Yablonsky[4] considered the hippie phenomenon to be the first American social movement that totally rejected the American social system. He described a number of hippie groups who built for themselves a style of life almost totally independent of the means, goals and values of 'straight' society. But when Yablonsky asked them what they thought of America, they tended to say things like 'It lacks something —like its original ideals and values' or 'It has stolen from youth the American dream.' Thus, even in the ranks of totally alienated hippiedom, admiration continued for the things that America was originally supposed to represent; it was the betrayal of basic values rather than the values themselves that the hippies objected to.

So America remained a fairly cohesive society throughout our period. There was little question, in the minds of most members and non-members alike, as to who were and who were not 'Americans' (though expatriate draft-resisters did pose a problem of definition). Most of those Americans who were disposed to challenge or disown some aspects of modern America would generally couch their criticism in the form of an appeal to traditional American values which, they would claim, had been eroded or betrayed. 'Americans' knew who they were and most of them thought they knew what 'America' stood for.

A stable society, as well as being predictable and cohesive, must also be efficient at transmitting attitudes and values from one generation to the next and from the society as a whole to the individuals who enter it. This is the process of socialization through which a society maintains its stability. There are several agents through which socialization is likely to take place but the most important are probably the home, the school, the mass media and the job. In post-war Britain and America, the socialization processes were generally perceived as operating successfully—as successfully, at any rate, as is likely to be possible in large, complex modern societies. Why should this have been so?

Most cultures have tended to resist the idea of change—

understandably because any alteration of the *status quo* is a
threat to the positions and values of those with an invest-
ment in it. America, however, in the words of Daniel Bell,[5]
is 'the first large society in history to have change and innovation "built into" its culture.' Britain, too, one of the first
really independent nation-states in post-Reformation Europe
and, three centuries later, first in the field in wholesale industrialization, has a long history of acceptance of and
adaptability to the challenge of new situations.

In modern times, this receptivity to the idea of change
assumed major significance. In some ways, it could make
a difficult situation worse. The parent or teacher would sometimes begin, for example, to imply to the child 'My job is to
prepare you for a world that has not yet arrived and for
which my own experience has not prepared me'—a message
that could hardly fail to help the adult to become speedily
obsolete, surpassed, and maybe discarded. The young could
suffer too in this process, for adults could no longer be the
sturdy models and exemplars that they had been for children
in earlier ages.

However, receptivity to change could also act as a buffer
by suggesting that one way to deal with it was to seek models
with rapidly shifting selectivity, sometimes admiring and em-
ulating person X, sometimes shifting attention to person Y.
This 'supermarket mentality', with its constant granting and
shifting of partial alliances, would have shocked earlier generations, but it helped people in Britain and America to sur-
mount the problems of coping with change more efficiently
than they could have done with a less dynamic set of values.

Thus, at a time of rapid change, the socialization processes
in cultures receptive to the idea of change, such as those of
Britain and America, were likely to be more successful than
those in cultures that resisted it.

Another reason for the success of the socialization processes in America and Britain concerns child-raising practices and beliefs. In primitive and traditional societies,
unthreatened by the exigencies of wrenching change, it is
probably true that 'authoritarian' child-rearing practices
lead to greater value-continuity than more 'democratic'
child-rearing practices. But in modern societies, the evidence

seems to point the other way. Those children most inclined
to rebel against the values of their parents, for instance, would
tend to come from relatively authoritarian rather than
democratic backgrounds. Children from more democratic
backgrounds, on the other hand, while they might grow up
and disagree passionately with particular opinions held by
their parents, would characteristically be less likely to reject
their parents' basic values.[6] In Britain and America in the
post-war decades, child-rearing practices and beliefs were
considerably more democratic or 'permissive' than for
example, in Germany, Italy, or Mexico,[7] so that sharp breaks
in value predisposition between the generations were probably less likely to occur in the USA and the UK than in the
latter countries. Thus, the socialization processes emanating
from the home were likely to operate over a period of time
with success in Britain and America.

For further confirmation of the success of the socialization processes and agents in the USA and the UK, one might
consult the views of social critics, people who would complain
that, for example, American and British children (or women or
the working class or non-whites) were 'brainwashed' into their
unenviable lot—were, that is, successfully socialized into it.

Here, for instance, is Ken Smeltzer, a high school student
from Elgin, Illinois:[8]

> We know only that we are supposed to come to class, do
> the homework, and work for a good grade. . . . Therefore,
> it is not a decision of joy which keeps us coming back for
> more. But most of us do come back. We have been brain-
> washed into thinking that the classroom is the only logical
> place for young people to be. The individual seems to
> ride along, waiting for society to tell him where to get off
> the educational merry-go-round.

Similar sentiments were expressed, in the late 1960s and
early 1970s, by articulate members of the women's movement. Kate Millett, for example, discussed the features of a
patriarchal society:[9]

> So perfect is its system of socialization, so complete the
> general assent to its values, so long and so universally has
> it prevailed in human society, that it scarcely seems to
> require violent implementation.

However, she argues, even totalitarian societies or societies with one-dimensional socialization systems tend to back up their values by the threat of force — and so it is in modern patriarchal society.

Comments like these suggest that society's most bitter critics could see its socialization agents as working successfully — too successfully. A similar view was maintained by social scientists who would generally find that, for instance, very high percentages of children agreed that 'the American [or British, or whatever] flag is the best flag in the world' or that 'America [or Great Britain] is the best country in the world'.[10] Nobody is certain from where British and American children would initially obtain these beliefs. But there is little doubt that, at an early age, they would tend to imbibe political values similar to those held in a more sophisticated way by their parents' generation.

This conclusion complements our earlier comments about social cohesion. After all, one of the prime values of any society — the one upon which its maintenance is most dependent — is that it does and should exist as a society. Once 99 per cent of children think that their country is the best in the world, the continued cohesiveness of the society is, barring sensational and unforeseen circumstances, firmly guaranteed. And once the children are successfully socialized, as they usually are in modern Britain and America, the basic institutions of society are likely to continue to operate reasonably predictably. All of which reinforces the contention that Britain and America were among the most stable of national societies in the post-war decades.

2 America

THE PURITAN ETHIC

So far, the relative stability of American and British society has been discussed against the time framework of the thirty years or so since the end of the second world war, and the main focus has been on the stability of society itself. However, this stability can be traced back through several centuries of history and has also tended to characterize people's attitudes and values. I am not convinced that there is much persuasive evidence for a sort of mystical bond between the inhabitants of a particular piece of territory from one generation to another, nor have the British—much less the Americans—been a race or shared a 'racial' unconscious. If there are unbroken themes running through the history of British or American social values, these are more likely to be found in the practical and continuous experience of the two peoples. The rest of Part I will look at the traditional values of the two societies, separately at first, and then each of the two sets of traditional values will be examined in the light of the other.

It is common to lump all seventeenth-century Americans together and talk of them as 'the Puritans'. In fact, the Virginians were, from earliest times, unlike the New England Puritans, and the Pennsylvania Quakers were unlike both. Even within a single section, such as 'puritan' New England, there were important variations of life-style and life-philosophy. But, with the exception of African slaves and native Indians, there were several things that most Americans of the seventeenth century and the first half of the eighteenth did have in common. For one thing, they were immigrants or the descendants of recent immigrants; in sharp contrast to the traditions of the transatlantic world from which they had come, they had deliberately uprooted themselves and were living three thousand miles away from the place in which their forbears had lived from time immemorial.

Secondly, they had made the decision to emigrate to America because they anticipated that they might be able to achieve something — material wealth, a society based on certain religious tenets, or whatever — that they had not been able to achieve where they came from. Thirdly, they maintained strong links with the society from which they had come (usually England) and tried in all sorts of ways to perpetuate in their various parts of North America some of what they took to be the best aspects of English society (witness, for instance, the determination of the Puritans — though not the Plymouth Pilgrims — to maintain their links with the Church of England). But, finally, they were conscious that, having made the break and left their homes, they *had* to make a go of it — and be seen by those around them and by those whom they had left behind to have made a go of it. Thus, the psychology of the immigrant was likely to include a powerful desire to achieve — and to be seen to achieve — material and spiritual success.

This psychology accorded well with the physical situation in which they found themselves. The problems faced by the Jamestown settlers in Virginia and, even more so, the first winter that the *Mayflower* Pilgrims survived in Massachusetts, have long since been incorporated into American mythology. Stripped of their romance and legend, these stories illustrate the acutely painful situation that any new immigrant was likely to face in early seventeenth-century America. In Jamestown, four-fifths of all the colonists who came between 1607 and 1624 died; some of those who survived did so as a result of cannibalism. Further north, at Plymouth, something like half the passengers who had arrived with the *Mayflower* in December 1620 were dead by the following spring; the Massachusetts soil was thin, the climate inhospitable, and, the celebrations of Thanksgiving notwithstanding, the native population was not always friendly. America in the seventeenth century was scarcity land and danger land. The immigrants may have hoped and expected that eventually they would, individually or communally, achieve abundance and security, but for the moment these were merely consummations devoutly to be wished. For the time being, the early settlers had no option but to adopt a series of values that would enable them to survive under conditions of extreme scarcity and danger.

These values tended to coincide, particularly in the area that came to be known as 'New England', with those epitomized by the Calvinist version of Christianity. Calvinism, which had been strong in parts of Scotland and, at the end of the sixteenth century, even in England, had never really become the predominant form of Christianity in Britain. Even after the civil war of the 1640s and the victory of the 'puritan' parliamentarians, England never became a Calvinist society. But in New England Calvinism thrived. It was a branch of Christianity that emphasized 'salvation by grace'; if you were one of the elect, one of the band who would, after death, land up in heaven, this was because God had long since decided this to be your destiny and there was nothing that you could do that would alter that decision. However, if you wanted to know whether you were one of the elect or not (and who could fail to be curious?) you could find out by trying to do 'good works' on this earth. If your earthly activities prospered and your faith in God increased (along with your certainty that He had chosen you for heaven), this in itself was a sign that you were one of the elect; if they did not, you were surely one of the damned. Although the good Calvinist knew that he could do nothing to alter God's plans for him, he could hardly have been blamed for working with immense zeal to prove to himself and to his neighbours that he was destined for heaven. This attempt to prove oneself one of the elect was an unending process; however well you were doing, you could never relax and live off your proven abilities—for the very process of giving up could be taken by your neighbours (and even by your own Calvinistic conscience) as a sign that you might not be one of the elect after all. And since only a small number of people were assumed to have been chosen by God for heaven, the process of proving that you were one of them tended to make for intense competitiveness.

This, of course, is something of a caricature and as one enters into the spirit of seventeenth-century America it becomes evident that strict Calvinistic mores were often more honoured in the breach than in the observance. Furthermore, even among firm believers, there was no unanimity regarding either the theological or the practical implications of Calvinism. Roger Williams quarrelled so bitterly with the authorities in Massachusetts that he split off from them and set up his own territory in what is now the state of Rhode Island. Anne Hutchinson was tried and banished for heresy and was eventually killed by Indians. Nevertheless, Calvinistic theology (and especially its emphasis on predestination and the idea of proving that you were one of the elect) did play an important part in helping to frame the value system of the early Americans. For it reinforced the values that were implicit in their material situation as achievement-hungry immigrants. Colonial Protestantism was harsh, and so were the economic conditions under which the colonial Americans had to live. Their religion and their practical circumstances combined to generate in them a rigorous set of values without the support of which they might have found it even harder to survive — much less prosper — as a society. To that set of values historians have attached the title of the 'Puritan ethic', or, more generally, the 'Protestant ethic' or the 'work ethic'.

The fundamental characteristics of the Protestant or Puritan ethic were not totally accepted by every inhabitant of colonial New England. Nevertheless, these values helped to give life in early colonial New England much of its peculiar style, and they remained as an important underlying presence in America long after the colonial period had become obscured in the mists of time.

At the core of the Protestant ethic was the idea that hard work was a good thing. In those difficult early days, hard work was not only a good thing but an absolute prerequisite of continued existence. You had to work hard in order to tap the meagre physical resources of crusty New England; if you and your neighbours did not work hard, you would possibly suffer the fate of your unluckier predecessors and die. Hunger, disease, and malnutrition were commonplace in early America, and hard work was an absolute necessity if you were to have even a reasonable chance of keeping them at bay. You not only had to work hard but also had to be seen to work hard. Everybody was in the same boat, and nobody

could be tolerated who did not pull his or her weight. Furthermore, this emphasis on hard work coincided neatly with the
requirements of Calvinistic theology. The authoritarian old
Genevan had never actually laid it down as theological
doctrine that people ought to work hard; but if you accepted
his idea that the one clear indication as to who were the elect
and who the damned was a person's faith which, in turn, was
likely to be strengthened by outward success, it followed that
everybody had a powerful religious incentive to back up the
needs of their society and work — and be seen to work — as
assiduously and successfully as possible.

From this need to work hard and to be seen to work hard,
there were a number of important offshoots. First, the
emphasis on productivity. You might know what a hard
worker you were, but, unless you had something to show for
your pains, nobody else would be convinced. The more you
produced, the more you justified your membership of the
precarious society in which you were living and reinforced
your faith that you were one of God's elect. Second, this need
to appear to be productive necessitated an element of competitiveness. The natural resources of New England were
limited and in any given village not all the land was good
and not every farmer likely to be equally productive. Since
there were no absolute standards according to which a person's
social worth or economic productivity could be assessed, the
one standard that could be used was a relative one. There
was a tendency, therefore, to rate people on a ladder of
social and economic usefulness. This, too, had its theological
as well as its economic overtones for, since only a limited
number of people was expected to be among God's elect,
there was a powerful motive for every able-bodied person to
prove that he or she was one of the lucky few; there is nothing
like the threat of everlasting damnation (unless it be the
prospect of imminent death by starvation) for making people
energetically competitive.

Since everyone was anxious to know where he or she stood
in the election-or-damnation sweepstakes, and since, in any
case, it was generally assumed that people were born sinful,
there was a strong tendency to pass adverse moral judgements upon those whom one considered lower on the ladder

than oneself. Those patently higher up the ladder would, by the same token, tend to be afforded lavish praise. This moralism was derived in large part from the Calvinistic heritage but here, too, it was subtly interwoven with the physical demands of the society. Only in a secure and affluent society, or in the upper reaches of one that is not, can people afford the apparent luxury of dispensing with moral judgements. Only in a Renaissance court in Elsinore can it be said that there is nothing either good or bad but thinking makes it so. In Puritan New England it was all too clear what was good and bad; that which minimized the problems of scarcity and insecurity was good, and that which did not was bad. Furthermore, since natural hardships (a drought, a heavy storm, an epidemic) could be unspeakably gruesome but would often be considered a necessary product of God's will and therefore not susceptible to moral assessment, the concepts of good and bad had to be saved up for one's fellows. And since, unlike their predecessors in the hierarchical medieval village, the colonial New Englanders could not use their lord or their serfs as outlets for their moralistic spleen, they tended to invent a constantly shifting moral hierarchy among their own peers. So the moralism of New England was, like its productivity, fiercely competitive.

Two further hallmarks of early colonial America were the emphasis on localism and on individual responsibility. There were many theological disputes regarding the level of authority to which one ought to defer. But politically the New Englanders had few doubts. They might have given lip service to a king three thousand miles away, but, in practical terms, they were often suspicious of any authority other than that which was local and visible and to which they had personal access. The mythologizers have probably made too much of the New England Town Meeting, but the myth arises out of a more or less accurate basis in fact. Town meetings did often take place and many of them did represent a considerable degree of local political autonomy. Here, too, economic and religious factors converge. In those days, when distances were great, means of transportation poor, and the population sparse, it would have made no sense for any political authority to have tried to impose upon New England the sort of political centralization that the Tudors and Stuarts—and even Cromwell—had been attempting in Britain. 'Government' was something distant and alien and, in practice, often not competent to deal with local problems. Theologically, this was not unlike the insistence with which Protestantism began, that the Papacy was not always right in all things and that a certain amount of local decision-making was preferable to an uncritical acceptance of the authority of the pontiff in Rome. It was consistent, too, with the Calvinistic resistance to the power of bishops. As in Calvin's Geneva, the society of New England was usually fairly authoritarian; once decisions were made, they had to be carried out and if they were not, severe punishments could often ensue. But the decision-making process was in many respects localized, and the individual generally expected to have access to it.

It followed that, if things went well for the community as a whole, each individual could share some of the glory; but it also followed that, since election or damnation was an individual matter, each person had to live with the responsibility of any failure either personal or communal. This social emphasis on individual responsibility was, of course, a useful way of encouraging every person to work as hard as possible; but it, too, followed from the Calvinistic assumption that election or damnation was a matter between the individual and God—something that each person, in his or her own heart, had ultimately to come to terms with.

These characteristics of the 'Puritan ethic' were dynamic rather than static. You could not work so hard or be so competitive or productive or self-reliant as to outstrip everybody else and then stop. For one thing, as has been pointed out already, the fact that you stopped could be taken as an indication that you were not, after all, a person of sufficient faith in God as to be indisputably one of His elect. But you would also be seen to be doing something that cut against the essential needs of the society. So the puritan values always included the element of change, of progress, of growth, of improvement—dynamic rather than static qualities. If you were doing well, you had to do better; if you produced a lot, you had to produce more. What it amounted to was a sort of primitive social Darwinism: if you deserved to survive successfully, you would; if your fortunes suffered, this was a sign that you did not have the wherewithal—God's grace or whatever—to do well in this world or, by implication, in the next.

In addition to the importance of hard work, productivity, competitiveness, moralism, localism, and personal responsibility, values without which survival would have been impossible, early American society subscribed to a further set of values. It was one thing to insist that everybody should work hard and be seen to work hard, but it was also vital for survival that the apparently scarce resources should be carefully husbanded. One set of social values, in other words, concerned the need for people to produce—as energetically as possible; but another set was more concerned with the ways in which people consumed the scarce resources that were available. Alongside the injunction to work and to produce, therefore, were values such as frugality: the desirability of living a simple and abstemious existence. Frugality was obviously necessary in conditions of economic deprivation; it was also a virtue preached by Calvinist theologians. The idea of thrift, too, represented a nice combination of the requirements of the theological and material universe. People clearly had to husband their economic resources with the utmost care, to spend as little as possible, and to try to ensure a good return on every penny spent. But it was also necessary to lend and borrow, both goods and services—and also money itself. Catholic theology had long been understood to prohibit the lending of money at a profit or, indeed, to sell anything for more than a 'just' price. But Protestantism in its various guises had made no such prohibitions. Consequently, the New England Puritans found both their religious beliefs and their physical surroundings inducing them to lend and to borrow, and to try to make a profit on the financial transactions into which they entered.

A judicious combination of theological and practical reasoning led, also, to the emphasis on extra-marital chastity. This was a way of trying to canalize sexuality away from directions that would provide society with unwanted infants; it was hard enough providing for those who were wanted. But it was also a way of inducing married couples to feel that children could and should be brought into the world in order to get on with God's work at the earliest possible opportunity.

The New England Puritan was also expected to practise charity—as much an exercise in enlightened long-term self-interest as a derivation from Calvinistic theology; and respect for the elderly—a good insurance policy for younger people to invest in if ever there was one!

So there were two prongs to the Puritan ethic. On the one hand, individuals had to work hard, be self-reliant, achieve their goals. But there was also a practical realization that resources were limited and must not be squandered and that some people who needed the bare essentials of those resources could not themselves perform the necessary work. So, along with the rough-hewn work ethic, tempered by the starkness of the physical environment and the austerity of the accompanying Calvinistic faith, there developed a dour but earnest charitableness.

These were two sides of the same coin. The theme that ran through both was the need for the individual to be personally responsible—primarily for his or her own earthly destiny, but secondarily for the destiny of the poor and the needy who were members of the same community. Personal responsibility meant much personal self-denial; if you enjoyed the here and now too obviously, you would not only be doing your hard pressed community a disservice but you would also be displaying (to others and to your own conscience) that you were one of those whom God had long since decided to punish in the hereafter. Gratification, as we say, or rewards, would come in their appropriate time and place. But the eventual gratification would be all the greater if you were able to defer it. Personal responsibility also meant that, when your neighbours had problems of which they could not remotely be considered deserving, it was your neighbourly duty—and not the duty of distant political authorities—to help them out as they would help you.

This set of social values helped to sustain the early white settlers in North America in their initial adversity and was to continue to guide the fortunes of their successors. It is not surprising that values derived from the exigencies of physical scarcity and the dictates of Calvinistic Christianity should have been so influential in North America in the seventeenth

and eighteenth centuries. What does require first a demonstration and then some explanation, however, is the contention that these values continue to survive in modern America.

THE PURITAN ETHIC LIVES!

One day, shortly before the November 1972 elections, I looked
in at a branch of the Republican State Central Committee
of California and picked up a number of leaflets. One of them
explained the difference between the Republican and the
Democrats. The cornerstone of Republican philosophy,
the pamphlet began,

> is the belief that each man is an individual who is respon-
> sible for his own place in our society. He is encouraged to
> work to secure the benefits of that society for himself and
> his family as well as for those who are unable to care for
> themselves.

Not a bad statement of some of the highlights of the old
Puritan ethic!

It would be nonsense, of course, to claim that these puritan
values somehow continued to hold unquestioned sway in
America for the three hundred and fifty years following the
arrival of the *Mayflower* and the *Arbella*, or even that they
were universally accepted during even the first thirty or
forty years. Indeed, as time passed, there was a gradual
relaxation of the grip of the forces that had moulded the
Puritan ethic in America — the Calvinistic theological heritage, the severe material scarcity, and the dangers provided
by a hostile native population. Nevertheless, anybody familiar
with modern America can easily identify institutions, behaviour, and attitudes that seem to be descended from the
values ascribed to colonial New England.

One of the most prominent and popular spokesmen for
puritan values — at least until his own moral authority became
so irreparably tarnished by Watergate — was Richard M.
Nixon. In 1971, President Nixon made a speech to the Knights
of Columbus. 'America', he said, 'became a great nation, a
strong nation, a rich nation because we have a competitive
spirit.' During the past quarter of a century, he felt, America

had often curbed that competitive spirit. But now, he went on,

> the time has come to be ourselves again — still compassionate, still with a sense of responsibility toward others in the world, still fair, still ready to help those who need help — but also determined to show what we can do, and to compete with other nations. . .

This competitiveness, for Nixon as for the early Puritans, ought to characterize both the individual and the society as a whole. 'A nation', he said, 'like a person, has to have a certain inner drive in order to succeed.'

That inner drive he called the competitive spirit — and he introduced his new economic policy of August 1971 in order 'to nurture and stimulate that competitive spirit'.

Nixon — like other American politicians but more conspicuously and (until Watergate) more successfully than most — gave expression to the continuing appeal of the puritan virtues in modern America. In an interview in the *Washington Star-News* just after the 1972 election, he said:

> The average American is just like the child in the family. You give him some responsibility and he is going to amount to something. He is going to do something. If, on the other hand, you make him completely dependent and pamper him and cater to him too much, you are going to make him soft, spoiled and eventually a very weak individual.

In his Second Inaugural address on 20 January 1973, a veritable thesaurus of resuscitated Puritanism, President Nixon said: 'Let us remember that America was built not by government but by people — not by welfare but by work — not by shirking responsibility but by seeking responsibility.'

And in a lengthy personality piece from the *Washington Post* at the time of the Second Inaugural, Nixon said that he had

> a strong streak of individualism which probably was more than anything else rooted in my family background. Not only at home but in church and school we had drilled into us the idea that we should if at all possible take care of ourselves and not expect others to take care of us. . . . Both my mother and father were almost fierce in their adherence to what is now deprecatingly referred to as Puritan ethics.

Throughout the post-war decades, American officialdom would often cloak its pronouncements in the language of the Puritan ethic — an indication not, perhaps, that the officials themselves necessarily subscribed to all of those harsh values but that they felt that an appeal to the doctrines associated with the early Puritans might elicit a more serious and admiring response from their listeners.

Evidence for the survival of various aspects of the Puritan ethic does not, however, come only from the voice of American officialdom. One finds it also in the slogans of advertisements. The idea of competitiveness is a case in point. Avis launched a stupendously successful advertising campaign with their famous statement: 'We're only Second in Rent-A-Cars. So We Try Harder.' The poster advertising National Library Week in the USA in 1973 featured the words: 'GET AHEAD. READ.' Then there was the old-fashioned localism that turned up in the advertisement for the giant ITT. 'Is small-town America really disappearing?' asked this commercial colossus. 'Not if 59,360 of us can help it.' There was evidence from opinion polls, too, of the persistent presence in modern America of some of the values associated with the early settlers. In November 1972, for example, *Better Homes and Gardens* published a survey on 'What's Happening to the American Family?' Two-thirds of respondents expressed views on chastity that were similar to those of their Puritan forbears and thought — well into the age of the contraceptive pill and the IUD — that premarital sexual intercourse was wrong. If one might legitimately doubt the society-wide applicability of the results of a poll conducted by a special-interest journal such as *Better Homes and Gardens*, the results of national surveys by organizations such as Gallup point in a similar direction. In October 1965, for instance, when Gallup asked whether contraceptive pills should be made available to unmarried girls, the overwhelming response (70 per cent of male respondents and 77 per cent of female) was 'No'.

God, cornerstone of the puritan structure of values, survived the vagaries of time with remarkable success — surfacing in modern America in the Pledge of Allegiance, mouthed by millions of schoolchildren daily; on the coinage;

in the rituals accompanying birth, marriage, and death; and, of course, in political rhetoric. Forest Lawn, the group of cemeteries (or 'Memorial Parks') in Los Angeles, made a survey in which they discovered that less than 50 per cent of those personally arranging funerals knew a minister of religion, but that 90 per cent wanted a religious service and the assistance of a clergyman.[1]

The heritage of the early Calvinists could be felt throughout modern American culture. Angry people would tell each other to go to hell, and, when excited, call upon the name of God or Jesus. There were important gestures of sexual modesty, too: dresses for women and shorts for men were never as short in America as they occasionally became in Britain.

Then there were the 'how it all began' tales, in the tradition of Horatio Alger, and, ultimately, of the self-reliance of the early Calvinists, tales with which visitors to successful business establishments would sometimes be regaled. Here is one (from a restaurant in Marina Del Rey, in Southern California); it was printed on the menu:

> Not so long ago there was a sandy-haired seven-year-old boy, with a red wagon and a big dream. Each day after school, he'd pull his wagon through the neighborhood selling his own specially fresh-squeezed lemonade, and candy. The kids loved to see what Burt had to sell, and it was they who inspired his dream of some day creating one of the most unique international restaurants in the world. So at the age of thirteen he got his first job after school as a dishwasher. Within a few months he was promoted, soda-jerk, waiter, to cook. He was a young lad with a lot of ambition for his dream, and he knew to accomplish it, somehow he would have to see the world for himself. . .

Today, by dint of abstemious hard work, an ability to save, and a determination to succeed, Burt has naturally achieved his dream of creating 'one of the most unique international restaurants in the world'.

The ability to save is a virtue that surfaces in the most surprising places. The idea of saving and of being saved is, of course, religious in origin; one of the central tenets of Calvinism, as has been seen, was the belief in 'salvation by grace'. The verb 'to save' still has religious associations in modern America; there are frequent signs to the effect that 'Jesus Saves'. However, the word long since acquired other meanings as well. In particular, the idea developed an economic and commercial aura that was, at most, only tenuously derived from the material exigencies of colonial New England. 'Buy more — and Save!' say the advertisements; Americans would talk of 'saving' (rather than, as in Britain, of 'collecting') Green or Blue or Pink trading stamps. Drugstore chains had names like 'Thrifty' and 'Sav-on'. The Californian State Messenger Service Envelopes in which for a while I kept part of the manuscript of this book, were inscribed: 'Costs are just as important here as they are in your home. Suggest a way to save.' Thus, while the idea may have maintained something of its early religious associations, it has also long been firmly harnessed to the economic imperatives of industrial America. Do you want to be one of the modern elect? Then show your initiative and guarantee your capacity to spend by 'saving'. The mixed message is splendidly encapsulated by the scribbled addition to the church notice: JESUS SAVES—*green stamps.*

   In view of this, it is hardly surprising to find that some vestigial traces of the values of puritan New England crop up — albeit in appropriately transmogrified form — in the language and slogans associated with that characteristically American institution, the savings association. When opening an account at one such institution, I was given, along with my pass book and a glossy booklet called The Freedom Collection (containing copies of the Declaration of Independence, the US Constitution, the Gettysburg Address, and so on), a little card. On it was written:

A New Day
This is the beginning of a new day.
God has given me this day to use as I will.
I can waste it or use it for good.
What I do today is very important because
I am exchanging a day of my life for it.

When tomorrow comes this day will be gone
forever, leaving something in its place.
I have traded for it: I want it to be gain —

not loss; Good — not evil; Success — not
failure, in order that I shall not forget the
price I paid for it.

A thought for each day from
MERCURY SAVINGS AND LOAN ASSOCIATION

Survivals of the Puritan ethic could be found, too, in universities. Shortly after I first went to the USA as a graduate
student in 1961, I bumped into one of my as yet very few ac-
quaintances on the Cornell campus and suggested that we
have a cup of coffee. 'Oh, no,' came the earnest answer, 'I
can't. I've got a term paper to complete.' I was used to an
atmosphere at Cambridge (England) in which nobody would
admit, in a social situation, that they had work to do, and as I
drank a solitary cup of coffee that morning I was convinced
that I had met a particularly virulent piece of Anglophobia.
But I soon came to realize that in the American context it was
much more acceptable for somebody to talk openly about
their work. A few months later, after I had allowed myself
to enter, in a leisurely way, the peripheries of the American
world of scholarship, one of my professor took me into his
office (it would probably have been called a 'study' at Cambridge) and, without a trace of humour, looked at me fixedly
and told me that if I wanted to get on I would have to learn
'to work twenty-five hours a day'. What I learned from those
two incidents was not necessarily to work for twenty-five
hours a day but certainly to present myself as though I did.

This American concern with hard work and the appearance of hard work continues to be widespread. Take, for
example, the professionalization of sports and the great
lengths in abstinence and training to which even high-school
athletes would subject themselves. Similarly, there are
surveys that demonstrate that despite automation and the
demands of American labour unions, people were actually
devoting longer hours to work and shorter hours to food
and sleep during the affluent 1960s than during the much
harder times a generation earlier.[2]

Productivity was often as important to the American in
the mid twentieth century as in the seventeenth. When the
nation's gross national product (or the productivity of a

particular business or industry) did not go up as much as was expected, people would worry. 'Any device or regulation', wrote Geoffrey Gorer,[3] 'which interferes, or can be conceived as interfering, with [the] supply of more and better things is resisted with unreasoning horror, as the religious resist blasphemy, or the warlike pacifism.' Think of the products that were advertised as bigger, better, new, or improved, or, indeed, of the seductive 'two for the price of one' that was the hallmark of so many transactions in modern America. Why was no car salesman satisfied at the prospect of selling exactly the same number of automobiles this year as last? Why, when the builders were about to get to work on the empty lot adjacent to my little cottage by the Pacific, thus ruining my view of the ocean, did my landlord react by saying, with breezy fatalism, 'Well, Dan, you can't stop progress you know'. These and similar questions can be answered, to some extent, by reference to the economic and social myths of modern America.[4] But the values that accompany, legitimize and perpetuate those economic and social myths are the spiritual descendants of the values of the New England of Winthrop and the Mathers.

The continuing presence of puritan-derived values in modern America is also evident in the so-called 'nostalgia boom'[5] of the 1960s and 1970s, for nostalgia can often be a disguised expression of belief in a traditional creed, a self-indulgent way of trying to prove that the values of the old days are still available if you wish to avail yourself of them.

Nostalgia for the values of yesteryear was widespread in modern America, particularly in the latter years of our period. The most popular television show of the early 1970s, *All In The Family*, began with Edith and Archie Bunker singing a few lines from 'Those Were The Days' — lines that included (from Archie) 'Guys like us, we had it made', 'Girls were girls and men were men', and 'didn't need no welfare state', and, from her, 'Songs that made the hit parade' and 'Everybody pulled his weight'. Part of Archie's attraction was undoubtedly that his old-fashioned bigotry corresponded, in a somewhat hyperbolic form, to the sort of things that millions of viewers were feeling (and wishing that they could say) as they watched him on the screen.

One of the most complete exercises in value nostalgia is a letter that appeared in a Texas newspaper in the 1960s. It was reprinted by Tom Wicker in his Introduction to the *New York Times* book *Great Songs of the Sixties*. Wicker refers to the letter as 'a cry from the American heart':

> Dear Mr Editor:
> . . . If you are a native American, and if you are old enough, you will probably remember when you could never dream our country could ever lose; when you took for granted that women and the elderly and the clergy were to be respected; when you went to church and found spiritual food; when the clergy talked about religion; when a girl was a girl; when a boy was a boy, and when they liked each other.
>
> You will probably remember . . . when you knew your creditors and paid your debts; when the poor were too proud to take charity . . . when songs had a tune; when you bragged about your home state and your home town. . .
>
> You will remember . . . when a man who went wrong was blamed, not his mother's nursing habits or his father's income; when everyone knew the difference between right and wrong; when you considered yourself lucky to have a good job, when you were proud to have one. . .

The values of Archie Bunker or the Texas letter-writer were not, of course, exclusively derived from those of colonial America. There is an element of nativism and of patriotism that the Puritans were in no position to share, while the new Puritans were not too worried about the tunelessness of modern songs or about the converging of traditional sex roles.

However, it is clear that the Puritan ethic was still deeply embedded in the values of modern America. The predominant values of a society are often in large part lubricants to the smooth fulfilment of its practical needs; how is it, then, that values moulded by the scarcities and dangers of seventeenth-century New England and by the religious tenets of those days, could turn up in the advertising rhetoric of an economic enterprise like ITT, the political rhetoric of

Richard Nixon, the menu of a Californian restaurant, or in the correspondence columns of a Texas newspaper?

WHAT KEPT THE PURITAN ETHIC ALIVE?

The answer to this question lies deep in the continuities of American history. Let us look at four developments that influenced the outline of American culture: the Revolution, the westward expansion, and the industrialization and massive immigration of the late nineteenth and early twentieth centuries. For each of these contained elements that helped to perpetuate some of the values associated with puritan New England.

The American Revolution was the first great modern revolution, the symbol of success for its French and Bolshevik successors. It was presided over by men who were intelligent, mature, and temperamentally conservative, most of whom cared as deeply about the problems of governing their fledgling nation as they had about obtaining its independence in the first place.

In certain ways, the American revolutionary leaders were markedly different from their forbears. If John Winthrop, Increase or Cotton Mather or Jonathan Edwards had written a Declaration of Independence or a federal Constitution, the name of God would certainly have received frequent and prominent mention; and they would not have dreamed of writing as the First Amendment to their Constitution a clause (which Roger Williams alone among the early colonials might possibly have countenanced) forbidding Congress from making any law 'respecting an establishment of religion or prohibiting the free exercise thereof'. Furthermore, it is unlikely that the seventeenth-century Calvinists would have chosen to list among man's 'unalienable rights' not only life but also 'liberty and the pursuit of happiness'.

To some extent, these were differences of style. In the late eighteenth century, educated men prided themselves on their rationality, and they had read their Locke and Montesquieu; a hundred and more years before, equivalent sentiments would have been expressed through the restricting filter of Puritanism. At a deeper level, however, the differences between the two periods were less striking than the similarities. The seventeenth-century settlers had refused to submit to the traditional authority of the society from which they had come and had taken the first steps towards setting up a new one. Many of them, even the most determined and aggressive, hoped to maintain their links with the society from which they had come, and tried to graft on to the new some of what they took to be the best features of the old. In this, the Founding Fathers of the late eighteenth century were the direct spiritual descendants of the Puritan leaders a century and a half previously. They, like their Puritan forbears, were aware that they were running major risks (if the men of the seventeenth century had failed, they would have died of starvation; the risk run by the revolutionaries was that they would be hanged as traitors). Like the Puritans, who were *émigrés* from a religious system that was intolerably autocratic, they were determined to resist a system, or at least the king who headed it, guilty (in the words of the Declaration of Independence) of 'repeated injuries and usurpations, all having in direct object the establishment of an absolute Tyranny over these States'. The revolutionaries were less concerned than the colonial American leaders with material scarcity (something from which many of them had been insulated by inherited wealth and education). But they were the direct spiritual heirs of the early Puritans in their sense of localism and self-reliance, and in their determination to establish a society that attached value to individual achievement.

A second formative development in American history was the experience of living on the moving frontier of the eighteenth and nineteenth centuries. As the 'west' moved westwards, Americans were less concerned than the New England Puritans had been with the ruthless God of Calvin and even more concerned with physical survival and, in time, with the possibility of great wealth as a result of the beaver, gold or silver, cattle, oil, or, in our own time, land. None the less, as millions of Americans, like their Puritan predecessors, tried to grasp a livelihood from land that had never been settled before, certain features of the Puritan ethic — for instance, the importance of hard work and the capacity to compete effectively for whatever visible rewards were going — seemed peculiarly appropriate.

Frederick Jackson Turner and his disciples attributed to the frontier experience whatever was peculiarly American about the American character. They have been criticized from many standpoints: some have argued that different types of frontier experience had different effects and have questioned Turner's geographical determinism (why didn't other frontiers sometimes develop 'American' characteristics?); others have quarrelled with his syphoning off of American values from their European roots, and have also expressed doubts about the 'democracy' that Turner alleges to have been provided for America by the frontier experience. But few (other than those who dispute the possibility of the existence of a 'national character' or 'culture') have taken serious issue with Turner's presentation of American values.

Stripped of its patriotic celebration of 'freedom' and 'democracy', Turner's message is that the major beliefs of the men of the frontier were that they were forced to be individually responsible for their fate, that they had to rely on their own resourcefulness rather than that of a distant and possibly impotent political authority, and that, to survive and flourish, they had to be ruthless and competitive. Turner does not attribute frugality and thrift to his frontiersmen nor does he see them as particularly chaste or charitable. But he does devote an essay to the idea that seventeenth-century Massachusetts was the western frontier of its day and that it was characterized by values that later, on a larger scale, were to characterize the whole area of western expansion.

The Turnerians were surely right in pointing to the westward movement as a main locus of subsequent American mythology. The frontier may have been closed in 1890, but it lived on, reinvigorated, in the stories that Americans told each other from that day to this. The cowboy (whose historical heyday lasted only from about the late 1860s to the late 1880s) became the central figure in twentieth-century American mythology. Again and again, especially on countless movie screens, the story was told of the intrepid loner, the man who would ride into town at the beginning of the story, keep in strict control of himself throughout, have a chaste love relationship with a doting blonde and, possibly, be chased by an unchaste brunette, put an end (single-handed and without the assistance of the official but unreliable law-enforcers) to some terrifying evil and the evil-doers—and then, at the end, ride off to some place else, alone. . . .[6] It was not only 'westerns' that tended to use this type of plot. Martha Wolfenstein and Nathan Leites[7] wrote an analysis of the major components of American film plots of all types. 'Winning', they said, 'is terrifically important and always possible though it may be a tough fight.' Also 'the hero, the self-appointed investigator and agent of justice, is able to set things right independently.' It is important, say Wolfenstein and Leites, that the hero (and, usually, heroine) should not only be all things virtuous but, at least by the end, should be seen to be so. 'They succeed in proving what they were all along. They emerge from the shadow of the false appearance. What has changed is other people's impressions of them.'

The formula of the tough self-controlled loner who grits his teeth and defeats the forces of evil has had a universal appeal, and was not, of course, confined to films or stories about America. But it was a myth that gained a boost from its associations with the opening up of the American West. It also tended to reinforce some of the American value traditions associated with the early settlements in the north-east. The frontiersman or cowboy, in myth as in reality, was less likely than the old Puritan farmer to make long-term plans or to worry about the hereafter; and, except for a few rather two-dimensional movie heroes, the man from the old west was quite prepared, as his New England forbear was not, to enjoy whatever wine and women were available. But both cultures were in part responses to scarcity of resources and physical insecurity. And in both one sees ruthless competitiveness, a need to fall back on one's own resources and resourcefulness, and a confident awareness that God (or whoever) helps those who help themselves.[8]

During the last years of the nineteenth century and the first years of the twentieth, America experienced one of the

biggest waves of immigration in history. Into a nation of
seventy or eighty million people, were pouring (by the
early 1900s) as many as a million newcomers each year—an
average immigration rate over twenty years or so of about one
per cent per annum.

What the new territory of the west had been to the pioneers
who opened it up in the nineteenth century, all America
was to its new immigrants: a tough, exciting new land of
boundless possibilities—so long as you worked hard and
competitively and were capable of putting off (often indefinitely) your enjoyment of the fruits of your labours. As
early as 1834, a German immigrant wrote home from
America to his parents:

> Nature has blessed this land abundantly. Here one fully
> enjoys what one earns, here no despots are to be feared,
> and honest citizens do not tolerate the least infringement
> or interference by human authority.[9]

Or in the words of two immigrants from Yorkshire writing
in 1872:

> I don't think we Could live in England know/we are yan-
> keys now/England is the place if you have plenty of money
> but America is the p[l]ace for a poor man to get a home/
> here is a home for every man if he is stedy/[10]

America appeared to be the land of limitless opportunity
—if you worked for it. This was the message sent back home
by the immigrant (who may have believed it—but who also
had a strong psychological incentive to believe it) and it was
a message eagerly lapped up in the old country by millions
who wondered about the possibility of making the journey
themselves. Carl Schurz wrote:

> The men in our family circle revelled in the log-cabin
> romance . . . and it wanted but little to induce the men. . .
> to try their fortunes in the New World.[11]

It was also a land in which religion, although not organized
by the government, was of consuming interest to its inhabitants. 'It will be necessary for me to attach myself to some
church', wrote a Polish-Jewish immigrant, anxious to make

himself into an 'American', 'since everyone these days wants
to know your religion'.[12]

One of the most famous of the later nineteenth-century
immigrants was also to become one of the greatest of all
American industrialists: Andrew Carnegie. He collected a
number of his writings in a little book called *The Gospel of
Wealth and Other Timely Essays*. In these pages, Carnegie
writes with a combination of religious and economic zeal of
the 'Law of Competition' and the 'Law of Accumulation of
Wealth' and says that 'civilization took its start from the day
when the capable, industrious workman said to his incom-
petent and lazy fellow, "If thou dost not sow, thou shalt not
reap".' Carnegie writes of charity, the main consideration
of which, he insists,

> should be to help those who will help themselves*; to
> provide part of the means by which those who desire to
> improve may do so; to give those who desire to rise the
> aids by which they may rise; to assist, but rarely or never
> to do all.... Every one has, of course, cases of individuals
> brought to his own knowledge where temporary assistance
> can do genuine good ... but ... he is the only true reformer
> who is as careful and as anxious not to aid the unworthy
> as he is to aid the worthy, and, perhaps, even more so, for
> in almsgiving more injury is probably done by rewarding
> vice than by relieving virtue.'

Carnegie was no New England Puritan, but the tough old
Scotsman had a philosophy that was not all that different
from theirs. 'Whatever I engage in I must push inordinately'
he wrote in 1868 when aged thirty-three. In his autobiogra-
phical sketch 'How I Served My Apprenticeship', he roman-
ticized the poverty which he had experienced as a boy; luxury,
he agrees, should be abolished, but not 'honest, industrious,
self-denying poverty'. Although Carnegie was to amass a
fortune of over three hundred million dollars, he never
lost his early belief in sustained hard work, diligent competitiveness, self-abnegation, and the eventual enjoyment
of those visible rewards that, as a result of steady allegiance

---

*cf. the view of John D. Rockefeller Jr that 'charity is injurious unless it
helps the recipient to become independent of it.'

to these virtues, were bound to come his way in the end.

Carnegie was a major force in helping to bring about the industrialization of late nineteenth-century America, a subject to which Turner, for all his concern with the frontier, also gave his attention. The scale of industrialization was staggering. Writing in 1910, Turner notes: 'Fifty years ago we mined less than fifteen million long tons of coal. In 1907 we mined nearly 429,000,000.' He goes on: 'the nation has produced three times as much iron ore in the past two decades as in all its previous history', and, a few lines later: 'the number of passengers carried one mile more than doubled between 1890 and 1908.' Railroad mileage in operation had increased spectacularly during the latter half of the nineteenth century:

Table 3   *Railroad miles in operation in the US, 1860-90*
with Index of manufacturing

	miles	Index of manufacturing (1900=100)
1860	30,626	16
1870	52,932	25
1880	93,262	42
1890	166,703	71

(Source: *Historical Statistics of the United States*)

Many of the industrialists who presided over this astonishing revolution tended to accept a view of life based, loosely, on an application of Darwin's theories of natural selection to the social and economic worlds. The great popularizer of 'Social Darwinism' — and of the *laissez-faire* economics with which it was so easily allied — was Herbert Spencer, and his *Social Statics* became one of the most widely influential books of the late nineteenth century. Spencer argued that, as in nature, the fittest survive. The American race (a word much beloved by Carnegie and many another) would survive — indeed, be strengthened — as a natural result of the consolidation of its fittest elements and the corresponding demise of its weaker members. This theory was applicable to the world community, to businesses, to communities, and to individuals. 'The fact that a man is here,' wrote William Graham Sumner, 'is no demand upon other people that they shall keep him alive and sustain him'. This sort of statement, while it may sound harsh or smug, was born of a powerful and optimistic patriotism — and is, of course, in a line of descent from the rough-hewn belief in competitiveness and individual moral responsibility of Puritan New England. Social Darwinism, in other words, was in part at least an application to the economic conditions of late nineteenth-century America of three ingredients: some of the comfortable theories of Adam Smith and other *laissez-faire* economists, the genetic theories of Darwin, and the less theologically tied of the values of early New England.

Thus, there were aspects of the American Revolution, the westward expansion, the immigration waves and the industrialization of America that tended to perpetuate that partly mythical but historically tenacious concept, the Puritan ethic. In colonial Massachusetts, as in Williamsburg or Philadelphia in the 1770s, on the western frontier, in Carnegie's steel mills, or in the immigrant sweat-shops of early twentieth-century New York or Chicago, there was a sense that you had to prove to yourself and to those around you that you had what it took to survive. The good Puritan knew that if he failed he could starve to death and in any case was probably one of those condemned to go to hell; the revolutionary knew that he would be hanged; the frontiersman that his fate could lie in the capricious hands of the elements; and the factory hand or sweat-shop worker knew that survival could depend upon the almost equally capricious nature of the boss. Ultimately, everybody was alone and the greatest virtue was, of necessity, self-reliance.

EQUALITY AND/OR LIBERTY

The seventeenth-century Puritans did not much talk of equality. Their traditions can only be called egalitarian in the limited sense that the fate of each soul was equally dependent upon the will of God (and perhaps in the more worldly sense that most people were equally likely to be forced back

on their own material resourcefulness if they were to survive).
Calvinism, with Lutheranism, may have struck a severe
blow at the Papacy. But in its own way it presented just as
hierarchical a set of dogmas and hardly promoted the social
and political egalitarianism that was espoused by later
Americans.

However, despite the harshness of both the theology and
the material conditions of Calvinist New England (and perhaps in part as a reaction to them), some of the seeds of that
subsequent social and political egalitarianism were sown in
early colonial times. In the religious separatism of Thomas
Hooker or Roger Williams, for example, or particularly
further south, in the idealistic nonconformism of William
Penn and the Quakers, there was contained the idea — later
to be enshrined in the First Amendment to the United States
Constitution — that an individual's religion should depend
not upon the territory in which he or she happened to live
but upon the right equally bestowed upon everybody to
choose his or her own faith. The idea of equality was no more
than hinted at.

Liberty, however, that other seminal value of later Americans, was more overtly appealed to by some of the separatists
and nonconformists of colonial America. Virtually alone
among seventeenth-century leaders, Roger Williams espoused both concepts; Rhode Island, he said, was founded
on the principles of 'liberty and equality, both in land and
government'. But even Williams fought more energetically
for liberty than for equality. In 1663, Rhode Island was given
a charter by Parliament that recognized that a 'most flourishing civil state may stand and best be maintained . . . with a
full liberty in religious concernments' and which declared
that 'no person . . . shall be in any wise molested, punished,
disquieted, or called in question for any differences in
opinion in matters of religion.'

In time, the idea of liberty was developed to incorporate
aspects of life other than religious liberty. In 1735, in one
of the milestone cases in the establishment of a free press,
Andrew Hamilton defended Peter Zenger in court with the
assertion that 'The loss of liberty to a generous mind is worse
than death' — a phrase that preceded by forty years Patrick

Henry's cry on the floor of the Virginia Convention 'Give me liberty or give me death!'

After about the middle of the eighteenth century, many Americans were coming to give equal place to liberty and equality as the twin pillars supporting the American value system. 'I believed that Liberty was the natural Right of all Men equally,' said the Quaker John Woolman in 1757.[13] Nineteen years later, in the Declaration of Independence, Thomas Jefferson was to write that 'all men are created equal' and to claim that liberty was one of the 'unalienable rights' with which all men were equally endowed by their Creator. Neither liberty nor equality was carefully defined by Jefferson — certainly not in the Declaration of Independence. But his palpable dedication to both was staunch throughout his remaining half century of life.

In the 1830s, shortly after Jefferson's death, Tocqueville tried to separate these two American values. Liberty, he wrote[14]

> is not the chief and constant object of their desires; equality is their idol: they make rapid and sudden efforts to obtain liberty, and, if they miss their aim, resign themselves to their disappointment; but nothing can satisfy them without equality, and they would rather perish than lose it.

Tocqueville went so far as to suggest, as Jefferson had never done, that liberty and equality could be mutually contradictory. If liberty were the primary value (which he considered it was not), then each individual would have been able to develop in his own directions and in his own way — and a society would have resulted in which nobody was in any way equal to anybody else. If, however, as Tocqueville believed, equality rather than freedom were the main American value, there would be a tendency for the society to impose its preferred types of belief and behaviour equally upon all its members. 'As a result,' he wrote, 'I know of no country in which there is so little independence of mind and real freedom of discussion as in America.'[15]

To Tocqueville, there was clearly an implacable conflict between the competing values of liberty and equality, a conflict that seemed to be resolved, in the USA, with equality as the winner. This is a view of America that has been widely accepted ever since John C. Calhoun wrote in his *Disquisition On Government* that it is 'a great and dangerous error to suppose that all people are equally entitled to liberty'. And, half a century later, William Graham Sumner was even more concise when he declared: 'We cannot go outside of this alternative: liberty, inequality, survival of the fittest; non-liberty, equality, survival of the un-fittest.' In our own day, the stark elitism of Calhoun and the social Darwinism of Sumner are largely discredited. Nevertheless, among the most widely influential books of popular sociology in modern America have been works (like David Riesman's *The Lonely Crowd*, William H. Whyte's *The Organization Man* and Vance Packard's *The Hidden Persuaders*) that have seemed to suggest, with Tocqueville, that American society is so egalitarian as to impose a more or less irresistible conformism upon the thoughts and deeds of its members.

But the Jeffersonian view, that liberty and equality are two sides of the same indispensable coin, is also one that has etched its way deep into America's self-image. In the Gettysburg Address, one of the three or four most famous statements of the American creed, and a document almost as familiar to American schoolchildren as their daily Pledge of Allegiance, Abraham Lincoln referred to the USA as 'a new nation, conceived in Liberty, and dedicated to the proposition that all men are created equal'. Thus, almost a century after the Declaration of Independence, the Jeffersonian vision was restated in a form that, in time, was to become almost as venerated as the original. And, in our own time, the two ideals have been jointly evoked by the movements demanding 'Freedom Now' for blacks or the 'Liberation' of women — movements whose political aims have generally been expressed as a demand for equal rights or equality before the law.

Thus, the relationship in American culture between the value of 'Equality' (variously defined) and of 'Liberty' (ditto) clearly repays careful observation. For in the tangled skein of this relationship lies much that is important about the ways in which Americans have envisaged themselves and their society.

The idea of 'equality' has been, for observers from at least the mid eighteenth century through until our own day, both there and good, both fact and value, both symbol and reality. A belief in 'equality' as in most social symbols, has been a sort of Rorschach test — you see in it what you want to see in it. And, like most such concepts, the idea of equality has, upon examination, proved to lend itself to many different and often mutually contradictory interpretations.

These have tended, at least in the traditions of American popular thought, to congregate round two broad approaches. Broadly speaking, there have been those, in what we might call the Jeffersonian tradition, who have regarded equality as meaning, in essence, equality of opportunity, and those who have (often without phrasing it in this way) preferred to see it as meaning something approaching what Tocqueville called equality of condition.

To the former, the Jeffersonian tradition, all people are created equal, they start life's race at the sound of the same gun and then it's up to them to run as best they can. An immigrant woman from Romania put it like this:[16]

> Everyone is equal here, and you can make a fortune or lose it, it matters not. You can start all over again with no feeling of failure or shame. . . . One day you are a street cleaner and the next you awake to find yourself a millionaire.

The idea of equality of opportunity in America has been applied with special fervour to the equal right of all to the ownership of property. Sometimes, as on the nineteenth-century frontier, property tended to mean land; sometimes it could mean a tractor or a car or stocks and bonds. Equality of opportunity developed social and political dimensions as well. America has often been described as an 'open' society, by which has been meant one characterized by more or less unfettered social mobility and also by political pluralism; everybody, that is, is adjudged as having an equal basic opportunity to gain (and to run the risk of losing) social status and political power.

The other tradition of equality, observed by Tocqueville, is less concerned with the running of the race of life. Indeed, its detractors would sometimes suggest that it is primarily interested in ensuring that all the runners arrive at the finishing tape together. But none of those to whom equality of condition is an attractive ideal would propose that a dull conformism be imposed upon all members of a society. On the contrary, the 'Tocquevillians', like the 'Jeffersonians', believe that there is something competitive about life and that people have different capacities which should be used to the full. But the Tocquevillians would typically be primarily concerned with ensuring that life's competitors be equally equipped to run their races to the best of their various abilities, that they should all start from the same place. The political emphasis, accordingly, has tended to be on a concern with adequate policies of social welfare.

By the twentieth century, the egalitarians of the first persuasion, professing a belief in largely untrammelled equality of economic opportunity, would nevertheless sometimes be the first to question the desirability of everybody having an equal opportunity to express their unedited and uncensored ideas on questions of culture and life-style. Conversely, those who advocated equality of basic economic conditions were, on questions of cultural expression, inclined to favour a philosophy of equality of opportunity. The modern descendants of the Jeffersonian tradition thus tended to hold views that were economically centrifugal but culturally centripetal; this was the basis of twentieth-century American 'conservatism'. The descendants of the second tradition, more inclined to hold views that were economically centripetal but culturally centrifugal, tended to find themselves at the heart of American 'liberalism'. The modern thrust of the two egalitarian traditions can be represented in the form of a diagram (see page 67).

Liberty (or its synonym 'freedom'), like equality, has meant several not always consistent things. In the culture of modern America, the concept was evoked in a variety of contexts. There was the 'Court of Liberty', for example, at the Hollywood Hills branch of the Forest Lawn Memorial Parks, or the 'Freedom Trail' in Boston which led from one Revolution site to the next around the city. Freedom, in the words of the song by Kris Kristofferson, is 'just another word for

(liberalism)	
equal rights of all to unfettered free speech (*cultural*) *equality of opportunity* centrifugal ←———————	removal of gross inequities of social and legal conditions (*economic*) *equality of condition* ——————→ centripetal
equal rights of all to unfettered economic enterprise (*economic*)	restriction on tasteless and dangerous expression of opinion (*cultural*)
(conservatism)	

nothing else to lose'. In the film *Easy Rider,* the young motor-cyclists are wondering what so irritates the 'red-necks' they encounter at the roadside café. 'What I represent', says one of them, 'is a guy who needs a haircut.' 'No,' comes the rejoinder, 'what you represent to them is freedom.' And inevitably, the commercial advertisers realized that freedom was a useful resource to tap. Talon, the zipper people, had an advertisement showing a sail-boat in the sunset — and the words 'When all that holds you is the horizon, that is called freedom.'

One distinction often made was between 'positive' and 'negative' kinds of liberty.[17] In his famous message to Congress on 6 January 1941, President Franklin D. Roosevelt listed what he called four essential human freedoms, two positive and two negative:

> The first is freedom of speech and expression. . .
> The second is freedom of every person to worship God in his own way.
> The third is freedom from want. . .
> The fourth is freedom from fear. . .

Essentially, the concept of liberty or freedom implies the right and the opportunity to make choices between real alternatives. Thus, it is closely intertwined with the concept of equality, for a society that values the right of its members to make choices between real alternatives will want to equip them equally with the right conditions and provide them equally with the necessary opportunities.

ACHIEVEMENT

Throughout much of American history, children were generally brought up to believe that they could 'do better', climb further up the social ladder, get a better education, make more money, marry someone more 'successful' than their parents had done.[18] The most famous statement of this achievement ethic was in the stories of Horatio Alger, and we have already encountered it in the saga of Burt and his wagon on the menus of the restaurant in Marina Del Rey.

The idea of individual achievement rests, in part at least, upon two preconditions. The first is that the society must be thought to be an 'open' one in the sense that there is little to prevent achievement-oriented people from following through their ambitions—a society, in other words, in which there is thought to be widespread equality of opportunity. Popular myths about people who go from Log Cabin to White House (or donkey-cart boy to restaurant owner) can hardly flourish in a society with, for instance, a rigid class structure or restricted systems of education or job recruitment. In a society that values individual achievement, importance is also likely to be attached to the need to guarantee certain minimal social standards from which individuals may set out to achieve their various ambitions; without this equality of basic social condition, ambition and achievement would more often be frustrated than fulfilled. Thus, if people are to take advantage of equality of opportunity, there must be some minimal equality of condition — and both types of equality are, in some degree, prerequisites in a society in which individual achievement is valued.[19]

Liberty is also a prerequisite of individual achievement. For not only must the opportunities be adequate and the conditions right, but people must also have the freedom to make use of those opportunities and conditions. Thus, the values of equality and liberty both provide support for what is possibly the quintessential American value, that of individual (and social and national) achievement.

Evidence abounds of the devotion of Americans from all periods and social strata to the idea of achievement. The most visible—and therefore most flaunted—yardstick of achievement was wealth, and 'successful' Americans were often inclined to display their riches as a way of publicizing their achievements. The archetypal American dream was to earn a fortune by dint of gruelling and sustained work and then to live luxuriously off the proceeds (which contrasts with the English dream of a country cottage with a small garden and a modest family saloon car[20]). Even America's 'failures', particularly white working-class males who did not have racial or sexual discrimination to fall back upon as an explanation of their lack of material success, would usually prefer to admit that they had not taken advantage of the opportunities for achievement that had come their way than to accuse the society of not having given them the opportunities in the first place. Thus, the belief that opportunities for achievement were potentially limitless in America could clearly be a cause of pride to those who were successful and of embarrassment and frustration to the 'under-achievers'.

The belief in achievement lay at the root of American optimism—the predisposition to assume that, if you set your mind to it, any problem could be solved. American optimism would characteristically contain an element of 'boosterism' or bragging. Also, it would often be focused on the latest cure-all or wonder-drug, with an inclination to believe that any technological or even artistic innovation might be the ultimate achievement of its kind. Foods and medicines, politicians and sportsmen, new weapons and rock stars, would be talked and written about in almost apocalyptic terms as the greatest that had ever existed. Why settle for less? was the message implicit in this type of cheerful hyperbole; why settle for the nursery slopes when you can have the whole mountain? Advertisers would tell you that this film or that whisky was the *ne plus ultra* of its kind; war-time slogans (the war to save democracy) and policies (unconditional surrender, the A-bomb) would often seem to correspond to a streak of 'totalism' in American culture. 'The difficult', it was said during world war II, 'we do immediately, the impossible takes longer.' There was an impatience to complete the job, and the certainty that the job could and would be achieved with total success. American optimism suffered some severe blows in modern times: the Russian launching of Sputnik in 1957 and the assassination of President Kennedy in 1963, the race riots of the mid-1960s and the Vietnam fiasco. By the late sixties, Jack Newfield wrote[21] that 'we are the first generation that learned from experience . . . that things were not getting better, that we shall *not* overcome.' Nevertheless, American culture continued to attach importance to the idea of achievement and to maintain its optimistic faith that the conditions and opportunities for achievement—and the freedom to take advantage of them—were still there.

THE INCORPORATION OF OPPOSITES

> *Do I contradict myself?*
> *Very well then I contradict myself*
> *(I am large, I contain multitudes)*
>   Walt Whitman

Equality and liberty can be defined in such a way as to seem complementary. However, American culture, while valuing both, has considered them as leading in opposite directions. The value of achievement contains elements of both. The Tocquevillians may be right; a clash may exist between liberty and equality. But the Jeffersonians may also be right, for America is characterized by its capacity to transcend and incorporate both of these conflicting values.

Any society depends for its dynamism in part on its capacity to tolerate diversity and inconsistency. A society characterized by a single set of values might be stable, but it would probably not be equipped to adapt and develop in the course of time. However, no other culture has been as tolerant of inconsistent and even opposite values as America. Its very inconsistencies might even have been one of its prime characteristics. 'It is clear to those of us who have made studies in many parts of the United States,' commented W. Lloyd Warner,[22]

> that the primary and most important fact about the American social system is that it is composed of two basic, but antithetical, principles: the first, the principle of equality; the second, the principle of unequal status and of superior and inferior rank.

Erik Erikson has written that 'the functioning American

bases his final ego-identity on some tentative combination of dynamic polarities' and he lists, among other examples of these polarities, migratory and sedentary, individualistic and standardized, free-thinking and pious.[23] Zbigniew Brzezinski, to take another example, talks of the challenges inherent in the changes being wrought by technology and electronics, notably the computer and television. 'The challenge in its essence,' he writes,[24] 'involves the twin dangers of fragmentation and excessive control.' Countless other observers have pointed to similar 'dynamic polarities' when trying to capture the essence of the American experience. Most surveys of modern American institutions, for instance, are likely to mention the pressures within many church organizations towards more local autonomy on the one hand and a broad across-the-board ecumenism on the other, or the demand for 'student participation' or 'workers' control' on the one hand and the move towards the 'multiversity' or the business group or chain on the other.

In colonial America, as in more recent periods, people often thought of their culture as imbued with sets of what Michael Kammen calls 'dualisms' or 'biformities'.[25] American civilization has always had the capacity to project a dual image. Geoffrey Gorer mentions two radically different but equally common modern symbols of America:[26]

> an extremely thin, tall, old man, his grey beard trimmed to an old-fashioned goatee, his clothes of a bygone era embellished with the stars and stripes of the national flag . . .
> and
> a portly, maternal female, dressed in flowing robes of classical style . . . crowned with a diadem, and holding a torch in one hand.

From puritan New England to the America of 'Radical Chic' and 'Hell's Angels' there are contradictory sets of values, forms of behaviour, or pairs of concepts that have somehow been strung together in an effective working alliance. All societies contain contradictions, but in America this characteristic is almost a definition. America, says Professor Kammen, is a 'contrapuntal civilization'. (Shades of Hegel. . .)

The fact of contradiction, and the ability to deal with it,

is part of the individual experience of every human being.
We are all likely, particularly during childhood, to have
come across a conflict between our desire to differentiate
ourselves from other individuals and an image of ourselves
as fused with our social environment. Thinkers from pre-
Plato to post-Freud have been convinced that the individual
soul or psyche is composed of various warring elements:
the intellect, the emotions, and the 'spirit', or, perhaps, the
super-ego, the id, and the ego. Some have suggested that
the personality develops in two clusters, one associated
with activity or 'doing', and one associated with passivity
or 'being', the former assigned by our culture to the male role
and the latter to the female.[27] The 'fulfilled' or 'adjusted'
person is one who manages to enable these potentially conflicting elements to operate in harness, to reinforce one
another; the person in whom one element is clearly too dominant, is, nowadays, thought to be 'unbalanced', 'immature',
'sick', or 'maladjusted'.

A huge national society is not an individual person writ
large, and it would be misleading to suggest that America is
a 'young' nation and therefore 'immature' or that Britain
acts 'phlegmatically'. However, a society, like an individual,
may be composed of potentially conflicting elements which
must reach a positive accommodation if the society is to function effectively.

If there is any truth in this thesis, it is especially applicable
to America which, to quote Erikson again, 'subjects its inhabitants to more extreme contrasts . . . during a lifetime
or a generation than is normally the case with other great
nations'.[28] Other cultures can generally be defined independently of the contrasts or biformities that they may
happen to contain; American culture can substantially be
defined by its biformities and inconsistencies and by the way
it manages to accept and incorporate them.

Take, for instance, the traditional American ambivalence
towards Europe. When Turner was writing his essays about
the influence of the frontier, he was partly motivated by a
desire to disprove the assumptions of the 'germ' theorists to
whom the European origins of America were all-important.
To Turner, all that was most characteristic of America was

home-grown, a product of a peculiarly American experience. The debate about the relative importance of America's European origins has gone on throughout American history, and attitudes towards Europe have fluctuated wildly, but perhaps the most common attitude is one that accepts Europe and rejects it at once. Here is a recent television commercial for Tuborg beer: the speaker is standing near the Statue of Liberty, and, as he talks, the sound of ships' horns can be heard in the distance:

> America welcomes class and this lady's seen a lot of it. People like Einstein, Knute Rockne. Our fathers showed a lot of class when they came over. And we think this new beer's got a lot of class. Tuborg beer. It's already one of the best beers in Europe and now it's made in America. It's still got a taste of the old country, but it's light like American and priced like American.

Here is another example, a commercial (spoken with an impeccable English accent) that appears to combine the aesthetic superiority often attributed to Europe with the economic expertise of America:

> All of the best melodies from the classics have been gathered by Columbia House into a big four-record collection. Yes, here are 120 of the greatest works of Strauss, Beethoven, Schubert, and many more, performed by Europe's finest musicians. Eh, it's a priceless introduction to the classics that will enrich every home. And it's all yours for only $6.98. But there's a great deal more. You also get this special collection of piano masterpieces. Thirty of the most beautiful melodies ever composed for the keyboard. So altogether you get 150 of the world's greatest music masterpieces for only $6.98. . . . Yes, here's a unique opportunity to own a complete library of the world's most beautiful music.

These commercial messages do not compromise between the putative virtues of America and Europe; they are attempts to have the best of both the old world and the new. They combine the appeal of the Europe from whence, indirectly or even directly, most Americans came (and of which they might feel in subtle ways deprived), and the America to which they or their ancestors emigrated. If America had cut itself off from its European roots—unthinkable to the seventeenth-century Puritans, the eighteenth-century Revolutionaries or the nineteenth-century immigrants—it would have been unrecognizably different; if, on the other hand, it had continued to think of itself primarily as a transatlantic branch of European culture, many of its characteristic achievements would have remained undone. Indeed, if either of these alternatives had occurred, America as a productive social experiment would have atrophied; it would have lacked the capacity to develop and change and to react to new circumstances. It is the capacity to incorporate the elements of apparently opposite outlooks that has given American culture its peculiar character.

This view is not as metaphysical as it may sound, for a society largely built up by immigrants was bound to learn the value of accommodating apparent inconsistencies if it was to survive and develop. 'Consistency', said Emerson, 'is the hobgoblin of little minds.' And, a few decades later, William Jennings Bryan surveyed the waves of immigration washing up on the shores of US society and said 'Great has been the Greek, the Latin, the Slav, the Celt, the Teuton, and the Saxon; but greater than any of these is the American, who combines the virtues of them all.'[29]

CELTIC CIRCLES AND ROMAN SQUARES

As one examines in more detail the many 'dynamic polarities', 'dualities' and 'biformities' of American culture, there emerges what might be called the 'Celtic' principle and the 'Roman' principle.

When the Roman armies landed in Britain in 43 AD, they found themselves in the south-eastern tip of a long, thin, triangular island inhabited by Celts. For the next four centuries—as long as the period from Elizabeth I or Ivan the Terrible to the present—these two peoples, the Romans and Celts, lived side by side in much of Britain (and, indeed, in parts of continental Europe) in uneasy coexistence. The confrontation of these two represented the confrontation of two substantially different attitudes towards almost all aspects of life. The products of Celtic culture were often characterized by curves and circles, the products of Roman culture by squares and straight lines. The Celts loved to talk vigorously and to burst into song; the Romans preferred more controlled and calculated forms of expression and spoke a language better equipped for the communication of logical thought than sentiment. The Celts sang poems; the Romans wrote laws. The Celts lived in round huts in the country; the Romans built towns which were connected by road grids. The Celts did everything with a fiercely individualistic passion; the Romans preferred to act in careful concert with one another. Celtic culture tended to be centrifugal and to permit and even encourage particular divergencies from general norms; Roman culture was centripetal and tended to induce convergence to norms.

Thus, when these two peoples confronted each other, that confrontation represented nothing less than a fundamental clash of cultures, a clash between the Celtic pressures towards cultural diversity, localism, and individual self-expression, and the Roman demands for cultural homogeneity, centralism and conformity. Celtic culture emphasized, as it were, the limbs, and Roman culture the central nervous system; or to use another analogy, the Celts were a little like the spokes of a bicycle wheel and the Romans more like its hub.

The precise historical accuracy of this dichotomy between Celtic and Roman cultural patterns is not important. What is relevant for present purposes is the symbolism of the centrifugal, divergent Celtic culture with its poetry and its curves, and the centripetal, convergent Roman culture with its laws and its lines. These two themes, or variations upon them, have characterized many of the dualities and divisions within American culture.

We have seen, for instance, how the idea of 'equality' helped to lead some (commonly called conservatives) towards an economic philosophy with strong centrifugal implications but a cultural outlook tending more towards centripetality (and 'liberals', on the other hand, towards the reverse set of predispositions). In general, the centrifugal forces within America have tended to induce greater unpredictability and heterogeneity, and the centripetal forces greater predict-

ability and homogeneity. The army of the centrifugals has
tended to be inspired by such political war-cries as 'States'
rights', and by such leaders as John C. Calhoun in the nineteenth century, George Wallace in ours, and, above all, the
pre-presidential Thomas Jefferson. Politically centrifugal
pressures were strong during the 'Era of Good Feelings' (the
years immediately after about 1815), the 'Gilded Age' (the
generation following the Civil War), and the 1920s. The
centripetal and homogenizing tendencies in American political history were generally in the ascendant when the nation
went through a severe crisis, and its special heroes have been
people like Lincoln and Franklin D. Roosevelt.

  Each of these two sets of forces has been present throughout American history. Sometimes they have been in a state
of equilibrium: usually they are to be seen wrestling with
each other; but there is no period when strong elements of
both could not be identified. Indeed, if the centrifugal and
heterogenizing tradition were ever to gain an unimpeded
upper hand, the nation would probably disintegrate, as it
virtually did in 1861. If the centripetal and homogenizing
tendencies were ever totally to dominate, on the other hand,
America would become impossibly drab. The constant
jockeying for position between manifestations of these two
tendencies has helped to give American history much of its
dynamism. When, in any particular respect, one of them
looked like being too dominant, the other would launch a
counter-attack. The Civil War was the result of one such
movement. In our own time, as coast-to-coast television networks and systems of highways and motels have been developed, they have been counterpointed by the increasingly
aggressive assertion of separateness and 'differentness' by
various 'life-style' groups or political groups such as the
Black Panthers, the Jewish Defense League, or the adherents
of the Red Power, Gay Liberation, and Women's Liberation
movements. These two traditions, the centripetal and the
centifugal, are not uniquely American. In any large and
evolving society—and particularly in a nation-state govern-
ed as a federation—there is likely to be a built-in conflict
between the interests of the central locus of the political,
cultural, and social systems and the corresponding peri-

pheries. But in America, land of 'biformities' and 'dynamic polarities', these centre-periphery conflicts have been particularly conspicuous.

Centripetal pressures often tend to produce cultural uniformity of various kinds, while centrifugal pressures tend to produce variety. Thus, many observers of American culture describe their centre-periphery 'paradoxes' in what is essentially the language of the conflict between the forces of uniformity (or homogeneity) and those of diversity (or heterogeneity). When, for instance, Erikson writes of 'open roads of immigration and jealous islands of tradition, outgoing internationalism and defiant isolationism, boisterous competition and self-effacing cooperation', or lists such 'dynamic polarities' as migratory and sedentary, individualistic and standardized, and free-thinking and pious, this is precisely the direction in which all his examples point—for in each of his pairs the first concept (centrifugal) has diversifying implications, and the second one (centripetal) contains what might be called 'homogenizing' implications. Brzezinski, in the article quoted, said that people were becoming 'simultaneously more unified and more fragmented'; and W. Lloyd Warner wrote of 'two contrary tendencies [that] operate in the symbolic behavior of contemporary America' — namely 'increasing diversity of symbols' (which result from 'a high division of social labor') and, at the same time, 'increasing generalization and standardization of public symbols'.[30] Other pairs of apparently contradictory American values with centrifugal-centripetal implications include: the distrust of bureaucracy and the inclination to bureaucratize; the assumption that one's own needs can be naturally satisfied and the assumption that other people's needs can be artificially stimulated; the attraction of the immediate, the material, and the practical, and the respect for the long-term, the spiritual, and the theoretical. In each of these polarities the more obviously decentralizing concept is placed first.

These and similar polarities may occur in most societies, but the conflicts between the interests of the centre and those of the peripheries seem to be greater, more recurrent, and the protagonists more equally matched in the United States than elsewhere, and American culture appears to take much of its quality precisely from its response to these conflicts. Why should this be so?

One possible explanation is that the American social system had elements of this conflict built into it from the start. Many of the first Europeans to settle in the American colonies were *émigrés* from political and religious systems which, in their view (a view subsequently enshrined in American mythology) were too centralized. The American Revolution, too, was fought, in part at least, over the issue of the abuse of centralized political power, and the debates that eventually produced the United States Constitution were preoccupied, again, with similar questions: what powers should be given to the federal government, what powers should be left to the individual States, and on what topics should no political body be permitted to exercise power? Further, there is the sheer size of America, both demographically and geographically. Any society with that many people and that many square miles is likely to have to consider the desirability or otherwise of permitting (or even encouraging) people in the localities to do things in their own separate and different ways. Even in the eighteenth century, when the USA had a population of four millions or so and was confined to the Eastern seaboard, it was already, in contemporary terms, large and populous and its centralizing forces ill-equipped to ride roughshod over those of the localities.

Finally, conflict between the forces of the centre and the peripheries is likely to occur in response to radical change. The United States had been ahead of most other societies in its preparedness and ability to accept innovation, and receptivity to innovation presents governments and peoples with the urgent question of control: how far should central authorities finance and administer and take ultimate responsibility for the diffusion of the latest discoveries and inventions and how far should control remain decentralized? The growth of the electronic media, radio and television, for instance, illustrates the ways in which the interests of the political, economic, and cultural centres and peripheries were gradually mediated in a way that was semi-satisfactory to all but wholly satisfactory to none. Coast-to-coast networks were bound to have a culturally homogenizing and centripetal effect, and the political and economic power that accrued to network headquarters was enormous; but local station ownership (and the strict limitation upon the number of stations a network or an individual could own, and upon the proportion of network material any given station could broadcast) could sometimes act powerfully in the opposite direction. A second example is the development of atomic power. On the one hand, the Manhattan Project and Hiroshima inaugurated the era of the 'military-industrial complex'. This network of elite relationships tended to direct and restrict the activities of millions of people and billions of dollars and to impose unprecedented central control over not only America's defence structure and those aspects of the economy directly related to it, but even over the raising and borrowing of funds by universities or the opportunities for certain types of freedom of speech and publication. On the other hand, the sheer size and range of the enterprises that the atomic age made possible meant that matters of considerable importance would often have to be delegated to authorities and to locales that would not hitherto have been consulted. In an age of atomic power and of the political and geographical devolution that this necessitated, there were people all over America who had some knowledge of what was being done in their name, and who might therefore have felt that much better equipped, as their relatively excluded forbears might not have been, to hold and express opinions about the saying and the doings of the elites for whom they were working.

As these two examples suggest, America's pre-eminence as a society bent on developing and spreading the fruits of technological innovation has been an important factor in keeping to the forefront of people's minds the conflict between the interests of the various centres in society and those of the corresponding peripheries. This creative tension between the 'Roman' and 'Celtic' forces in American culture has been valued through much of American history and its recurrent presence has consistently contributed to the dynamism of American culture.

3   Britain

MYTHS AND ELITES

In some ways, the traditional and historically-based values of British culture should seem easier to identify than those of American culture. Britain, after all, has a far longer history than the USA, a more traditional culture, and a more compact and homogeneous society. However, in at least one respect, namely the use of historical myth,[1] the quest for traditional social values is easier in the case of America than in that of Britain. American history contains pivotal epochs, events and persons from which have been developed important myths concerning the origins of the most revered values of American society; British history may also have yielded to generations of mythologizers, but in a less revealing way.

The British can hardly feel, as Americans might, that the roots of their society can be traced back to a small number of fixed and definable events and periods in the past. There are no equivalents in Britain—at least since the Norman invasion—of such historical foundation stones as the white colonization of North America in the seventeenth century or the Revolution at the end of the eighteenth, epochs from which generations of later Americans believed their own social and cultural roots to have been derived. While the British, like the Americans, certainly mythologized many events and persons from their past, the British myths—unlike those about the New England Puritans or the cowboy—were generally concerned with the defence and maintenance rather than the foundation of the society or the nation. Thus, while the mythologizing of the historical past (or even the legendary past—witness Adam and Eve or Romulus and Remus) can help to provide a chronological starting-point from which to explain all that followed, this function was performed better by myths in America than by those in Britain.

Another function of an historical myth (of a positive one at least) is to act as a symbol of values later espoused by society

80

as a whole. The mythologizing of the early American Puritans is again instructive. In the opening section of Chapter 2 there was little reference to what the Puritans may actually have said, done, or believed, but a great deal to the mythologized picture of puritan values as pieced together by later generations. This subsequent reconstruction helped to provide later Americans with a basis for their own partially neo-puritan values. Again, no equivalent myths exist within British culture, no stories about Fathers (whether 'Puritan' or 'Founding'), no legendary events or figures from whom a corpus of subsequent values and behaviour could be derived.

The problem is not that the British have no historical myths. On the contrary, they have, if anything, too many. The British past is full of people who, between them, can lead the historian in every possible direction. Should one look to the early Celts for guidance to later British values? Well, yes, in some ways; it may be that their supposed love of words and song (not to mention drinking) pointed out by people like Gildas, Diodorus Siculus, or Giraldus Cambriensis, filtered down through the centuries into the culture of modern Britain. But what of the Romans, with their cool and disciplined administrative skills, their hierarchical social system, and their love of the straight line? Or the Angles and Saxons? Or the Normans? There are great mythologized individuals, too, such as King Arthur and King Alfred—the former almost entirely invented, the latter a real historical figure, but both of them endowed during later centuries with elements of both the absent-minded aesthete and the hard-nosed military hero. Later on came the large and pugnacious Henry VIII (a forerunner of 'John Bull' and of the already partly mythologized Winston Churchill) and his supposedly virginal daughter, Queen Elizabeth I. There is the rural and left-wing Robin Hood who ends up (according to some versions) with a peerage, and there is Prince Hal who is most at home in tavern society, and even as king on the eve of Agincourt, chooses to mingle, incognito, with his troops.

Some historical myths function as clear-cut symbols of subsequent social values, and the mythologizing of American history gives out a clearer message than does the mythologizing of British history. But there are also historical myths that represent, for the later generations who write and read about them, symbolic conflicts or disputes that prefigure similar disputes in their own times. Here again the contrast between American and British experience is instructive. American intellectual debate has been much exercised with such questions as whether the Puritans were embryonic democrats or even civil libertarians, or the extent to which the Founding Fathers were primarily responding to philosophical or material considerations. These are problems to which the modern historian of America is almost inescapably drawn, the mythical milestones upon which an interpretation of American history is bound in part to have to rely. British history is longer and relatively free of conflicts of a partly symbolic nature. Did the Angles and Saxons and Jutes civilize or barbarize? Was the erosion of royal power in later medieval England volunteered from above or forced from below? Was the Reformation primarily motivated by religious or political factors? Did Britain acquire an Empire in 'a fit of absence of mind' or as a result of practical policy? Questions such as these are of some academic interest. But unlike their American equivalents these issues are hardly likely to arouse partisan passions among non-historians.

In sum, American history can be seen as having started, both socially and politically, at a more or less definable time, with a set of suitably mythologized persons and events that provided a set of symbols upon which later generations of Americans were able to elevate their social values and define the terms of their own social disputes and debates. British history, by contrast, is more commonly interpreted as having been (certainly since 1066 and perhaps for much longer) by and large an uninterrupted continuum, its myths being dispersed over time, and their symbolic value, in consequence, largely diluted.

The reasons for this contrast lie to no small degree in the respective 'facts' of American and British history. But the past cannot be perceived except through the more or less distorting prism of the present. American society in the twentieth century is most commonly pictured as a mixed multitude of immigrants and the descendants of immigrants, people from all parts of the world, carrying with them almost every imaginable sort of cultural baggage. Consequently, America has developed a series of myths designed to act as cement to hold together the extraordinarily disparate elements that compose it—hence the concentration on the origins of the society, and the convergence on events and personalities that symbolize social and national unity. In modern Britain, by contrast, the supposedly uninterrupted homogeneity and cultural unity of the society (until our own times, at least) have been largely unexamined and even unquestioned. British historical mythology, consequently, has emphasized not the origins or the unity of the culture so much as its continuity. In America, the Puritans or the Revolutionaries are most commonly seen as people who interrupted the flow of history and started something new; most British myths, from Alfred and the Danes, Drake and the Armada to Churchill and the Battle of Britain, concern people and events that succeeded in enabling the uninterrupted flow of history to withstand disrupting influences from-outside.

SELF-RESTRAINT

'Reserve is so natural to the English. Feeling is interior.' Hubert Saal, writing in *Newsweek* about Janet Baker (1974).

'If you really care passionately about something, if you are working very hard or trying your best at some game, it is unlikely that you will admit this publicly.' J. D. R. McConnell on the boys of Eton (*Eton — How it Works*, Faber 1967).

In some ways, British social values have probably changed substantially over the past couple of centuries or so. The 'jingoistic' patriotism of Victorian Britain, the uninhibited public displays of aggression and cruelty during the eighteenth century, and the traditional respect of the young for their elders—these already seem, from the perspective of the last quarter of the twentieth century, to have been largely relegated to the irretrievable past. However, the modern social values of the British are not entirely unrelated to those that held sway during earlier periods.

For example, British culture has long emphasized the virtue

of self-restraint and has tended to applaud the understatement, the double negative, the qualifying phrase, the ability
to try to keep calm under fire. 'Unflappable' was the epithet
used when this quality was attributed to Prime Minister
Macmillan; it was the maintenance of a 'stiff upper lip' that
was admired.

The classic instance in modern times of this quality being
displayed on a nation-wide scale was the cool and efficient
way in which the British people responded to the potentially
devastating challenges of World War II. In the years 1939-42,
Britain was faced with the strongest challenge for the highest
stakes in her history. The most admired response was one of
calm and rational dedication, an inclination to understate
the depth of the crisis and the size of the problems, and a
cheerful refusal to express any but the most mundane emotions. These qualities were particularly lauded at times of
retreat and apparent defeat[2] — times when other people
in similar historical circumstances have often been known
to panic or to look for scapegoats. Dunkirk was not a victory
but a costly retreat but the 'spirit of Dunkirk'[3] went down
almost immediately in British mythology as an instance of
the British personality not only at its best but also at its most
characteristic, and it provided an image of indomitable
courage to which British political leaders would appeal
whenever things got tough.

This 'Dunkirk spirit', the capacity to turn a calm and confident face to even the most hazardous circumstances, was
clearly something that the British cultivated and were proud
of during the darkest days of World War II. It is not easy to
separate myth from reality. Subsequent memories (as well
as written and filmed accounts) of the period were often filled
with cheerful Spitfire crews always at the ready, quiet but
indefatigably dogged inventors, soft-spoken but incontro-
vertibly authoritative BBC announcers, and an entire nation
resolutely devoted to the task of victory over 'Jerry' or the
'Hun' or the 'Bosch'. In fact, of course, a great deal of outward
calm would often be no more than a momentary and necessary disguise for something not far removed from panic or
even hysteria. Angus Calder tells what he says is a 'true, and
chilling, anecdote':[4]

One elderly woman refused to leave her stewpot and stayed on in her blasted home in a huge area of devastation. A stretcher-bearer, to humour her, asked to taste her cooking, and found the pot was full of plaster and bricks.

The myth making was by no means the exclusive invention of subsequent generations. On the contrary, reality, as ever, fed myth; but myth went straight back to feed reality. There genuinely were cheerful Spitfire crews, dogged inventors, authoritative BBC announcers and the rest, people who willingly and easily played roles that had been created for them partly by the external exigencies of the war but also by their own already partly mythologized performances.

In the early 1940s, many foreigners in Britain were impressed by the national mood. General de Gaulle[5], in London immediately after the fall of France, (a time when, by the logic of events, the British mood might reasonably have been expected to show signs of panic or even of a resigned fatalism) found that London had

a look of tranquillity, almost indifference. The streets and parks full of people peacefully out for a walk, the long queues at the entrances to the cinemas, the many cars, the impressive porters outside the clubs and hotels, belonging to another world than the one at war.

Tranquillity, almost indifference . . . The determination to remain unflappable could, on occasion, lead people to appear to be almost insanely indifferent — not to the course of the war but to any fate that the war might have in store for them personally. Alongside the woman with the stewpot full of bricks we should, perhaps, place the man who (anticipating the satirical spirit of *Beyond the Fringe* by twenty years) asked, on the second day of the war: 'Pardon me, but have I time to get to Victoria before the devastation starts? I have to get a train for Haywards Heath.'

People would expose themselves to danger asserting with resignation that 'if your number's on it, the bomb'll get you'. Others held the absurd belief that the same place would never be bombed twice — an assumption that wove a meagre thread of safety around the appearances of the King and Queen — and above all the mercurial Winston Churchill — in areas that had only just been the targets of enemy bombardment.

During those early days of the war, the British displayed a pride in their traditional capacity to distance themselves from the emotional enormity of a crisis, a capacity in contrast to the understandable but often irrational panic that gripped many West Coast Americans during the aftermath of Pearl Harbor.

This quality had long been emphasized by the observers — and mythologizers — of British character. Among the capacities listed by Kipling in his poem *If* . . . as prerequisites for manhood were the capacity to 'keep your head when all around you/Are losing theirs' and also the ability to 'meet with Triumph and Disaster/And treat those two impostors just the same.' In Kipling's terms, perhaps the greatest 'man' of the nineteenth century would have been the Duke of Wellington. The Iron Duke is supposed to have talked of what was arguably the most significant battle of the century, Waterloo, as though it had been an athletics race. It has, he said, 'Been a damned nice thing — the nearest run thing you ever saw in your life. . . . By God! I don't think it would have done if I had not been there.' Would Hitler have said to his generals at Stalingrad what Wellington is supposed to have said to his at Waterloo? 'Hard pounding this, gentlemen; let's see who will pound longest.'

Prior to the late eighteenth century, the British were sometimes considered (by themselves as well as by observers from abroad) to be quick and intense in the expression of such emotions as anger, fear, resentment, or vindictiveness, or those of friendship, affection, and love. But the values commonly inferred from British history would rarely highlight the expression of powerful emotions. On the contrary, the most graphic stories with which British children would be inculcated — particularly with the onset of mass literacy in the nineteenth and twentieth centuries — were those emphasizing the emotional restraint of the British, often contrasted with the self-defeating expressiveness of foreigners. There was, for instance, the myth of Sir Francis Drake, busily playing bowls at Plymouth Hoe in 1588, being told that the dreaded Spanish Armada was at that very moment sailing up past the Cornish coast. Drake, or so the story goes, insisted that he and his men finish their game of bowls — and only then would they go and finish off the Spaniards, which naturally, they duly did. In an earlier period there was King Richard the Lionheart who, imprisoned in a European castle in the 1190s, was eventually located by his faithful minstrel Blondel after the two of them — the King in captivity and Blondel outside the castle walls — recognized each other's voices as they sang in duet a French folk-song. This story is encrusted in layers of chivalric mythology and has come to us through a filter as much French in origin as British. But the fact that, like the story of Drake and the bowls, it continues to find its way into story books for children is testimony to its continued popularity. Richard, like Drake, was able to keep his cool in the face of crisis, a message that still seems to have a special appeal for the British.

The British were often inclined to identify themselves by reference to their response to crisis and to infer their most laudable characteristics from the way in which they dealt with it. The Englishman, said Stanley Baldwin in 1924,[6]

> is made for a time of crisis, and for a time of emergency. He is serene in difficulties but may seem to be indifferent when times are easy. He may not look ahead, he may not heed warnings, he may not prepare, but when once he starts he is persistent to the death and he is ruthless in action. . . .
>
> It is in staying power that he is supreme, and fortunately . . . to some extent impervious to criticism — a most useful thing for an English statesman. That may be the reason why English statesmen sometimes last longer than those who are not English.

The Englishman might typically 'lose every battle except the last'; or, in the words of a less militant cliché, he would always 'muddle through'. Not for him the ideologies, the logical systems, the statements of principle so characteristic of continental Europe.[7] Nor would he copy the Americans and adopt a written Constitution full of carefully premeditated checks and balances. The Englishman, in fact, was no intellectual.[8] But though he might display some indolence he would distinguish himself by his ruthless tenacity when crisis made this necessary. Thus if the Englishman would never shoot until he could see the whites of his enemy's eyes, he and not his hot-blooded opponent would be more likely to shoot straight.

These idealized self-images were not, of course, universal among the British at any period of their history. It may be doubted whether, for instance, the rural worker faced with the threat of enclosures, or the factory-hand in the early nineteenth century really experienced the self-restraint that they so often felt obliged to display.[9] Self-restraint was, nevertheless, a virtue which generation after generation of British children learned to admire, and the roster of popular British heroes is full of figures who knew how to deal calmly with crises and, in general, to keep their nerve.

The British, even in modern times, were ruled by a relatively small, intimate social and educational elite whose members tended to feel that they had a duty to govern their compatriots to the best of their ability. The majority of the British people generally seemed prepared to accept this and to show more deference towards their political and social elites than did their American counterparts.[10] They might sometimes laugh at their kings and dukes, their generals and cabinet ministers, and they might draw them with funny faces and call them rude names. But even the most outspoken expressions of popular discontent in Britain rarely included such obvious elements of political egalitarianism as a determination to get rid of the monarchy, the system of hereditary (and often landed) peerages, or the entrenched position of the Anglican Church. Piecemeal reform, maybe; but a cry for outright abolition — hardly ever.[11] To this day, it would be an unusual Englishman (though not so unusual an American) who would suggest that, for instance, universities should offer courses to anyone wishing to attend or that political candidates should everywhere be chosen, not by selection committees but by open 'primary' elections. The British, but not the Americans, maintain official titles of respect and honour. It has even been said that at elections the British would normally vote for candidates whom they considered capable of looking after their public life for them, while the American voter was more inclined to cast his ballot for somebody whom he perceived as being the epitome of himself and his peers, someone with whose activities he could identify. 'The Conservatives are better suited to running the country,' said one working-class Tory after the 1959 election, 'they're gentlemen born, I think they're made for that sort of job!'[12] An American voter, on the other hand, surveying the Republican Dewey and the Democratic Truman in 1948, decided to cast his vote for the latter, because 'Harry Truman, running around and yipping and falling all over his feet — I had the feeling he could understand the kind of fixes I get into.'[13]

Not only were the British inclined to be more deferential towards their supposed superiors than the Americans; they were also more inclined to respect the privacy and institutional exclusiveness of their elites. The American visitor to Oxford or Cambridge was often surprised to discover that, as with many of London's more exclusive clubs, there were no names outside the various colleges; either you were already one of the initiated or else you did not need to know.[14] This commitment to the ideas of privacy and exclusiveness, like so many other elite values in Britain, could be found throughout the culture. Many British people liked, if possible, to live in a house completely detached from other buildings as though the modern grassy (or stony) equivalent of a moat could enable today's house to confer the privacy and exclusiveness of yesterday's castle. The people of twentieth-century Britain (the south-easterners above all) were a by-word for their reluctance to talk to strangers in buses or trains, and they could be offended if their newspaper was being read by the person sitting next to them. The Londoner (some of whose taxis had smoked windows) was less inclined than the New Yorker to fill in forms about himself or to talk frankly to pollsters or even to friends about his domestic life or his income. Nor (unlike Americans and most other people) would the Englishman generally put a return address on the outside of a letter.[15]

The press and, in modern times, the broadcasting media, were to some degree inclined to undermine the secretiveness and the exclusiveness within which the ruling elite would normally operate. Every now and then, they would make much of the fact that (Britain's strict libel laws, the Official Secrets Act, and the D-Notice System permitting), they had published some hitherto strictly-guarded piece of proscribed or 'secret' information. But the media tended to be in the hands of people who shared the values of the ruling elite; there was scarcely an editor or senior reporter in Fleet Street or the BBC whose cultural background did not correspond closely to that of the political leadership of the day — a contention that was less obviously true in the United States. As a result, the extent to which the British media would really be prepared to probe, prod, and expose the sayings and doing of those in positions of official leadership was more limited than in America, not by political or legal censorship so much as by the self-censorship arising out of commonly shared values. It is arguable, for instance, that Watergate could not have happened in Britain; partly (let us fondly imagine) because British elites would not do things like that; partly because, if they did, the facts would more probably have remained hidden because those in the know would have retained a silent group loyalty; but above all because British journalism lacked the investigative and muck-raking tradition that in the USA, was able to produce a Woodward and a Bernstein who, encouraged by a courageous editor and publisher, were prepared to take on the very apex of their country's pyramid of power.

Thus, the relatively homogeneous British ruling elite was normally able to work in comparatively uninvaded secrecy, exchanging information only with other selected members of the small and trusted circle. The majority of the population were informed (or maybe not even informed) that this or that policy had been implemented for reasons considered by those in leadership positions to be important, and it was not characteristic of the British to want to push things further.[16]

CONTROL OF AGGRESSION

Another manifestation of the self-restraint so characteristic of British culture is the concern displayed over the subject — or, more typically, the 'problem' — of aggression. Geoffrey

Gorer, in his book *Exploring English Character,*[17] suggests
that historically the English have in fact been a fairly violent
lot. However, for at least two centuries, the ability to control
aggressions has been a source of pride to the British. Britain
indeed, has been described as one of the most tolerant and
even gentle of societies, a place where people actually seemed
to like waiting patiently in queues, the receptive haven—
and probable neutralizer of political and social extremists. Modern Britain, in conspicuous contrast to the big
cities of North America, had unarmed police and no substantial gangsterism; in the major British cities, muggings
and street robbings were relatively rare.

The emphasis on the absence — or at least the determined
control — of aggression might have been (at least according
to Gorer) an expression of the awe with which the British
subconsciously regarded the strength of their own aggressive desires, as well as a convenient means of keeping in
check the presumably equally powerful aggressive desires
of others. The social formality and coolness that many have
attributed to the English is attributed by Gorer partly to this
assumption: better to seem unfriendly and un-neighbourly
than to run the risk of unleashing within (or towards) oneself
powerful feelings of aggression.

This argument, at least as summarized here, begs a lot of
questions. Do the English have more potential aggression
than other people, and if so, why? Do people, in any case,
contain natural reserves of aggression? And how can you be
sure, from the observation that English people seem to be
anxious to keep their aggression (and that of others) under
strict control that they really have (or think they have) not
less but more powerful aggressive impulses than people
in other societies? However, it is an argument that helps
to make comprehensible a great deal of evidence (from
Gorer and many others) that might otherwise be hard to
appraise.

In Gorer's discussion of marriage, for example, he reports
on the answers of his married respondents to a question about
their reactions if they discovered that their spouse was being
unfaithful. Only a small group claim that they would resort
to violence. On the contrary, the replies, he writes,

illustrate that aspect of English behaviour which is called 'civilized' by those who admire, and 'cold' or 'unemotional' by those who dislike it. A sense of fairness and a most lively conscience are, for the majority, far stronger than passion, either passionate love or passionate jealousy.

Gorer also has a chapter on law and order which documents the overwhelming English admiration for that symbol of the control of aggression, the police.[18] This attitude was in part of a form of moral self-congratulation, like the pride in being 'law-abiding'. The police, after all, not only protect you from the aggressions of others but also, by their very presence, help to keep in check the repercussions of your own aggressive impulses. To the British, there was often almost a direct equation of the force of law with the control of aggression. George Orwell even said in one of his essays that the majority of the British assumed that 'against the law' was a synonym for 'wrong'. Anything that is within the law, conversely, they tended to think of as 'right'. He gave a delicious example:[19]

During the worst of the London blitz the authorities tried to prevent the public from using the Tube stations as shelters. The people did not reply by storming the gates, they simply bought themselves penny-halfpenny tickets; they thus had legal status as passengers, and there was no thought of turning them out again.

This admiration for the institutions and guardians of the law is a further instance of the way in which the British were impressed by the need to keep things under control. Gorer cites a couple of trivial examples—the English love of pets[20] and of gardening, two activities that depend upon 'mastery', and also mentions the old imperial admiration for those who 'tamed' other continents. He might have written, too, of the attempts to 'conquer' the South Pole or Mount Everest, or to 'defeat' various ideologies or diseases. In each case, the tamed or mastered or defeated object was considered potentially aggressive, something to be controlled; it was as though one's own aggressions were imputed to an external object and that object were then subjugated by the paramount desire for control.

This seemed to correspond closely to the way many British parents would regard their children. The typical English view of the nature of children, writes Gorer,[21]

> is that the young child is inadequately human and that, unless the parents are careful and responsible, it will revert to, or stay in, a 'wild' or 'animal' state, aggressive, destructive, without proper respect of property or sense of shame. To transform the child into a proper human being, a good English man or woman, undesirable or retrogressive tendencies must be eradicated by appropriate punishment.

And what of toilet training, an activity generally taken to symbolize (for trainer and trained alike[22]) the control of aggression? Seventy-eight per cent of Gorer's respondents thought it would be worse for the child if toilet training began too late; only 22 per cent, that is, thought that the child could come to more harm if toilet training were begun too early. In general, a huge proportion of respondents felt that children should get more discipline (and that it should start earlier) than was generally the case. Finally, when Gorer asked 'If you were told that a small child. . . had done something really bad, what would you think the child had done?', no less than 86 per cent of respondents identified 'badness' with the expression of aggressive impulses.

This emphasis on the value of discipline (primarily as a means of controlling—and perhaps canalizing—the expression of aggressive impulses) is found again and again in the culture of the British. Early in 1967, an opinion poll revealed that the only recommendation of the Plowden Report on children in primary schools to be more criticized than approved (by 47 per cent to 41 per cent) was the abolition of corporal punishment. In 1970, ten years after the abolition of compulsory military conscription, the reason most frequently cited by those who wanted it reintroduced was that it would help to discipline Britain's young men. Jeremy Seabrook, in his book *City Close-Up*,[23] quotes Alan, the Blackburn caretaker, who says 'I'd like my kids to do two or three years in the Forces and learn a bit of discipline in that way. . . . Kids definitely don't have enough discipline these days.'

This desire to keep strong and aggressive feelings under

control could take many forms. Sometimes, the British would affect a certain docility or even laziness—a useful insurance policy against the possibility of getting into heated discussions or fights. Indeed, among the higher echelons of British society, a certain studied laziness—the appearance, at least, of casualness—was long a widely cultivated mannerism. This mannerism was often aped by other elements within British society and it could even create that impression of indifference noticed by de Gaulle.[24]

Another device was to appear aloof (though this could also surface as shyness). The visitor from France or Italy (but less often from, say, Sweden) could be amazed to discover that one could travel for hours with the same people in a railway compartment and not exchange a word. Gorer, while acknowledging that Northerners would often be more neighbourly than Southerners, sums up the typical relationship of the English to their neighbours as one of 'distant cordiality'.

Another manifestation of the restraint of aggressive impulses so prized by the British was their inclination to apply to even the most contentious circumstances the criterion of 'sportsmanship' or 'fairness'. Occasionally, it almost seemed to matter less who won—not only in games but even in political or economic or military struggles—so much as that the 'game' had been fairly played. If the sides had been unevenly matched, British sympathies (particularly if Britain herself were not directly involved) were likely to be on the side of the underdog. It was even said that the British sometimes seemed to *like* to lose games, or to win them only after a hard-fought contest, if only to show what gallant protagonists they could be. In the political and diplomatic spheres, the predilection would characteristically be for compromise—a solution admired by the pragmatic British as giving some justice to everybody but in the event, sometimes representing a betrayal of both sides in a vital argument. Rupert Wilkinson, in his book *The Prefects,* shows how the British reluctance to go for the jugular and the predisposition to give the other side the benefit of the doubt was a prime factor in the diplomatic disaster that led from Münich to the outbreak of world war II.[25]

In war itself, British commanders would often find sporting metaphors and references coming readily to their lips
as ways of exhorting their troops or of explaining their
actions. Montgomery, for instance, wrote of 'hitting Rommel
for six' or 'knocking the enemy out with a "left hook".'[26]
The courtesy was not infrequently reciprocated by the sporting world. 'England Repulse German Attack' was a newspaper headline referring not to war but to football, while
cricket tours were talked about as 'campaigns'. The *Sunday
Times* profile on the English cricket captain, Len Hutton
(16 August 1953), said that 'he has the makings of a splendid
general, by temperament more a Montgomery than a
Rommel'.

The English language as written by the British may have
been full of the metaphors of sport and battle. But as spoken,
British English—particularly elite British English—was
interspersed with euphemisms and prevarications enabling
the speaker to avoid the expression of strong feelings. If the
Englishman wanted to disagree with somebody—particularly when on his best behaviour in front of others—he would
often begin by saying something like 'I may be wrong, but. . .'
or 'There is just one thing in all that you have been saying
that worries me a little. . .' If he was well brought up he would
tend to be effusive with his apologies, his 'I'd be awfully
grateful ifs' and his 'Thank you very much indeeds'. If he
wanted to enthuse about something, he would probably
resort to double negatives and say, with a smile of
pleasure, that something was 'not bad' or that so-and-so
had 'a not inconsiderable talent' or that he 'wouldn't mind'
doing such-and-such; Margaret Mead noted that, in Britain,
directions were often given with the postscript 'you can't
miss it'.[27]

The public gentleness of the British, their apparent indolence and aloofness, their sense of 'sportsmanship' and
fair play, their predilection for compromise, their disinclina-
tion to express strong feelings—all this might simply mask
the fact that they really did not have anything much to get
worked up about, or that they were intellectually lazy and
emotionally insensitive. After all, British society did generally seem to run more smoothly than most, the political system

did have a uniquely long run of acceptance and, materially, the British were able to enjoy a standard of living substantially higher than that of most other people.

However, there are deeper reasons why these qualities were characteristic of the people of Britain. In order to identify these reasons, it is necessary to look further, as was done in the investigation of traditional American values in Chapter 2, at the mythologization of historical experience and at some of the traditional institutions of socialization in Britain.

INSULARITY

Great Britain is a long, narrow island stretching off the top left-hand corner of the map of Europe, at the 'edge of the earth' as England's Latin-derived names have sometimes been taken to suggest. With its temperate climate and (except in the far north and west) its gentle topography, Britain often seemed to visitors from abroad to nurture an atmosphere of moderation and of independence from extremes of belief and behaviour. On the other hand, the people of Britain had always been inclined to look somewhat superciliously at the supposedly immoderate thoughts and actions of their continental neighbours, preferring to treat the narrow stretch of water between them as a major psychological barrier. Nothing in modern history, not even the advent of almost universally available television or jet travel, or Britain's eventual membership of the European Common Market seriously dented this insularity. On the contrary, it was frequently reinforced. 'Fog in Channel' read the apocryphal headline, 'Continent Isolated'. Listerine, the mouthwash people, ran an advertisement congratulating their British clientele on their discriminating taste (and excellent breath); 'everyone has got the message', ran the text in the Tube stations, 'except maybe that guy standing next to you with the continental fumes'. Or, in the inelegant cliché of the British tourist, 'Wogs begin at Calais'.[28]

The inclination towards insularity dates back, no doubt, for as long as Britain was an island, into the misty reaches of pre-history. But insularity as a social value was strengthened by aspects of British history. The experience of repeated invasions for over a thousand years, from the Romans to the Normans, probably helped to induce British people to regard outsiders with distaste or suspicion, while the presence of a sea-coast within seventy miles of any spot in Britain may have helped to strengthen a conception of separate (and, in time, superior) national identity. By Tudor times, a sense of British nationhood had been firmly established and the attitude to continental Europe was now inclined to be not so much fearful as condescending. Official policy was usually to maintain a balance of power on the Continent so as to free England from worries and threats from that quarter, while popular stereotypes of foreigners took on something of the belittling quality that was maintained into the twentieth century. In their disregard or disdain for continental Europe, people in Tudor England may have displayed the narrower aspects of their insularity. However, they also seemed determined to make a virtue of their physical and psychological insularity and to show the land-locked continental Europeans just how freely they could expand their interests into other parts of the globe.

Another indication of the independence of Tudor Britain from the thinking of much of continental Europe was England's rather special brand of Protestant Reformation. The motives that underlay the process by which England left the Roman Church and eventually became reconciled to the Lutheran theology and the temperate atmosphere of Anglicanism are numerous and complex. The desire—or new-found capacity—to assert national independence was but one among many. But the Protestant faith (with its refusal to accept the authority of a foreign religious leader, its scepticism regarding metaphysical beliefs or ritualistic practices, and its emphasis on the opportunities afforded to the individual for the performance of good works and, eventually, for the achievement of heavenly salvation) and the way in which it was adopted in England were to play an important part in moulding the social values of the British people in later ages. For instance, Anglicanism was avowedly a *via media*, a compromise (by which England, unlike France, avoided a period of bloody religious wars) between the extreme demands of Puritanism and Catholicism. This capacity to avoid a major ideological or even military collision by means of a practical compromise was one by which, centuries later, the people of Britain would still be characterized.

The insularity of the British led them to concentrate more than most societies on their nautical skills. British ships and British sailors developed a status that could only be achieved in an island or a peninsula, and their great heroes included people like Sir Francis Drake and Sir Walter Raleigh, men whose principal claim to fame, to their own generation and to those who mythologized them later, lay in their skills as fighters, conquerors, explorers, and economic expanders— at sea.

By the late eighteenth century, when Britain was well embarked upon the extraordinarily wrenching social and economic process that historians call the Industrial Revolution, her dependence upon ships and the men who sailed them grew more intense. Her economy largely depended on the 'mercantilist system' whereby Britain's newly-acquired colonies and client states around the world had to do virtually all their trade through the 'mother country'—much to the economic benefit of the latter. With heavy industrialization, the rapid growth of towns and cities, and the spectacular rise in population, this system became all the more necessary for Britain and all the more oppressive for some of the colonies overseas. A British (that is, combined English and Welsh) population of between four and five million people in 1600 or something like six million by 1700 could only survive if there were substantial imports of food and raw materials from abroad; already by Stuart times Britain could not easily have been self-supporting even had her leaders wanted this. By 1800, with a population of eleven million, a self-supporting economy would have been absolutely out of the question. Britain may have led the world as a manufacturing nation, but by now she was no longer able to provide for the more basic needs of her increasingly urbanized and rapidly expanding population (which was to rise to twenty-two million by 1850, and thirty-eight million by 1900). She needed to make colossal imports. Hence, the heavy reliance of the British on their sea-power.

While the new industrialization was imposing its demands, Britain faced a number of external threats. For one thing, the mercantilist system was being challenged with a new intensity, primarily by the colonists in North America. The Treaty of Paris in 1763 had given the colonists something like a sense of military security, and some began to turn their attention to the economic inequities they suffered at the hands of the British. Those economic grievances, exacerbated by dramatic and often crass measures in London, led eventually to the independence of the United States of America. If American independence was a huge blow to British pride, to the British economy, and to the British belief in the invincibility of her armed forces, it was also an unmistakable indication that British sea-power was no longer in a state to guarantee the inviolability of British interests around the world.

The point was put even more forcefully at the turn of the eighteenth and nineteenth centuries. For almost two decades, with one short gap, Britain and France were at war. For a while the war took the form of an attempt by Napoleonic France to impose an effective blockade against Britain—a policy which, if successful, would have destroyed Britain's capacity to survive except on France's terms. In order to counter this policy, Britain was dependent for her very existence on her navy. British ships and sailors were at a premium. Shipboard life was often almost unbearable, and there were several mutinies, notably at Spithead and the Nore in 1797. Men were press-ganged onto the ships and even seized, after the most flimsy excuses, from American and other foreign vessels. On the other hand, wages on board ship were, if not princely, often better than on land, and if you happened to participate in (and survive) one of the great sea battles, you were left with no doubt that you had played your part in the most heroic and patriotic activity available to anybody in your position.

Sea-power, long an important component of the British self-image, became paramount at the turn of the nineteenth century. The various factors that we have been discussing—

industrialization (with its by-products of a great increase in population and urbanization), the threat to mercantilism, American independence, and the wars with France—all combined to give to the people of Britain even more strongly than before a sense that national survival depended upon their nautical skills. The greatest hero of the day was Admiral Nelson. Songs were written to the effect that 'our men' and 'our ships' had 'hearts of oak'. And, from that day to this, through tragedies (such as *Billy Budd*), comedies (*HMS Pinafore*), poems ('I must go down to the sea again. . .'), royal sailors, films, monuments (Nelson's Column at Trafalgar Square), the clichés and metaphors of daily life (keeping the office 'shipshape', not rocking the boat, all pulling together), nicknames (Jack Tar, Limey), and, above all, by sea songs and shanties ('Heave away', 'Tom Bowling', 'What shall we do with the drunken sailor?', and the rest), the myth of the great but grim days of British sea-power has been perpetuated. The Navy, wrote one of its most effusive advocates, the historian Arthur Bryant,[29]

> touched mystic chords in the English heart that went deeper than reason. The far sails of a frigate at sea, the sight of a sailor with tarry breeches and rolling gait in any inland town, and that chief of all the symbolic spectacles of England, the Grand Fleet lying at anchor in one of her white-fringed roadsteads, had for her people the power of a trumpet call.

Sea-power is an adjunct of insularity. Indeed, a ship is itself a sort of island. If Britain's dependence upon sea-power was derived in part from her geographical position and shape, the national values associated with insularity could be observed clearly enough, writ small as it were, on board ship.[30]

There was the self-image of being part of a (literally in each case) watertight community and the necessity of loyalty to the command structure—mutiny, like its national equivalent of treason, was normally considered the most heinous of crimes. There was the sense of pride in one's own supposed superiority to one's rivals and enemies. And there was the sense of freedom to spread one's influence over large tracts of the earth's surface—a freedom denied to individuals and nations locked in by land rather than liberated by the proximity of sea. Seaboard existence made indispensable a system of clearly understood and scrupulously obeyed (but often merely customary and implicit) rules, an efficient and respected system of enforcement, and a corresponding system of punishments for wrongdoers. There were hierarchies of power and authority, hierarchies that people on the lowest rungs might theoretically be able to climb but which tended in practice to be reflections of pre-existing status relationships. One had duties and responsibilities and also, under special and carefully defined circumstances, privileges; all three were to be discharged with the utmost solemnity. One's loyalties and responsibilities were to the group as a whole rather than to oneself or to one section of the crew. Opportunities for individual self-expression—certainly for genuine and unrestrained emotion—were rare on board ship and almost eliminated at times of crisis. Homosexuality was probably reasonably common on board ship but officially frowned on; emotional alliances and enmities were ubiquitous but officially ignored. 'Discipline' was a major virtue, something with which you tried to impress your superiors and a quality you tried to instil into yourself and your inferiors. Intellectuality or special expertise were less esteemed than practical versatility; the 'jack of all trades' was the most valued member of a crew. Even physical versatility was a major virtue—the person was admired who could drink a great deal one night and work hard the following day; the capacity to withstand the acute physical deprivations and irregularities of shipboard life was a quality that any successful sailor would have to be able to display. In general, you were admired for your adaptability and flexibility, your capacity to deal intelligently with any crisis as and when it arose.[31]

This catalogue of virtues is familiar and, as has been suggested, was by no means confined to life aboard ship. Rules and punishments, recognized command hierarchies, duties and privileges, subordination of individual desires to group norms, no officially acknowledged sexuality, discipline, versatility. . . . Values such as these were also the characteristics of that repository, crucible, and generator of British elite values in the later nineteenth century and beyond — the British public school.[32] In many ways, life at a public school would resemble life at sea. The differences (notably in the distribution of such social factors as age, class, wealth and so on) are obvious, and the actual quality or style of life was far from the same in each type of institution. Nevertheless, the values associated with each were similar and derived in part from the fact that each society, the man o'war or the public school, was a closed system, a social island. The values in each case were those of insularity.

There were other British institutions that, like the ship or the school, embodied social values characteristic of the wider society. There were, for example, organized sports, notably the 'King of Games . . . the game which links an Empire'[33]: cricket. Virginia Cowles, in a book explaining the English to the Americans, wrote[34]:

> The reasons for the pre-eminence of cricket are typically English. It is a game with a history, having been first played in the seventeenth century. It is an aristocratic game, for it has always been played by the gentry; yet it is also played in every village and in the back streets of every town.

Sir Neville Cardus, in the Prelude to his book *Cricket*, summed up the atmosphere of this most English of games and, like Stanley Baldwin describing the typical Englishman, picked upon its sudden galvanization by crisis as its most characteristic quality:[35]

> The game . . . is a capricious blend of elements, static and dynamic, sensational and somnolent. You can never take your eyes away from a cricket match for fear of missing a crisis. For hours it will proceeed to a rhythm as lazy as the rhythm of an airless day. Then we stretch ourselves on deck-chairs and smoke our pipes and talk of a number of things — the old'uns insisting that in *their* time batsmen used to hit the ball. A sudden bad stroke, a good ball, a marvellous catch, and the crowd is awake; a bolt has been hurled into our midst from a clear sky. When cricket burns a dull slow fire it needs only a single swift wind of circumstance to set everything into a blaze that consumes nerves

and senses. In no other game do events of import hang so
bodefully on a single act. In no other game does one little
mistake lead to mischief so irreparable.

Many games have rules; cricket, the game traditionally
so beloved by the supposedly disciplined, hierarchical,
deferential and 'fair-minded' English, has 'Laws'. The laws
of cricket, writes Cardus,[36]

> tell of the English love of compromise between a partic-
> ular freedom and a general orderliness, or legality. . . .
> If everything else in this nation of ours were lost but
> cricket — her Constitution and the laws of Lord Halsbury
> — it would be possible to reconstruct from the theory
> and practice of cricket all the eternal Englishness which
> has gone to the establishment of that Constitution and the
> laws aforesaid.

An exaggeration no doubt, but one containing an important kernel of truth. The gentle anti-intellectualism of the
British also surfaces in the writing of Cardus:[37]

> Possibly our young cricketers ponder the theory of the
> game more than is good for them. Only think long enough
> about the mysteries of spin and swerve and you will dis-
> cover a dubious problem in every ball sent to you by the
> bowler. Ponder . . . the intricate adjustment and readjust-
> ment that goes on in the muscular organization as you
> alternately play forward and play back, and the thought
> of all the complications may overawe you to immobil-
> ity. . . . It is indeed significant . . . that in a period which
> is more attentive to the theory of cricket than ever it was,
> young players are said to be growing less audacious. The
> giants of old . . . did not strike you as men from whose eye
> shone the light of intellect; they were children of the sun
> and wind and grass.

In cricket, as on board a ship or at a Victorian public school,
it was the all-rounder who was most admired. Team loyalty
was never to be overtly questioned and nor were the decisions and orders of one's 'captain' (at cricket or on a ship) or
one's 'master' (in the classroom or again on a ship). In all three
institutions there were uniforms to enhance the dignity of
the little community of which one was part and to reduce

the visible individual differences between oneself and one's peers. All three were essentially single sex preserves, male institutions within which females tended to be regarded (more or less happily) as an absent distraction. And in all three, the group was encouraged to be intensely competitive, and yet at the same time, to be anxious to give its rivals a fair chance — a pair of aspirations whose inherent inconsistency is admirably illustrated by an incident in that perennially popular story about the fantasy life of a group of upper-crust English children, Peter Pan. Towards the end of the novel based on Barrie's play, Peter comes face to face with his arch-enemy, the evil Captain Hook:

> Peter was just about to stab the captain, when he saw that Hook was lower down the rock than he was. So he held out his hand to help his enemy up, that they might fight fair. And the ill-natured Hook bit him!
> Peter's hand was hurt, but his feelings were much more hurt. It was so very unfair of Hook. Though, of course, you wouldn't expect a man like that to behave nobly. Anyhow, Peter was so taken aback that he was quite helpless. And while he stared at his dreadful enemy, Hook clawed him twice with the iron claw.

Peter Pan obviously knew how you ought to behave towards an adversary. So did the cricketer Lindsay Hassett at the England v. Australia Test Match at the Kennington Oval in 1948 when Denis Compton slipped while running between the wickets. Hassett, who had already gathered the ball and could easily have run Compton out, held on to the ball until Compton had regained his posture so as not to take unfair advantage of his opponent.

There are other sports and other institutions in which the British values that we have been describing have manifested themselves over the years. Not just in cricket but in rugger, too, and (more recently) in soccer; not just in the navy, but in the army, too, and (more recently) in the air force. Anybody who knows the atmosphere within most of the older Oxford or Cambridge colleges, the clubs in and around Pall Mall in London, or the administrative levels of the Civil Service will be familiar with most of the values that we have been discussing. In fact, wherever males have gathered together—particularly when they have been members of the social elite—they have tended to build up around them institutions that depend for their atmosphere if not their very existence upon the sort of values discussed above, values essentially derived from the fact and the concept of Britain's insularity.

4 Anglo-American Mirror Images

THE PURITAN ETHIC IN BRITAIN

The traditional cultures of America and Britain have much in common. Strong traces of the Puritan ethic have long been present in Britain; the British, scarcely less than the Americans, have valued the concept of liberty (Britons, in the words of the song, not only 'rule the waves' but 'never, never, never shall be slaves'). Americans, for their part, have often displayed a streak of insularity (the 'isolationism' of traditional American foreign policy being an obvious expression of this) and espoused the person or policy that seemed to express the virtue of cool self-control at times of crisis. In order to assess the similarities and the dissimilarities between the two traditional cultures, it is necessary to examine each in the light of the other. What, first, has been the role of some of the traditional American values in British culture?

The 'Puritan ethic' is a convenient but imprecise expression for a loose combination of various different qualities and values. At its core it is a 'work ethic' or what one might better call an 'earn ethic'. It was suggested in Chapter 2 that the Puritan ethic was in part a response to the physical dangers and economic scarcities of seventeenth-century New England and that, theologically, it was an indirect derivation of the teachings of Calvin.

The nearest the British came to adopting Puritanism as an official theological position was at the end of the civil war in the mid-seventeenth century. Cromwellian England was hardly a haven for the values that the settlers in New England were then developing; indeed, historians have shown that at this period in English history, sexual and artistic expression for instance, were in some ways regarded in a less austere light than before. Nevertheless, there was always considerable receptivity in Britain to some aspects of the

Puritan ethic and this receptivity was by no means confined to the 1650s.

Central to the Puritan ethic was the idea that one should work hard and productively—and be seen to be doing so. Attitudes towards work, like the definition of the term, varied greatly from one period to another and between the various strata of society. This was true in Britain as in America. Bosses, for instance, would often try to instil into their workers the desirability of hard and productive work, a position about which workers themselves would often be, so to speak, less puritan and more cavalier.

In pre-industrial England, many adults were economically responsible primarily to themselves. Money was scarce but goods were fairly cheap and people would often feel little need to satisfy any but the more basic demands. Consequently, despite the long and hard hours that would often be worked and the appallingly restricted financial and material rewards of many jobs in sixteenth-, seventeenth- and eighteenth-century Britain, it is remarkable how often and with what impunity and guiltlessness people would take time off from their work. For a start, every Monday ('Saint Monday') was widely recognized as a more or less legitimate holiday.[1] In late medieval and early modern England, there were in addition between thirty-five and fifty official holidays (many of them 'holy days')—in addition to Sundays—every year.[2] And there is a lot of evidence that substantial numbers of people took even more time off than this from their work. If you worked, you'd earn; if you took time off, you would earn less. People were often chided for taking time off from their work, and periodic grand pronouncements such as the Statute of Artificers of 1563 would imply official concern at this and try to do something about it. Nevertheless, in an age in which most people worked for themselves or for their own tight-knit little local family unit, there was precious little that the state or the society as a whole could easily do to imbue intransigent citizens with a belief in the virtue and sanctity of work or productivity as such. If you were a baker or joiner or shirtmaker and your work and productivity dropped off, your customers might have had to do with less new bread or furniture or shirts. But they could fairly easily do without these items for a while, or get them from someone else, or produce them (or substitutes) themselves.

With the coming of industrialization, however, and the urbanization and division of labour that accompanied it, this situation changed drastically. As the individual worker became a link in a lengthy chain, his own contribution, however menial and uncreative it may have been, became increasingly indispensable. As the bread or furniture or shirt became the end product of a longer and longer process, the pressure on each person taking part in that process intensified. If someone took time off from work, whole factories might be slowed down or even brought to a standstill. Consequently, greater pressure was placed on people than before to get a job and to work at it with total and unmitigated dedication. This was a stick and carrot operation. The stick was represented by the severest sanctions: if you did not work flat out in the post-industrial but pre-union days, you could literally be left penniless — a contingency that might have been just tolerable in the simple (and often communally-minded) agricultural economies of the farm and the village, but which, in the new industrial cities, was emphatically not. And the carrot? This took the form of an assurance that there was nobody so virtuous, so likely to receive the smile and blessings of his master and his God as the man (or woman or child) who worked long and hard. This grafting of a strong moral sanction onto the performance of hard work (reinforced with appropriate references to the Bible) was certainly present in pre-industrial Britain, but not until the Industrial Revolution did it become a widespread social value, commonly espoused — at least verbally — by workers and masters alike. In America, on the contrary, it was a major social value pre-dating industrialization by two centuries.

There had always been at least two clusters of attitudes to work; those held by people who had to do it and those held by people who did not. In neither Britain nor America would people obtain much moral gratification from labour that they found unpleasant, and which they had not chosen. To most workers in both societies at most periods, the work ethic was probably a myth to which they subscribed, if at all, as a means of keeping their employers at bay or perhaps for the sake of a crumb of psychological comfort in the midst of a life largely lacking in material or spiritual rewards. Nevertheless, invocations of the work ethic by working people in the seventeenth and eighteenth centuries were probably more common and more acceptable among Americans than among the British.

What were the attitudes of British and American elites towards the concept of work? American society has always been less obviously stratified than British, and its elites, therefore, harder to pinpoint. In the USA opportunities for social mobility were often believed to be more extensive than in Britain (see pp. 116-120), and a society that permits many people to raise their social station thereby places its leaders at best on a somewhat shaky pedestal. British society might never have been quite as stratified as myth would have it;[3] nevertheless, people tended to see substantial social mobility as more of an exception than a rule, the occasional product of chance rather than the rightful implementation of an agreed social philosophy. There was a further difference between the two societies. America had always presented to its socially ambitious a number of only roughly parallel ladders to success; you could marry up one ladder, educate your way up a second, and climb a third by your financial or political skills. While success on one ladder often implied or contributed to success on another, this was by no means as frequently the case as in Britain where the various ladders would often merge into a single social hierarchy.

These two differences—greater perceived social mobility and more status paths in America than in Britain—tended to reinforce slightly different attitudes to work among British and American elites. In America, your moral worth was partly indicated by your capacity to climb various ladders and to stay on as high a series of rungs as possible; if you let your grip slacken, if you allowed yourself to sink into a smug acceptance of your social status quo, there was a danger that you would be displaced by others. You had to work to raise or even maintain your status. Work of one sort or another thus became in itself an indicator of virtue. In contrast, there was a tendency for members of the relatively secure and homogeneous social elite in Britain to feel that they could live a leisured life and even afford to look upon the concept of 'work' as beneath them.[4]

If you were one of the more earnest members of the British upper classes, you might work very hard indeed or devote to your hobby the assiduous and untiring attention that the lower orders would supposedly be devoting to work. But 'work' itself you would probably not want to be seen to do. For work was what men (and at certain periods some women and children too) were forced to do, not something that anyone would normally do out of choice. If one was part of the regular work force, this was supposedly a product of one's economic and social dependence. Anyone who was economically and socially independent—or had more important things on his mind—would not, in theory at least, need to work.[5]

One way of managing to work without appearing to do so was to cultivate the *persona* of the 'amateur'. This word has at least three connotations. In the first, literal sense, an amateur does something because he loves it; the second sense is that of a person who does a job voluntarily and not for payment; and the third is of a person who lacks both the discipline and the training of the 'professional'. Today, we use the word loosely in all three senses and tend to think of, say, amateur painters or singers as people who paint or sing in an obviously enthusiastic but untrained fashion, people who are not good enough to be paid properly for what they do but whose inadequacies are counterbalanced by their love of the relevant activity.

In the past, the word 'amateur' was less ambiguous and generally had a positive and complimentary connotation. Take, for instance, the revealing world of sport—revealing because a society is often likely to display some of its fundamental attitudes through its leisure activities. Cricket, that quintessential English sport, was once dominated by amateurs (in all three senses) known as 'gentlemen'. Until as recently as 1950, it was still unthinkable to some that an England team should be captained by a professional,[6] and amateurs were still afforded courtesies, such as having their initials printed *before* their names on some score cards, that were denied the professionals or 'players'. From the early nineteenth century until 1962, there was even an annual 'Gentlemen v. Players' match held at Lord's, the Mecca of cricket. Virginia Cowles wrote that one respect in which cricket was so typically English was precisely the fact that it 'is one of the few games in which players of the highest class can still be amateurs'.[7]

This emphasis on the virtues of the amateur gradually gave way, in cricket as elsewhere in British life, to streamlined professionalization. English sportsmen and their supporters came to learn the lesson that 'Nice Guys Finish Last'.[8] The Wimbledon tennis championships, long the preserve of amateur players, were opened in the later years of our period to the world's tennis professionals as well. From 1974, the word 'amateur' was written out of the Football Association legislation. But the traditional status of the amateur in British sports had reigned supreme for decades if not centuries; it was not prepared to die without a fight and it took some painful knocks as it gradually became outmoded. In an amusing footnote to an *Encounter* article on Britain's amateur tradition Dwight MacDonald wrote in 1956:

> The old-style British athletes were appalled by the fact that competitors from upstart regions like Australia and America actually trained for an athletic contest, sometimes going so far as to make a study of technique; the shock was not lessened by the fact that the upstarts usually won.

It was no longer possible, evidently, to work without appearing to do so. The attitude of the British to work was, at last, almost indistinguishable from that of the Americans.

Historically, a further difference between the traditional social values of Britain and America—one related to their respective approaches to work—is the attitude towards money. In colonial America, one's material prosperity was a proof of one's virtue. The early settlers, it has been said facetiously, came to America to do good and stayed to do well. Money came to be one of the chief criteria of social

status and many of the popular myths that sprang up concerned the occasional spectacular acquisitions—and losses—
of private fortunes. In Britain, particularly in the upper
reaches of society, where wealth was more likely to have been
inherited than in America and where the cult of the amateur
was so strong, it would often be assumed that you did not
need to get paid for whatever work you did. Indeed, a
member of the British elite could even consider the very
mention of money (though not its possession, in the form of
land and property) as something distasteful. 'Pursuits that
were unremunerative—classical study, voluntary service as
a magistrate—conferred prestige by the very token that they
were unremunerative', says Rupert Wilkinson on the subject.[9]
And Simon Raven, discussing the ways in which British
social values were derived from a reading—often a misread-
ing—of Ancient Greece, writes of the English gentleman
and of his putative Greek predecessor:[10]

> If he was reduced to earning his living, that was his mis-
> fortune and he was to be pitied: even so he must not sell
> himself sexually or politically, engage in the meaner forms
> (that is, practically any form) of commerce, and on
> no account must he work with his hands. . . . Basically,
> the rule was that no free citizen might engage himself to
> any enterprise in order to make a monetary profit.

Here, as elsewhere, the difference between British and
American cultures is less marked now than formerly. In
modern America, the actual presence of money is minimized
and sometimes avoided altogether by the ubiquitous use of
credit cards, while in Britain many hitherto amateur and
unpaid spheres of work (particularly in the social services)
nowadays recruit and pay trained professionals. But it was
never thought as distasteful in America as it still widely is
in Britain to discuss openly the size of another person's (or
even one's own) income or bank account, to haggle over a
fee, or to display one's riches through the acquisition of
conspicuously expensive goods. Americans visiting Britain
have sometimes noticed what they understand to be a dis-
inclination by the British to accept or talk about money at
all, unless they actually have to. Stan Cohen, a New Yorker

who visited London for the first time in 1970, described on a BBC radio programme how a clothing salesman had seemed almost reluctant to sell him a jacket unless he was absolutely sure that it was just the jacket he wanted. 'In a men's clothing store in the United States,' said Cohen, 'they would sell you a one-sleeved coat—if they could.' Allowing for the euphoria of being on holiday abroad, there is clearly some truth in the contrast of attitudes towards which this story points. In the same broadcast, Cohen talked about his London hotel (one of the best) and 'the embarrassment of the person who serves you your food or the bellhop at receiving a tip'. He contrasted this to the American situation where 'if you're a little slow going into your pocket, there's not the slightest suggestion on the part of the bellman or the service person of walking out of the room.'[11]

Another puritan virtue closely allied to work was that of competitiveness. This is by no means a quality that the British lacked ('if you want to get ahead, get a hat', said the advertisements). However, it has sometimes taken a different form on the two sides of the Atlantic. The competitiveness derived from early American Puritanism was essentially that of individual against individual. Your loyalties and your responsibilities were to yourself (and, perhaps, your immediate dependants). In the field of international sport, for instance, America produced a series of champions in fields emphasizing the virtues of individual competitiveness —notably tennis, athletics and boxing; but in internationally recognized team games dependent upon carefully groomed group discipline and loyalties (as opposed to strictly home-grown sports like baseball or American football) America was often conspicuously less successful.

Competitiveness in British culture, on the other hand, was traditionally more likely to be on behalf of one's group —one's ship, one's school house, one's team, or one's nation —against another. (For many years, British radio sponsored a weekly programme, *Let the People Sing*, in which choral groups from around the world competed with one another. It is hard to imagine a weekly choral competition gripping the attention of listeners in America, though American FM radio might well have contemplated a series of solo contests.)

This contrast between an individual and a communal orientation is one that crops up in other aspects of the two cultures as well. Take, for example, another offshoot of the American Puritan ethic, self-reliance. Self-reliance was a traditional British value, too, widely adopted by the ruling elites and often by those lower down the social hierarchy; but it was frequently allied to a concept of service to those less fortunate than oneself. Not the individual but the wider society was expected to be self-reliant. The 'Tory Democracy' of Disraeli, for instance, was essentially a hands-across-the-classes alliance between the traditional pillars of British society (which were quite happily able to thrive with a fillip from no one but themselves) and those in the lower strata of society in return for whose respect and political loyalty they would effect various social reforms.[12] A similar spirit would often pervade the English public schools. J. D. R. McConnell, in his book *Eton — How It Works*, wrote;[13]

> The crux of a young man's education and the most important single lesson he has to learn at school is this: that when you receive most then you must give most, that when you reach the top position in your society, be it house, firm, department or area, then is the moment when the emphasis on service must be greatest.

There are other traditional American values derived from the Puritan ethic that could be discussed in a British context. There was the tendency towards localism, the intense moralism, the sense of the dynamism of life, of change, progress, growth, improvement. There were also the virtues of frugality, thrift, chastity, charity and respect for one's elders. All these values were to be found in Britain too, as in most societies. In so far as people in Britain suffered from the inadequate fulfilment of their material needs, they too, like people in economically less developed societies all over the world, would praise the resource-conserving values such as frugality. And, partly because the British, like the Americans, tended to be conforming (and often believing) Christians, they too lived in a culture imbued with a strong streak of moralism. When roads were poor, telecommunications unknown, and the population relatively sparse, the British, like the Americans, would concentrate much of their moral pride not on their nation but on their locality.

But there were differences and these tended to revolve, again, around the orientation to oneself (in the American case) or to one's group (in the British). The frugality, the moralism, the localism and the rest were, in American culture, values that were primarily inspirations for individual behaviour—it was the individual who was supposed to act frugally, to apply moral judgements, to identify himself or herself by local affiliations and loyalties. In the British case, these values would commonly be embraced by and on behalf of one's social grouping.

EQUALITY AND LIBERTY IN BRITAIN

There is one Mrs Macauley in this town, a great republican. I came to her one day and said I was quite a convert to her republican system, and thought mankind all upon a footing; and I begged that her footman might be allowed to dine with me. She has never liked me since. Dr Johnson

Egalitarianism ... is a creed which, at its unacknowledged heart, resents the diversity of talents and abilities in man. ... The victory of egalitarianism ... would be a basic fundamental defeat for political liberty. Ronald Butt (article in *The Times*, 12 July 1974)

The British, with their feudal past and relatively stratified society, were traditionally less devoted to the idea of equality than the Americans. Despite early egalitarians such as the Levellers or such twentieth-century developments as universal adult suffrage or the welfare state, there was rarely in Britain any really passionate or widespread belief in equality. Tom Paine, one of the few radical egalitarians produced by England, was far more influential in France and in his adopted America than in Britain. 'Men are made by nature unequal', wrote the nineteenth-century historian J. A. Froude: 'It is vain, therefore, to treat them as if they were all equal.' In our own century, Aldous Huxley said: 'That all men are equal is a proposition to which, at ordinary times, no sane individual has ever given his assent.' To the American, equality inhered in the condition of human life; to the Englishman, equality was achieved either in an intolerably

bloody state of nature which men made contracts to avoid
or else in the grave. Thomas Hood wrote (in his 'Ode to Rae
Wilson' :

> One place there is—beneath the buried sod,
> Where all mankind are equalized by death. . .

Or, in the words of the sporting Lord George Bentinck, all
men are equal—on the turf or under it.

Equality can mean several different things: in Chapter 2
the distinction was drawn between equality of opportunity
and equality of condition. These two types of equality could
lead in diametrically opposite directions, but American
culture tended to espouse both. In Britain, however, the
path to the door of equality was less enthusistically trodden.

One of the most telling indications of a society's devotion
to the concept of equality is in the provisions it makes for
social mobility. In particular, the opportunities that people
have—or believe they have—for rising (and falling) in social
status provide an indication of the value their society bestows
upon the concept of equality of opportunity. Much work
has been done on social mobility in the United States, rather
less in Britain, and very little of a comparative nature.[14]
The evidence tends to suggest that in the USA it has almost
universally been believed that opportunities for some mobility exist and that any American can, with effort, climb up
the social ladder a little—but might also, if he or she is not
careful, fall back somewhat compared with the other climbers.
Mobility has generally been thought to be towards the middle rungs, and this remains true in our own time. 'The process of "Middle-class-ification",' writes E. C. Banfield,[15] 'is
undoubtedly continuing at an accelerating rate and will in
a few decades have reduced the working class to a very small
proportion of the whole population.' Banfield's prediction
may be open to serious reservations, but there is little question that, at least when asked to assign themselves to a class,
Americans have often been strongly inclined to place themselves in the 'middle' class (though the figures will vary from
one period to another and according to such factors as the
number of class categories respondents are offered).

In Britain, opportunities for social mobility were never

thought to be as high as in America. Even in modern times, despite changes that seemed to democratize many aspects of Britain and despite the increasingly wide distribution of identical and mass-produced material comforts, many prestige institutions were still run in the 1970s by the children of the sort of people who had run them a generation before. This may have been partly because of inertia on the part of those who were excluded; it has been argued, for instance, that the sons and daughters of working-class parents, particularly in the north of England, did not generally want to go to university or to enter the professions. More important was the fact that British elites still tended to be fairly restrictive in their recruitment policies. Whatever the reasons, most people still considered genuine and widespread social mobility to be strictly limited in Britain a generation after the introduction of the welfare state.[16]

Even where children from working-class homes did climb up the affluence ladder or the job-prestige ladder, it was often true—as it generally was not in the United States— that they would cling to aspects of the culture of the class or status group from which they had risen rather than try to adopt wholeheartedly that of the social grouping into whose ranks they might otherwise have been moving. Donald Nicholl, a working-class boy from Yorkshire who became a university professor, has written:[17]

> My first term at Oxford I was really miserable, but for a long time I never understood why. And then I realized that for weeks I had not heard a single warm voice; the voices around me were all false, as though whatever warm impulses the people may have had got congealed on thin hard-frozen vocal chords. And I longed for our back-to-back home, with its warm fire, the dog on the hearth and neighbours coming in who called me 'luv' and 'lad' and not that ridiculous 'sir'.

Peter Willmott's adolescent boys of East London were not sure that they wanted to rise through the social ranks at all even if they had the opportunity. 'I don't want promotion,' says one, 'I just want to stay ordinary.' And another adds, 'Plumber's mate now, expect to be a plumber, and if I could choose, that's what I'd like to be.'[18] This attitude was well evoked in the famous David Frost sketch in which three British men, a very tall one, a middle-sized one, and a short one, stood in a line. The tall one looked at the middle-sized one and said 'I look down on him because I am upper class'; the medium one looked at the tall one and said 'I look up to him because he is upper class but' — looking at the short one — 'down on him because he is lower class'; and the short one said 'I know my place.' One of the many reasons why a Labour Party developed in Britain but not in the USA was that the British worker was often proud to identify himself with the group or class of workers of which he was part and was prepared to help to build up a political party ostensibly devoted to its interests, while the American worker was more likely to try to identify with people on the next rung up the social ladder.[19]

This approach contrasts with American attitudes towards mobility, about which David Riesman used an instructive analogy from the world of sport:[20]

> As tennis or golf players keep looking for those whose game is just a little better than theirs — but a game to which they can lift themselves by effort — so this mobility allows us to look for those whose life is in significant respects just a little better but whose 'lifemanship' is still within our potential grasp.

Riesman, talking about the middle class, summarized the major transatlantic differences by suggesting[21] that

> whereas in England and Europe generally [a] person is constantly confronted with aristocratic standards and behavior, to which to aspire or against which to hold firm, the American middle class is more ambiguously challenged by life-styles and taste-gradients developed by its own experimental and traditional wings.

American parents would characteristically prepare their child for a sort of race; they would perceive their job as being, primarily, to enable their child to get as far up the various social ladders as possible.[22] British parents, by contrast, would be more inclined to inculcate into their child the idea that his or her main aim in life was to fill their shoes. The American child would more probably expect to be admired

in proportion as he or she had travelled up the various social
ladders. One of Riesman's faces in the crowd is a bright
young graduate student with a lower-middle-class background. He is asked 'Do you expect to attain a position
which, compared with that your father holds, or has held,
is higher, lower, about the same, or don't you know?' His
sanguine and revealing answer is 'Well, I'm not sure whether
you mean in terms of service to mankind or salary or deference granted, etcetera—but anyway, higher.' And we can
safely assume that his father would have been proud of the
boy's answer. A British father, of about the same period,
Mr Jones of Bethnal Green, was full of critical resentment
towards Harry who has 'got his own business at Fulham and
has bought a big house and is too busy with his business to
bother about us'.[23]

More importance was attached in America than in Britain
to 'keeping up with the Joneses'. The USA was a society of
many graded classes and status groups and considerable
apparent freedom to move from one to another. In so flexible
a social system, people would pay careful attention to the
outward symbols of class and status and learn which symbols
would most enhance their own status.[24] In British society,
with its relatively clear class lines, people would typically
find these symbols less worthy of note. The British, whose
values tended to be oriented towards groups, might have
been more class conscious; but the Americans were more
inclined to be observant of the outward signs of personal
status.

Thus, whatever the genuine opportunities for social
mobility might have been in Britain, many people, particularly those lower down the ladder to start with, tended to
perceive them as strictly limited and to assume that it would
in any case have been somehow inappropriate to try to take
much advantage of them. In the United States, on the con
trary, people often felt that there were *more* mobility opportunities than actually existed and that one should try to
better oneself by means of them.

Similar differences emerge if one contrasts the attitudes
of the Americans and the British with those just *below* them
on the various social ladders. In both cultures, there was

considerable status insecurity, and nowhere more so than among the small and challenged bourgeoisie, the members of the traditional lower middle class. These people—the small shopkeeper, the artisan—were less and less valued as society depended increasingly upon mass production and mass distribution; and they lacked the skills (rapidly being learned by their children and even by the children of unskilled manual workers) that *were* in demand in an increasingly automated consumption-and-service-oriented economic system. In the United States, these status insecurities could take strident forms. Much unjust and inhumane behaviour in modern American history was in part the product of the fears of one group of people (the poor whites in the south, the Poles or the Irish in the big cities of the north-east) when they felt threatened by groups just below them. If you lived in a society where you might easily move up the socio-economic ladder, the groups a rung or two lower down might as easily climb up and displace you. In Britain, on the other hand, despite some white working-class resentment against non-white immigrants in recent times or occasional grumblings by members of the middle-class professions at a high pay award to unionized manual workers, the more common assumption was that everybody in society had his place. Just as you would not try to displace the group above you, you would not be seriously in danger of displacement by those below. This attitude was a modern variation on the feudal assumption that everybody had a more or less immutable place in society and that the best that anyone could expect to do—whether king, lord, yeoman or serf—was to know his place and to fulfil the demands that it imposed.

Thus, while American culture regarded equality of opportunity—at least of social opportunity—as a major virtue, in Britain this fundamental type of equality was afforded far less approval or even attention. Much the same would be true of the other types of equality of opportunity—economic, cultural, and political—that were mentioned in Chapter 2.

It would be true, too, of that other type of equality—equality of condition—and of the relationship of both with the concept of liberty. In the American tradition, equality of

opportunity and of condition were both intricately bound
up with the idea of liberty. In Britain the two concepts were
more easily separated. Indeed, they were often treated as
polar opposites. There were those, as we have seen, who
dismissed equality as practically unattainable and even
morally undesirable. Liberty, however, was long accorded
a central place among British social values.[25] It was not
always carefully defined as to either meaning or applicability, nor was it generally given explicit legal or constitutional
guarantees. But its importance was rarely in doubt.

Liberty was particularly valued if not taken to excess.
'None can love freedom heartily but good men,' wrote
Milton; 'the rest love not freedom, but licence.' And Burke,
over a century later, thought that liberty without wisdom
and virtue was 'the greatest of all possible evils; for it is folly,
vice, and madness, without tuition or restraint'. The only
liberty that he applauded was 'a liberty connected with
order'. His compatriot George Bernard Shaw made a similar
point with his observation that 'Liberty means responsibility. That is why most men dread it.'[26]

In their determination not to let freedom be taken to
excess, the British were sometimes prepared to gainsay
certain liberties that were sacrosanct in America. The first
of President Franklin D. Roosevelt's 'Four Freedoms', freedom of speech (see p. 67), was guaranteed by the First Amendment of the US Constitution but was not generally considered
a basic principle in Britain. British laws concerning libel
and official secrets, for example, were more restrictive of
free speech and publication than their American counterparts and yet were rarely challenged. Nor did the British
attach fundamental importance to the second of Roosevelt's
'Four Freedoms', religious liberty and the separation of
church and state, though this too, was guaranteed in America
by the First Amendment.

On the other hand, the two 'negative' freedoms listed by
Roosevelt, freedom from want and from fear, corresponded
more closely to themes in the British tradition. British culture has been inclined to regard liberty as a negative virtue,
a desirable lack of restriction. Hobbes called liberty 'the
absence of external impediments: which impediments may

oft take away part of a man's power to do what he would' and
John Stuart Mill, in his essay *On Liberty*, considered that the
only freedom which deserves the name 'is that of pursuing
our own good in our own way, so long as we do not attempt
to deprive others of theirs or impede their efforts to obtain
it'. Liberty implies not only the right but also the opportunity to make choices between real alternatives. If you are
seriously lacking in nourishment or in adequate clothing or
warmth, or if your options are restricted by the intrusion of
an external force, you can hardly be said to be free to choose
between such alternative positive courses of action as might
subsequently present themselves to you.[27]

The British record in providing people with the basic
necessities of life from which to make their positive choices
is a patchy one. Until the nineteenth century, few governments considered it a part of their duty to ensure that everybody had adequate food and shelter;[28] the most they would
normally do would be to lay down regulations about working
conditions or wages, or set up prisons and poor-houses for
those whose destitution had become personally and socially
intolerable. It is true that after the dissolution of the monastaries had robbed the poor and needy of their major source
of free provisions, an enlightened poor-law system had
evolved in Elizabethan England and was administered with
efficiency and compassion by the early Stuarts, but the civil
war and Restoration saw an erosion of these policies. By the
beginning of the eighteenth century, while Vanbrugh and
Capability Brown were creating the spacious glories of
Blenheim Palace, institutions like Bridewell were packing
together, in the most dire and abject conditions, and generally undifferentiated by age, sex, or condition of physical or
mental health, thousands of impoverished wretches with
whom the society could not otherwise cope. During the tense
and repressive period of the wars with France at the turn of
the eighteenth and nineteenth centuries, the 'Speenhamland' system left it to local JPs to award poor relief on a scale
tied to the fluctuating price of bread, but the Poor Law
Amendment Act of 1834 brought poor relief back under the
supervision of the national government where it has stayed
ever since. In the heyday of Victorian 'voluntarism' and

'self-help', several bills were passed which, while they did not give food or shelter to people who did not have them, raised the standard of these basic commodities for those who did. But it was not until the National Insurance Act of 1911 and the nationalized health and welfare services of the Attlee government after world war II that most people in Britain were guaranteed the basic physical necessities of life. Whatever the inadequacies of the laws and their administration, whatever the tricks played on some by the caprices of the national economy, the people of Britain, progressively after about the 1870s and substantially by the mid-twentieth century, were guaranteed a degree of 'freedom from want' that compared well with most other societies.

Roosevelt's fourth freedom was 'freedom from fear' and here, too, British culture was not unresponsive. The fear of arrest by the powers of the state—often for transparently political reasons—has besmirched the quality of life in many societies, and in modern times the interests of the state and the means available to it for promoting them have been greatly extended. Britain and America, even in recent decades, have seen their share of this sort of activity; witness the treatment occasionally meted out to 'reds' and blacks in America, for instance, or to members (or alleged sympathizers) of the Provisional IRA in Britain. But fear of the arbitrary power of the state has not generally been as common or as justified in these two societies as elsewhere. It is a fear from which most people in America and Britain have usually considered that they can take their freedom for granted.

In the USA, a fear that did bubble up to the surface from time to time in different guises was that of 'tyranny' or 'dictatorship'. America's earliest white settlers became mythologized by later generations partly on account of their resistance to theological authoritarianism, and the Founding Fathers earned their capital Fs partly for having fought a successful war against political tyranny. The Declaration of Independence was expressly aimed at King George III for 'having in direct object the establishment of an absolute Tyranny over these States'. In 1787, when the new federal constitution was being worked out at Philadelphia, debate was often peppered with references to the autocratic form of government so recently shaken off. And throughout subsequent American history, any president who conspicuously asserted or augmented his executive powers was almost automatically accused by his critics of trying to build up a personal dictatorship.

Tyranny was not generally a major fear of the people of Britain. Indeed, on occasion (for example, under Cromwell) many even appeared to court it, and the *symbol* if not the reality of an autocratic monarch continued to appeal to the British throughout much of modern history.

If one type of fear seemed particularly characteristic of the British, it was that of being dominated not by a single powerful and autocratic ruler but by foreigners. 'The rhetoric of liberty,' wrote E. P. Thompson,[29] 'meant . . . first of all, of course, freedom from foreign domination.' The British had liberty and foreigners did not. The fear of domination by foreigners, consequently, was tantamount in many minds to a fear of losing one's freedom. This theme was particularly powerful in times of war and was given a new lease of life in the 1940s in the speeches of Winston Churchill and the writings of people like the historian Arthur Bryant (who wrote about what he called 'Freedom's Own Island'). But it far antedates Sir Arthur Bryant. In June 1850, Lord Palmerston, the 'personification of England',[30] defended the dubious claims of Don Pacifico—a British subject because he had been born in Gibraltar—against the government of Greece, and ended a passionate parliamentary speech with the words:

> As the Roman, in days of old, held himself free from indignity, when he could say 'Civis Romanus Sum', so also a British subject, in whatever land he may be, shall feel confident that the watchful eye and the strong arm of England will protect him against injustice and wrong.

Historically, British elites often tended to gravitate towards two clusters of attitudes towards foreigners. Either the foreigners would be regarded as rivals and therefore enemies (and probably white)—in which case they had to be outwitted or defeated. Or they were malleable (and often enough non-white)—in which case their land could probably be colonized. Either way the British were reluctant to familiarize themselves with the languages, styles of food and clothing, or social customs of the foreigners with whom they came into contact. Instead, they would characteristically resort to the lazy way out and simply think of foreigners as poor benighted people who did not enjoy the benefits — and in particular, the freedom — that were the very birthright of the British.

Behind the bombast and the condescension and, above all, the sheer ignorance, however, there could often lurk a streak of fear. The unknown can easily be frightening, particularly if it is something which you refuse to try to understand except in the most rudimentary way while, at the same time, you bring yourself into constantly renewed contact with it. This fear of the superficially familiar but fundamentally unknown frequently lay at the heart of British perceptions of foreigners. The response was often to resort to military conquest and/or economic domination. These attitudes doubtless contributed to the attempt, in the days of Queen Elizabeth I, to play various European powers off against each other, and may still have been present in the ambivalence shown in our own day towards the European Economic Community. In between, there was the rise and fall of the British Empire which, while obviously not just the outcome of an irrational British phobia about foreigners, probably had this element among its contributory factors.

The phobia was not applied to all foreigners, and some, like William of Orange or the Hanoverian monarchs, were even welcomed as leaders. But the idea of involuntary subordination to the will of a foreign nation was peculiarly worrisome to the British. Perhaps this had something to do with long memories of the indignities supposedly suffered at the hands of the Roman, Saxon or Norman invaders — generations of English people were brought up to believe that the 'Norman yoke' was one of the most degrading impositions to which their ancestors had been subjected. It may possibly have resulted in part from a subconscious projection onto foreigners of British desire for aggressive conquest of others. Whatever the cause, this fear of domination, like much else in Britain, was often expressed in the

positive form of the determination of the British people to
retain their freedom.

Thus, British culture was more receptive to the idea of
liberty as a social value than to that of equality. Many British
egalitarians, indeed, would clothe their views in libertarian
language in order to obtain a more favourable hearing.
G. D. H. Cole, for instance, wrote a massive socialist tract[31]
in 1947 that was, in essence, a call for sympathetic support
of the Labour policies of the day. Although most of those
policies were designed to eliminate glaring social inequities,
egalitarian arguments rarely surfaced in Cole's thousand-
and-more pages. But he waxed eloquent about British ideas
of freedom, referred to them as 'the Englishman's idea of his
birthright', and considered that one should be prepared to
wage total war for freedom (but not for equality). 'In the
name of freedom', wrote Cole, 'it is necessary for us to get
Socialism, even if we have to take quite a number of high-
handed steps in order to get it.' The pronouncements of
political pamphleteers and popular philosophers in Britain
over the centuries appealed to similar sentiments. 'To all
real lovers of Liberty' read a broadsheet in the 1790s:

> My friends, you are oppressed and you know it. Lord
> Buckingham who died the other day had thirty thousand
> pounds yearly for setting his arse in the House of Lords
> and doing nother [*sic.*]. Liberty calls aloud, ye who will
> hear her voice, may you be free and happy. He who does
> not, let him starve and be damned. He who wishes well to
> the cause of liberty let him repair to Chapel Field at
> Five O'Clock this afternoon, to begin a glorious revolu-
> tion.

The inclination of the political left to cloak its egalitarianism in the guise of libertarianism is a further indication that
British culture was probably more receptive to the idea of
freedom than to that of equality. If you wanted to advocate
the latter, it seems that it was worth sounding as though you
were advocating the former.

This concealment of one value under the guise of another
suggests a further feature of the traditional culture of Britain.
This is its predilection for the implicit and the understood.
Sometimes, this could appear to take the form of deceptive-

ness; 'perfidious Albion' was the phrase used. More commonly, it expressed itself in the understatement, the euphemism, the double negative. American culture, with its written Constitution, its colourful profanities and its 'WRONG WAY' highway signs, was often more explicit and direct. If Americans wanted to advocate something they would be less inclined than their British counterparts to beat about the bush.

This was certainly true of American egalitarianism. Equality was more highly valued in American culture than in British, and although it had its opponents, it was a concept to which a direct appeal could usually be made with safety. Something of the same was true of the value of achievement. This presupposed a degree of equality of opportunity and was a quintessential part of American culture. In Britain, where equality was less valued, achievement held a less prominent place among the hierarchy of traditional values. While British culture might encourage you to strive to do your best within your particular sub-culture, it was commonly understood that the boundaries of your achievement would normally be drawn by the social sub-culture into which you had been born. Whether you were a member of the landed aristocracy, a young eighteenth-century spinner, or a nineteenth-century factory hand, you might try to do what were considered your proper tasks as proficiently as you knew how and some economic and social advance might even result. However, the possibility of achievement in the rags-to-riches or log cabin to White House sense was never part of the picture of society that people in Britain generally drew for themselves. Indeed, the real climber, the person who *had* transcended the restrictions of his own sub-culture and risen through the social ranks as a result of his own achievements was likely, in Britain, to be not so much revered as laughed at or scorned. Self-help was all very well — so long as you 'knew your place'. It was surely overdoing things, and therefore worthy of lampoon, if you pushed yourself up from being 'an office boy to an attorney's firm' to being the 'Ruler of the Queen's Navee'. In Britain, social stratification was at once more visible and more accepted than in America, and members of all strata tended to feel that they should keep to — and be loyal to — the social stratum or group of which they were part.

SELF-RESTRAINT IN AMERICA

Self-restraint, the lynch-pin of the traditional British value system, is a virtue to which Americans would also appeal, but with a number of differences. Traditional American culture was more heavily overladen with the bequest of Puritanism and more inclined to be moralistic. So Americans would tend to emphasize the virtue not only of emotional or physical self-restraint but above all of moral self-restraint. The myths of Britain and America alike would spotlight people who did not panic or lose their capacity for cool judgement however great the provocation. 'Unflappability' was a virtue in both cultures: George Washington and Abraham Lincoln, like King Arthur or Sir Francis Drake, were venerated for, among other qualities, their capacity to remain calm at times of crisis. But British mythology also included people such as Robin Hood, Henry VIII, Wellington, or that symbolic invention John Bull, who enjoyed various sensuous pleasures and expressed their enjoyment with gusto; Nelson's love-life or Churchill's brandy and cigars were part of the myths that grew up about them. On the other hand, the philanderings of 'Ben' Franklin or 'Tom' Jefferson were long ignored or excused or winked away while that epitome of American heroes, the cowboy, was often presented as spectacularly able to withstand the temptations to which ordinary mortals succumbed.[32] In Britain, when Disraeli heard that the elderly Lord Palmerston was said to have a mistress, his immediate reaction is alleged to have been 'Don't tell anyone or he'll sweep the country'; that was far from the attitude of the incumbent Republican leadership in America to the news of the sexual indiscretions of their Democratic rival Grover Cleveland.

Deference was a characteristically British expression of self-restraint — the feeling that people should display a distant respect for their putative superiors and try to derive their social values from their example. This attitude was far from unknown in America, too, but the differences between the two cultures were striking. At British soccer matches, for example, the crowd would accept that it was up to the referee to blow his whistle when, according to his own watch (and mathematics if there was injury time to be added) the game had to come to an end; at an American football game, there would generally be a huge clock, visible to everybody at the ground, which would be stopped if there were any injuries, and which would register — for everyone individually including the referee—the moment when the game was due to finish.[33] In America, revelations of official duplicity (in the Pentagon Papers or over Watergate, for instance) would be treated by many people as gloomy endorsements of what they had long suspected; similar revelations in Britain (even assuming that they would ever surface) would probably be received with almost universal shock or incredulity. Many Americans (but hardly any people in Britain) would find it hard to believe that bodies like the Arts Council or the University Grants Committee could receive money from the British Government but that no Government would interfere substantially with the use to which the money was put. My exam books at Cornell used to have printed on them a formal instruction the burden of which was that you weren't allowed to cheat — a rubric that suggested that the popular mistrust of authority in America might well have been reciprocated.

The differences in deference between the two cultures were also thus differences of trust.[34] Like so many other differences between the two cultures, this too related to the fact that British society was more obviously stratified than American. In Britain, it was generally thought to be easier than in the USA to assign people to specific social groups and to be confident that people would act according to the norms of the group of which they were part. Members of one social group could generally trust those of another to act in a way expected of them. In the USA, a socially more fluid society, it was harder to be certain of the exact identity and motives of others and, therefore, mutual trust was sometimes at a premium. Furthermore, American culture tended to attach greater value than British culture to the building of bridges between individuals rather than of moats between social groups. In America, consequently, personal inter-course would less often fall into patterns arising out of the habits of group deference and the maintenance of a polite distance, and would more frequently take the form of the search between individuals for themes of mutual interest.

British culture was also more secretive than American and would stress the rights of people to keep to themselves, to have their own rituals and secrets, to refrain from grant-ing access to their secrets to others. This, too, was related to the virtue of self-restraint which was taken in Britain to imply that you did not encroach upon the territory — including the psychic and social territory — of others. To Americans, self-restraint may have been a virtue, but greater value was normally attached to the right of the individual to have access to other people and to the facts about them. Journalists in America would be more prepared than their British counterparts to delve into, for instance, the financial and domestic problems of public figures. The exposé journalism inaugurated by Hearst and Pulitzer took a generation to cross the Atlantic, while the muck-raking tradition that descended from Lincoln Steffens and Ida Tarbell and people like Drew Pearson to the Watergate investigations of Bob Woodward and Carl Bernstein had no parallel in Britain. Individual privacy was inevitably breached by writers such as these — often in the name of the right of other individuals to know what was going on. In Britain, conversely, the secre-tiveness of the elite group would not infrequently enhance the privacy of its individual members.

A further difference between the two cultures concerns the distinction between class and status. In any society, certain forms of social stratification are inevitable; a completely egalitarian society is impossible in either theory or practice. But the dominant forms of stratification developed by a society are an important indicator of the type of society it is. Britain, with its long-standing class structure, was character-ized by the relationship between its members and the pro-duction and distribution of its economic resources. America was less a class society and more a status society; one charac-terized above all by the relationship between its members and the ladders of esteem and praise. A person's class is a group of people with whom he or she is identified; status, on the other hand, is more an individual matter, a question of the esteem or praise that a person receives or feels entitled to. In America, consequently, the characteristic emphasis was traditionally on individual opportunities for mobility while British culture was more inclined to stress the immobilizing effects of one's membership of the social group. In America, far more than in Britain, status ladders were commonly thought to be available to all who wished to try and climb them, and the individual would not normally consider it in any way inappropriate to try and acquire, for himself and maybe his family, but hardly for any wider social group, any increase in social esteem to which his exertions entitled him.

The greater 'openness' of American society than British had implications too, in the political realm. The American was, for instance, more likely than the person from Britain to feel that he or she had a right (maybe a duty, potentially a real opportunity) to try to leave a mark on things. People in America would traditionally feel less restrained than people in Britain when contemplating involvement in some national or local pressure activity. Almond and Verba found that 51 per cent of American respondents thought that the ordinary man should be active in his local community, a view shared by only 39 per cent of British respondents. When respondents were asked whether they felt that they could 'do something' about national regulations of one sort or another, an affirmative answer came from 75 per cent of Americans but only 62 per cent of the British.[35] Most Americans, of course, were not actively involved in pressure politics, while, in Britain, a pressure movement such as the campaign to stop the 1970 visit of South African cricketers to Britain could be successful. Nevertheless, the American was more likely than the Englishman to believe that he might be able to influence the views and policies of his leaders and was also less likely to feel restrained when opportunities arose for acting on that belief. Americans were more inclined than their British equivalents to take literally the rhetoric of representative democracy and to pick up the telephone and try to get hold of the Congressman or mayor or judge or even the bishop or editor or television pundit; or indeed, to organize a 'spontaneous' write-in campaign to achieve some desired political end.

In a number of ways, then, the openness of American culture implied an absence of some of the restraints characteristic of British culture. The value of self-restraint, so important to the British, was not unknown to Americans; but it tended to be modified in a number of ways. First, American culture would often attach greater value to the sayings and doings of the individual than did that of Britain which was more stratified and group-oriented. So while in Britain self-restraint might often have implied the subordination of one's individual emotions to the interests of the wider group of which one was a member, it was more commonly a purely personal virtue in America. Second, in a relatively open culture like that of America, the social values were likely to be spelt out and institutionalized; if there were few inhibitions upon your social mobility or your rights and opportunities to communicate with others, the few restrictions that were imposed had to be made particularly clear. In Britain, things could characteristically be left unsaid, with the understanding that members of the various subcultures would never normally question or challenge the universally-known rules.

CONTROL OF AGGRESSION IN AMERICA

It was suggested in Chapter 3 that one of the distinguishing marks of British culture, at least since the early nineteenth century, was the extent to which aggressive feelings were held in check. In American culture things were different. American boys would often be brought up to admire frontier heroes whose chief claim to fame was their capacity to win fights. Violence ('as American as cherry pie', said Rap Brown in 1967 in a phrase that became famous) was often officially frowned on but everywhere expected. The rhetoric of American foreign policy had long been full of the language of standing up to bullies and aggressors. And it was almost part of the ritual of displaying his manhood[36] for an

American boy to prove that he could get into fights (which, of course, he would never start) and then win them quickly and easily. 'My manhood was profoundly connected with dissent,' wrote Dotson Rader in *I Ain't Marchin Anymore.* 'Violence was wanted. I hungered for it. I wanted to fight in front of my chick.'

Until recent times, observers tended to emphasize the value of social consensus as the basis upon which America operated. But in the 1960s, many social scientists, politicians, students and journalists claimed that American society was characterized more by social conflict than by consensus. In those years, many sensed a growing feeling of polarization, an increasing predisposition among Americans to see any given issue in terms of confrontation and even potential apocalypse. It was the decade of the civil rights movement, the Vietnam war, the student revolt. It was a decade of great violence. 'The general impression seems to be,' wrote Sheldon G. Levy,[37] 'that the United States is currently in one of its more violent periods, if not its most violent.'

What was new in the 1960s was not only the scale of the violence but also the popular and scholarly preoccupation with the subject. By the late 1960s, there was scarcely a college in the United States that did not boast at least one course on some aspect of violence. Intellectuals like Hannah Arendt burst into print on the subject. Creative writers like Truman Capote wrote semi-fictionalized accounts of violent events. In 1967 President Johnson set up the National Advisory Commission on Civil Disorders (the Kerner Commission) and a year later, after the killing of Robert F. Kennedy, the National Commission on the Causes and Prevention of Violence (chaired by Dr Milton S. Eisenhower, the brother of one of Johnson's predecessors).

This flowering of concern about violence was the outcome of a number of factors including, no doubt, a peculiar combination in many people of both their stated revulsion and their possibly unconscious attraction towards violence. There were, of course, a number of inescapable manifestations of violence to trouble any but the most complacent: in the public and political sphere, several extraordinarily wrenching political assassinations, a series of spectacularly destruc-

tive urban riots, a peculiarly grisly (and unsuccessful)
foreign war, and at the private and social level, a homicide
rate that was the highest for any developed nation and
which continued to rise. Similar trends were discernible
in other Western, heavily urbanized and technologically
sophisticated societies, including Britain. But by the end of
the 1960s, murder occurred something like forty-eight times
more often in the USA than in England, West Germany,
and Japan combined. According to United Nations statistics,
the average number of deaths per 100,000 population resulting from murder in 1960 was 0.6 in Britain, 1.0 in West
Germany, 1.9 in Japan — and a staggering 4.7 in the USA.
Rates of non-homicidal violence in America were also high
and climbing during our period, though here the figures
for Britain and other countries did not lag quite so smugly
behind those of America. A decreasing proportion of murders
and other violent crimes in America was committed within
familial and friendship structures and more and more crimes
were impersonal, arbitrary and even indiscriminate.

There were many attempts to explain away the American
trends. The apparent rise in the rate of violent crime, said
some, was in part a result of better reporting by the public
and of greater efficiency by the police; furthermore, some
violent crimes were more severely punishable in the United
States than in other countries and, therefore, less likely in
those other nations' statistics to appear as part of an upward
spiral of violent crime. It was also argued that the increase
in spectacular robberies with violence was, in a perverse way,
a reflection of growing affluence, an evil spin-off from an
otherwise welcome development. But none of these explanations could hide the fact that the rate of violent crime in
America was exceptionally high and that America was
dramatically ahead of any similar society in these unenviable
stakes.

The American preoccupation with violence was, however, more than the rational response to a specific social
development. After all, other societies experienced similar
trends without developing so consuming a passion for the
subject of violence. The riots in Paris in May 1968 were every
bit as violent as those in Chicago three months later, but,

Jacques Ellul notwithstanding, no violence 'industry' developed in French intellectual life. Similarly, the homicide rate in Mexico or Colombia and the political assassination rate in Guatamala or Tunisia were higher than in the USA. But the extent of the preoccupation with violence was a peculiarly American phenomenon.

In order to understand why this was so, let us look once again at earlier American history and at the wider culture of which attitudes towards violence are but a part. Just as American history had helped to perpetuate some of the values associated with Puritanism or with liberty and equality, it had also moulded a culture in which the expression of aggressive feelings was valued more positively than in Britain. In the volume on *Assassination and Political Violence* submitted to the National Commission on the Causes and Prevention of Violence, the authors summarized some of the historical factors that appeared to them to have contributed to the high level of violence in America:[38]

> The frontier tradition, with its emphasis on the individual's often violent assertion and protection of his rights, is one explanation. The high level of immigration and the resulting friction between the newer and more established groups is another theme found in the analysis of violence within American society. Slavery, the Civil War, and the Reconstruction period eroded faith in legal processes as the chief means of resolving social conflict. Violence by groups seeking to direct attention to their plight and to force the political system to respond to their needs is another frequent theme. Violence is identified with the recognition of trade unions, the periodic revivals of the Klan, and the recent riots in urban areas.

These historical explanations, the authors recognize, need to be complemented by explanations of a cultural nature. There is, for example,[39]

> a predominant emphasis on achieving specified ends or goals, with less consideration given the means for such achievement. . . . American folklore has also emphasized direct action and individual initiative. . . . In many respects, the American cowboy, a powerfully attractive figure in American folk culture, has proved an amalgam of these

themes. It is noteworthy that the heroes have been individuals who acted on their own to achieve their ends—Billy the Kid, Jesse James, and the classic portrayal of the Western sheriff.

The authors also point to the American emphasis on freedom of conscience, a goal in the pursuit of which Americans have traditionally been prepared to suffer ostracism and employ unconventional, even potentially violent, means.[40] And, like all writers on the subject, they also mention the prevalence of privately owned firearms. For these and no doubt other reasons, American culture was less inclined than British to induce people to control their feelings of aggression or to condemn others for failing to do so.

In the discussion of British culture, it was noted that the British characteristically seemed anxious to try to control their aggressive inclinations, to prevent their aggressions from surfacing except when they were satisfied that it was absolutely legitimate for this to happen. One reason for this, it was suggested (pp. 91-2), might be that the British, far from being inadequately endowed with aggressive feelings, were in fact afraid of the strength those feelings could attain if unleashed. The fear of one's own aggressiveness is often projected as a fear of other people's aggressiveness and, correspondingly, the fear of what would happen if one did not control one's own impulses can be projected as an inclination to control the feared impulses of others. Hence, it was suggested, the enormous respect of the British for policemen.

If there was any truth in this psychological interpretation of British attitudes to aggressiveness, it helps to place American attitudes in a new and not altogether unhealthy light. For while American attitudes were certainly related to broader historical and cultural factors, they also suggested that Americans might have been more confident than the British that their aggressive feelings would normally remain within acceptable bounds. Like the parent who knows that the child will not want to stray too far into the realm of the forbidden even if permitted to do so, American culture was more prepared than that of Britain to tolerate aggressive feelings and permit them a fairly full rein. The American, according to this interpretation, was often more confident than his transatlantic counterpart that he knew how to deal with his own aggressiveness and was less inclined therefore, to hunt for means of restraining it. Britain may, as a result, have been a more violence-free society than America; but it was also one in which opportunities for the expression of aggressive feelings were substantially more restricted.

There is probably little relationship between the way a person uses language and the extent to which he expresses or analyses or bottles up his feelings or aggression. However, it may be interesting, as a footnote to this section on aggressiveness, to take note of the restrained and reflective way in which the British would enjoy using the English language in contrast to the more gritty muscularity of American English.

The section on British social values mentioned (p. 95) the euphemisms and prevarications, the 'I may be wrong, buts' and 'I'd be awfully grateful ifs' so beloved of the British. The American inclination, on the other hand, was to use over-direct or over-emotional language, to reduce the value of superlatives by constant use, to use shorter and more dynamic phrases, the occasional 'thanks' and the even more occasional 'please'. 'U-TURN OK' said the short and sharp American road signs; or, more discouragingly still, 'WRONG WAY. DO NOT ENTER. SEVERE TIRE DAMAGE.' In Britain, politicians were said to 'stand' for office, in America to 'run'. In journalism school', said a New Yorker on a BBC radio programme in 1970 when visiting Britain for the first time,

> you were taught to keep sentences short; twenty words or fewer in a lead, thereafter no more than thirty words to a sentence. English papers run the sentences much longer. They use more adverbs, they use more adjectives. A New York City paper describing a difference between two Congressmen—a serious difference—would say that one Congressman 'charged' the other Congressman with trying to deceive the public, where I think an English paper would say they 'indicated' that he might be misleading the public. English newspapers say that one person 'opposes' the other when a New York paper might say he 'blasts' him or 'rips' him or 'scores' him.

New York, as the cliché goes, is not America. Nevertheless, the differences in journalistic styles give an accurate insight into the different speech patterns used on the two sides of the Atlantic. For further examples, compare the following:

Seen in USA	*Seen in Britain*
No dogs allowed.	We regret that in the interests of hygiene dogs are not allowed on these premises.
Please keep hands off the doors.	Obstructing the doors causes delay and can be dangerous.
Official business. Penalty for private use $300 (on Veterans' Administration envelope).	Under the existing regulations staff are allowed to use the BBC telephone system for private purposes within reason subject to the condition that business must always have priority (from BBC Internal Telephone Directory).
Radar controlled.	Notice: In the interests of our regular customers these premises are now equipped with central security: closed circuit television.

Americans would sometimes resort to long and convoluted words and phrases, of course, particularly on formal occasions or for academic publications. However, this was not generally because they wished to avoid expressing strong feelings so much as because they wished to add prestige and grandeur to an otherwise banal job or thought or social position.

One can hardly infer aggressiveness from a predilection for shortness and sharpness of language. Some of Britain's most loquacious orators—Disraeli for example, or Churchill —were also among the most aggressive, while the most flowery and unaggressive members of the 'love' generation of the later 1960s would often talk, if at all, in monosyllables.

None the less, the language in which people choose to speak and write is one indicator among many of the type of sentiments that they commonly wish to express. A culture like that of America, relatively tolerant towards the expression of aggressive feelings, encouraged the use of sharp and dynamic language; the lengthy and prevaricatory language more characteristic of the British was often better suited to concealing than to revealing the most abrasive edges of aggressive sentiments. American culture applauded the explicit, the expressive, the direct; British culture was more favourable towards the implicit, the controlled, the subtle.

INSULARITY IN AMERICA

The USA has lengthy land boundaries to the north and south, and the continent of North America as a whole is so gigantic that it would be preposterous to consider its inhabitants as ever having lived on an island (or peninsula) except in the strictest cartographic sense. None the less, some of the attitudes associated with 'insularity' can be found in American culture.

The early colonists tended to think of the world as divided into two halves. Such maps as were available to them would picture the oceans in surrealistic proportions and would reinforce their impression that the Atlantic was a sort of Great Divide, like the River Jordan in the Old Testament, between the Old World and the New. The fact that America was physically separated by water from almost all other societies is a theme reiterated time and again by some of the most admired and influential of America's early leaders. George Washington, in his Farewell Address, talked slightingly of immediately post-Revolutionary Europe and went on to say 'Our detached and distant situation invites and enables us to pursue a different course.' Thomas Jefferson, in his First Inaugural Address, used stronger language and referred to America as being 'kindly separated by nature and a wide ocean from the exterminating havoc of one quarter of the globe'. And in a letter to Baron von Humboldt (6 December 1813), Jefferson wrote proudly of 'the insulated state in which nature has placed the American continent'.

The knowledge that America was physically remote from most of the rest of the world did not prevent some Americans from developing an active interest in events elsewhere on the globe. Just as Britain could hold in disdain the affairs of relatively close neighbours while entering actively into those of some more distant ones, Americans would often show a blithe disregard for the affairs of Canada or Latin America while becoming deeply immersed in the activities of societies further afield. The foreign policies of Britain and America have each been referred to as 'isolationist' at periods when they were also economically 'interventionist'. This apparent contradiction meant that, in both cases, the governing elites tried to avoid strong commitments to other countries and felt themselves all the more free therefore, to conduct an unimpeded and often actively imperialistic foreign policy. (For example, Britain in the 1890s, America in the 1920s.)

Despite the 'isolationism' of US foreign policy, however, the element of 'insularity' played a more important and pervasive role in British culture than in American. One of the products of insularity in British culture was the importance attached to the image of ships and the men who sailed in them. Shipboard life was a metaphor for the island existence that everybody in Britain shared and was an exemplary locus of many of the social values the British admired. Americans (until the last decade of the nineteenth century at any rate) were generally less interested in ships and sailors. There were the occasional mythologized maritime heroes and exploits: these ranged from the *Mayflower* to Commodore Perry, Admiral Farragut, and the *Monitor-Merrimack* duel. But images such as these were relatively rare in America.[41]

To Americans, shipboard experience was primarily derived from the fact of immigration. From Columbus to the huddled masses struggling to catch their first glimpse of the Statue of Liberty, the mythologized images of ships and the people who sailed in them were associated not so much with noble battles or distant and exotic adventures as with the crossing of the harsh and inhospitable Atlantic. Shipboard life was not a metaphor for life in America; on the contrary, it was essentially transient, a means of crossing from the old existence to the new. And for black Americans, the transatlantic ship had transported their ancestors to the most cruel and abject slavery. So Americans were less inclined than the British to romanticize ships and sailors or to elevate them into a heroic representation of society's most admired values. In both cultures, the presence of the sea was important and helped to create a sense of distance from people who lived on the other side of it. But the centrality of the immigration experience to American culture — an experience almost totally absent from British history — helped to give the quality of insularity important associations in American culture that were largely unknown in Britain.

The Westward movement, too, had its effect on this aspect of American culture. To Americans, with their mammoth uncharted territories, the nearest equivalents to Drake and Raleigh and Nelson were people like Daniel Boone, Andrew Jackson, and Davy Crockett. For 'Hearts of Oak' the Americans would be more likely to sing a song about the West — 'Home on the Range' or 'Red River Valley'. For the fear and the challenge of the seas, Americans had the fear and the challenge of the frontier. Just as the young Raleigh and countless generations of adventurous young Englishmen might have been thrilled by the outstretched hand of the old sailor pointing out to sea, so the young American would be inspired by the outstretched hand of Horace Greeley urging him to go West.

The fear and dislike of foreigners — those who lived abroad (xenophobia) and those who had come to America (nativism) — was an important and even passionate presence in America from time to time, particularly at periods of large-scale immigration and at times of war or social unrest. The reasons for this peculiarly unattractive form of cultural and even ethnic insularity are complex and include religious bigotry of various sorts, the losing battle for a homogeneous culture, the anticipation of economic competition, and various political fears and resentments. One partial explanation may well lie in the sheer size of the Atlantic and the great physical and mental cost and effort involved in crossing it, for once you had made the crossing, you had a strong incentive to convince yourself that the people in your newly-adopted society were

better than those living elsewhere — an attitude projected
with particular venom by relatively new arrivals in America
against those who had made the crossing even more recently.

This distaste for foreigners was not totally unlike the
xenophobia of the British. In both cases, for instance, the
various negative emotions would often take the pseudo-posi-
tive form of super-patriotism. But there were important
differences. The British might make jokes about foreigners
and their accents and customs, and they were deeply committed to resisting any attempts, real or imagined, by foreigners to dominate them. Their attitudes to individuals
from abroad would often resemble those of adults towards
children: superior, condescending, tolerant, amused, sometimes even kind, rarely angry or cruel, and usually carefully
controlled. By contrast, the super-patriotism, xenophobia,
and nativism of Americans could take more direct forms.
There was the widespread idea — enshrined in the title of
one of the best-known and feared of Congressional Committees — that a person or idea or action could be 'un-
American', and there were periodic attempts to tighten up
the immigration laws to prevent this or that group of immigrants from following in the footsteps (or the holds and
cabins) of their fathers. Above all, there were occasional
bouts of extreme insensitivity and even brutality — for
instance, the anti-Irish bigotry of the Know-Nothing Party
of the early 1850s, the anti-Chinese atrocities of the 1870s
and 1880s, the anti-Semitism of Tom Watson and others,
or the viciousness with which many German-Americans
were treated during world war I and Japanese-Americans
during world war II.

In many languages, the word for 'foreigner' is also the
word for 'stranger'. The way a culture deals with foreigners
is often an indication of the way in which it deals with the
strange, the unfamiliar, the unexpected, the unusual.
American attitudes towards the 'different' and the 'strange'
varied according to a number of social factors. Those in-
tolerant of unfamiliar values and ideas, for instance, tended
to be people from smaller towns and rural areas, older and
retired people, and those distinguished by high religious
commitment (particularly to Roman Catholicism) and low

educational level and occupational status.[42] Historical factors entered the picture too; tolerance of social diversity was probably less enthusiastic and widespread at times of social and economic tension and crisis.[43]

In general, however, American culture was probably more receptive than British culture to the strange and the different. American cultural insularity was more aggressive but less frequent or widespread. Americans were generally more inclined than the British to smile upon at least the idea of cultural pluralism if not all of its practical implications, and to despise the cultural 'monism'[44] that they associated with the societies of Europe. The national motto of the United States of America, *E Pluribus Unum*, one out of many, encapsulated the idea that national unity should be forged not from the exclusion of diversity but by incorporating it. James Madison in the tenth *Federalist* paper, makes the famous declaration that the first object of government is the protection of the 'diversity in the faculties of men'. A century and three-quarters later, President John F. Kennedy, in his posthumous book written to press for a liberalization of the immigration laws, argued that America's immigrants had enriched the flavour of American life by the 'interaction of disparate cultures'[45] that their presence had produced, and he went on to quote Whitman:

> These States are the amplest poem,
> Here is not merely a nation but
> a teeming Nation of nations.

THE CENTRE AND THE PERIPHERIES RE-VISITED

American culture, despite an occasional display of narrow-minded insularity, was generally fairly receptive to people and ideas from elsewhere. British culture, by contrast, tended to be somewhat less tolerant of diversity and more obviously dominated by its social elites. In Britain there was much concern with, discussion about, interest in, resentment of, admiration for, and attempts to locate the idea of the centre, and less of an orientation towards the peripheries. In America, on the other hand, the orientation tended to be more equally divided between the centre or centres and the peripheries.

British culture, that is, was predominantly centripetal while American culture retained strong elements of both the centripetal and the centrifugal.

Like America, Britain was always characterized by conflicts between the interests of the centre and those of the periphery. However, being a smaller, more compact and more homogeneous society, the forces of the centre usually showed a greater tendency to predominate. This tendency was probably accelerated and facilitated by the forces released by the Industrial Revolution. 'Do you not think that the present tendency of this country is towards centralization?' asked Tocqueville of John Stuart Mill in the 1830s.[46] Mill agreed that this was the case but when pressed, was confident that things would not be taken too far. 'Up to now' said Mill, 'centralization has been the thing most foreign to the English temperament. . . . The taste for making others submit to a way of life which one thinks more useful than they do themselves is not a common taste in England.'

Mill's slightly smug optimism was justifiable, perhaps, particularly in a conversation with a French aristocrat. But the belief in the predominance of the political centre in Britain at the expense of the peripheries is one that goes back far earlier than the 1830s. For at least three hundred years, Britain has been dominated by her large cities and, in particular, by London. Culturally, socially, economically, the great southern conurbation acted as an almost irresistible magnet to anyone with substantial ambition and talent, and to many with neither. The centripetal tendencies were not, however, only geographical. British history — particularly in modern times — is full of amalgamations of business firms, government departments, schools, police forces, newspapers and so on, and bears frequent witness to the constantly increasing scope of the activities of these and similar institutions.

Centrifugal tendencies had also long been a feature of the British cultural landscape and they too were present in modern Britain as well. In recent decades, Scottish and Welsh nationalists obtained representation at Westminster and made important headway in various other ways. The 1960s saw a Prime Minister with a North Country accent, and a television serial (*Coronation Street*) set in Manchester that broke audience

records. The decentralizing tendencies, too, were not exclusively geographical. For instance, there was set up a Parliamentary Commissioner (or Ombudsman) whose job, albeit
severely circumscribed, was to investigate complaints emanating from individual citizens, of governmental maladministra-
tion. The same period saw the enactment of important laws
on homosexuality, abortion and divorce, all designed to en-
large the freedom of action of people whose sexual inclinations did not comply with the predominant cultural norms.
And there grew up a vibrant youth culture (copied by, as well
as from, that of the USA) which gave many in the orthodox
cultural centre the feeling that the very foundations of their
world were being shaken by a phenomenon which, since they
did not fully understand it, they felt inclined to condemn.

So British culture, like that of America, was characterized
by a conflict between centripetal forces which tended to
accentuate the homogeneous elements and centrifugal ones
which tended to accentuate the heterogeneous ones. However, the contest tended to be more even (and often more
ferocious) in the United States than in Britain where the
centripetal forces generally appeared to have the upper
hand. The polarities whose perpetual rivalry gave American
culture so much of its dynamism did exist in Britain, but
the dumb-bell was less evenly weighted and the conflict
often less vehement.

In the discussion on the centre-periphery tension in
American culture three of its causes were identified (see
above, pp. 18-19): the important role of this kind of conflict
in the founding myths of American culture, the sheer size
of America, and the constant confrontation with the implications of technological change. In British culture things have
been different.

Britain, unlike the United States, did not have a centre–
periphery conflict built into the great myths of its history.
On the contrary, almost all the great personages and land-
marks of British history as taught to generations of youngsters tended to further the idea that attachment to the nation
as a whole or to those in authority superseded sectional or
factional loyalties. Figures such as the major Tudor monarchs, Nelson, or Queen Victoria and her prime ministers

might have had their equivalents in American mythology; but there were no British heroes to correspond to Davy Crockett, Kit Carson, or Robert E. Lee. The great British explorers were courtly figures such as Drake and Raleigh; Britain's rebel-in-chief, Oliver Cromwell, was certainly no believer in the rights of political or cultural peripheries against those of an authoritative centre. As for the really mythical rural figures, Johnny Appleseed could never have ended, as Robin Hood had done by the early modern period, as the Earl of Huntingdon, or its American equivalent.

The great demographic and geographical size of the United States also forced people to consider the legitimate scope of central and local authorities of one kind or another. Throughout its history, white American culture contained greater social diversity and covered more space and contained fewer good means of communication than in Britain at any given period. In Britain, with a more densely packed and more homogeneous population largely untouched by immigration, potential conflict between the interests of the centre and the peripheries would often tend to be resolved, almost by default, in favour of the former.

The third factor that was mentioned as a partial explanation of the incessant rivalry between the centre and the peripheries in the United States was the constant need to adjust to technological innovation. Britain, despite a relatively unbroken social history going back for centuries, the fairly homogeneous nature of her population, and a political and social system largely dominated by a central elite, was none the less a pioneer of certain types of change. Her insular position enabled her, at the time of the Tudors, to be one of the first countries to develop independent nationhood and to throw off allegiance to Rome and, two hundred and fifty years later, she was first in the field with massive industrialization. In the later nineteenth century, she developed a system of responsible government that was later adopted in many other parts of the globe. So Britain was hardly a society that shied away from change and innovation. But the changes were evolutionary, slow and pre-emptive. They were, by and large, the result of a response by the ruling elite to an ongoing situation, a gradual adaptation to apparently inexorable processes, a means of preventing the inexorable processes from coming—if come they must—as too great a shock. And since the British proved peculiarly adept at this type of pre-emptive change, their social and governmental system was, generally speaking, remarkably immune from shock. Things may have looked like falling apart, just a little, from time to time; but the centre never really failed to hold. So, to the extent that the centre-periphery question is raised by the need to confront the demands of change, this factor, too, helps to explain why centre-periphery tensions often seemed less salient in British culture than in American.

In Chapters 2 and 3, the discussion centred on some of the traditional values of British and American culture. Chapter 4 went on to consider ways in which one of the two cultures would respond to some of the values more characteristic of the other. Throughout, the emphasis has been on immutable and omnipresent facts such as those of geography and on the continuity of certain traditional values over time. The data for the argument so far has come primarily from the past, or the subsequent mythologization of the past.

However, the immutable and the continuous do not constitute the sole element of human experience. Indeed, the history of most societies and most individuals tends to be a record of discontinuity, of change. And it is to the partially changed values of modern British and American culture that it is now necessary to turn.

PART II

5   An era of change?

CAUTIONS

Say, Dad, is it true you were born before jet airplanes, the atomic bomb, TV, and everything? *New Yorker* cartoon (July 1974)

The Times They Are A-Changin' Bob Dylan

'We are living through an era of unprecedented change!' How often have we heard sentiments like that during the years since World War II! There has been almost unanimous agreement among social commentators that our age is characterized above all by the scope, extent and speed of change.[1]

The chorus of change-sayers grew louder as time passed. Theodore H. White, for instance, found himself grappling with the fact that 1968 had been one of the most bloody and divisive years in American political history. With some reluctance, White attributed the spectacular and painful events of that year to what he called[2]

> the cliché of change — not the sudden ripping apart of an ancient system in instant crisis, but the cracking of a system under previous strains and temptations, finally bursting into the streets.
>
> Raw, dislocating change has been moving in America at such speed and with such force that in 1968 it reached the point of overpowering American understanding. . .
>
> If change was what caused the cracking of dreams in 1968, the new dynamic was the very pace of change itself. The accelerating rhythm of new perceptions, new technologies, new knowledge had been churning out new opportunities, new appetites, new temptations, new capacities too fast for the folk-wisdom to grasp, for dreams to adjust.
>
> . . .Change is the law of history itself, moving slowly or rapidly through every era; but in ours it has come almost ungoverned.

In 1970, Alvin Toffler published his best-selling book *Future Shock*. His message was that we might as well accept the fact that we are doomed to continue to live face to face with ever-increasing types and rates of change, and that if we do not want to become nervous wrecks or individually obsolete, we should do our best to move with the times.

A year later, the BBC's Reith Lectures were given by Donald Schon who argued that change was not only universal but that it had been progressing at an exponential rate over the past century or two. 'Currents of change', Schon later wrote,[3] 'roll through every domain of society... *No established institution in our society now perceives itself as adequate to the challenges that face it.*' (Schon's italics.) He went on:

> Institutions formed in the late years of the nineteenth and earliest years of the twentieth centuries find themselves threatened by complex changes now under way. In some instances, the very success of their adaptation to the period before World War II, or even to the forties and fifties, makes them inadequate now. There is nothing parochial about this phenomenon. It cuts right through society.

At other times and places than ours, people have been convinced that they are living through a period of especially significant change. There are doubtless many reasons for this recurrent attitude, but it seems to be related to a search for some degree of stability. People seek out, and even invent, a certain amount of change almost as though they wanted to display to themselves their capacity to deal with it. For example, in the age of superbly-serviced air-conditioned centrally-heated suburban homes, individuals go camping and ski-ing and mountain-climbing; part of the enjoyment is in the process of surviving the physical risks and uncertainties involved, of capturing the experience — taming it, neutralizing it — in the memory and in photographs. In much the same way, societies expose themselves to limited and more or less manageable encounters with new and unfamiliar pressures. History is full of international confrontations provoked by leaders of relatively newly-established countries and of the rhetoric of national revival mouthed by those of older ones. In exercises such as these, the real risks are small but the psychological rewards are considerable. This occasional tendency for fundamentally stable individuals and societies to seek out superficially challenging novelty situations in order to reinforce their own sense of stability is one reason why the assertion that our age is one of radical and unprecedented change should be treated with some caution.

There is a further reason for scepticism. Much of the rhetoric of change, particularly in recent times, was in part the hyperbole of people bemused and confused by a huge barrage of messages. The psyche can take only so many new and diverse inputs at once. When we are bombarded with too many, we are inclined to impose uniformity upon them, to attribute everything to some simple concept like 'change'. Armed with this comforting piece of intellectual laziness, we feel better equipped to deal with inexplicably inflationary bills or incomprehensible and threatening new tax forms; school curricula for our children that we would be unable to master, or works of so-called 'art' that we do not understand but are too shy to criticize; styles of clothing and popular music that are beyond our capacity to judge but which we learn to tolerate, even like, or methods of love-making which we may successively condemn, dismiss, ignore, tolerate, accept, try and even enjoy. Are one-way streets and motorways a good thing? Or city centres that are kept free of private cars? Are electric toothbrushes and fluoride and KL37 and MFP good for your teeth? Do waterbeds help you to sleep better or to develop a stronger spine? Is jogging good for your lungs, the hula-hoop for your waist, and cycling for your legs? Do isometrics help your finger muscles, and honey (or milk) your capacity as a lover?

An intelligent response to most of these questions requires a certain amount of knowledge and thought, more of each than we are generally prepared to focus on them. None the less, they are indisputably and often intrusively 'there' and cannot be easily dismissed. Since we are baffled at the prospect of having to make a separate assessment of every single one of them, we tend to try to find ways of lumping them all together under a single more manageable category so that we only have to work out our orientation towards *one* sort of thing rather than many. And one of the most convenient and popular of such categories is that of change.

A third reason for caution is implied by the arguments in the earlier sections of this book. In Part I it was shown that the fundamental values of American and British societies remained *un*changed in many essentials over a long period of time.[4] The American tradition of work and self-reliance and individual achievement, for instance, was reinforced by the beliefs and material circumstances of colonial America, the Revolutionary period, the expansion across the frontier, and the industrialization and immigration of the late nineteenth and early twentieth centuries. Similarly, the self-restraint, unflappability, insularity, and centre-orientation of British culture were also products of geo-historical forces that can be traced back over the centuries.

Nevertheless, it would be foolish to dismiss the view that the post-war world has seen more than its fair share of change. If there are enough parking meters, frozen foods, aerosol cans, synthetic fibres, electric toothbrushes and spin dryers, the quantitative changes they represent can amount to a qualitative one. In any case, if people believe that theirs is an age of exceptional change, this belief may in itself be of more direct relevance to their social values than whether or not they may be right. Part II will consider, therefore, first such changes of indisputable quantitative significance as have been peculiar to modern times and, second, the new configurations in social values to which they might have helped to give rise.

THREE MAJOR CHANGES AND THEIR EFFECTS

One important modern change concerns technology: not so much the *number* of technological inventions that have been made as the *rate* at which they have been diffused (and then often superseded). Previously societies could usually adjust to the diffusion of technological changes by the natural processes of birth and death. Any of Gutenberg's contemporaries who might not have been keen on his new-fangled printing press, for instance, would have died long before they would have had a chance of seeing many printed books. And if the existence of television (or anything else) should ever make books obsolete, nobody from Gutenberg's day will know. Occasionally, the diffusion of technological change was fast and opposition to it heated: for instance, the machine-breakers in early nineteenth-century England. But, in general, history rarely contained periods of sixty or seventy years in which too much technological change occurred to be comfortably absorbed by one person or at least by the children of the generation by which it was first developed. And innovations were generally not widely superseded by later ones until a decent interval had passed.

However, the rate of technological innovation and of its diffusion experienced by anybody born at the beginning of the twentieth century was unique. For a person to have lived from the age of gas lighting and the horse-drawn omnibus to that of instantaneous international television, and interplanetary travel is an experience beyond all comparisons. 'In times gone by' wrote Theodore H. White in the final chapter of *The Making of the President 1968*,

> decades, centuries, ages were permitted to folk-wisdom to adjust to the pace of novelty. It was sixty years between James Watt's invention of the steam engine in 1769 and Stephenson's first practical steam engine in 1820; and another generation before the social laws of England caught up with what steam power did to industry and industry to people. It was forty years between the time that Einstein announced $E = mc^2$ and the demonstration of that fancy in the sky over Hiroshima in 1945.

Nowadays, things happen faster than ever before. In the single decade preceding 1968, wrote White, the world saw: the dramatic development of America's moon programme from the mere promise (by President Kennedy in 1961) of a manned landing to a point where a manned landing would be only a few months away; a radical change in sexual mores in America as a result of the widespread marketing of the contraceptive pill 'releasing the ecstasy of sex from the discipline of love and parenthood'; the change in air travel from the introduction of the first commercial jet flight to the introduction of the 747 or 'Jumbo'; and the change in the international status of Japan from an American satellite to a major rival of America.[5]

In order to demonstrate how the rate of change has been

increasing, Donald Schon suggested that if you plot any technological parameter (velocity, propulsive force, the strength of materials) over a period, you discover that the curve is exponential: each further position on the curve is a multiple of the preceding.[6] Any of these curves may appear to approach saturation point and you might then expect it to level out. But at that stage a new technology comes along and incorporates into a new curve all that preceded it. This applies not only to technological novelty itself but also to the speed at which technological innovation is diffused through the society. This assessment could easily be seen to apply in many other areas: the speed at which new words enter and leave our vocabulary,[7] the speed at which clothing fashions or news stories or popular celebrities become part of, and then drop out of, the common culture, and so on. If instances of this sort could be plotted on a graph for the past century or so, it would probably show that the rate at which innovations became minted, diffused, and then superseded was constantly on the increase and often exponential.

There are many different types of technological innovation the rise and diffusion (and eventual superseding) of which were peculiar to the twentieth century. Some were in large part extensions of previous technologies. But those most characteristic of recent times were the innovations that made use of a new technology: electronics. Notwithstanding the splitting of the atom and the discovery of the DNA molecule, our age will probably be looked back upon as, above all, the first in which people had the means to process vast quantities of data more or less instantaneously. In the 1940s, television, transistor radios, computers, photo-copying machines and magnetic tape were at various stages of relative infancy and their processes and potentialities were known to few. By the mid-1970s, however, these inventions and their effects were commonplace in Britain and America. There was hardly a home without a television set or a transistor radio, an office without a photo-copying machine, or a major business without a computer. And it looked as though tape recorders were fast on the way to becoming equally commonplace.

Table 4   Electrical appliances in American homes 1952-71,
and percentage of homes with appliances

	1952		1960		1965		1971	
	millions	*%*	*millions*	*%*	*millions*	*%*	*millions*	*%*
Dish-washers	1.3	3.0	3.7	7.1	7.8	13.5	19.4	29.6
Blenders	1.5	3.5	4.2	8.0	7.5	13.0	26.2	40.0
TV (black & white)	19.8	46.7	46.2	89.4	55.9	97.1	65.4	99.8

(Source: *Statistical Abstract of the United States*)
Between 1965 and 1969 the value of shipments of computing machines almost doubled from just under $3 billion to just under $6 billion (*Statistical Abstract*).

A third major characteristic of our own times is that, for the first time, people lived in a society in which universally available abundance was assumed to exist. Poverty was thought to afflict not the majority but the minority — an achievement without parallel. There were, of course, major pockets of material deprivation in Britain and America, but it was widely believed that existing poverty was largely the result of the inequitable distribution of abundance rather than its absence. The harsh facts may on occasion have appeared to indicate the contrary; by the early 1970s, for instance, it was increasingly clear that supplies of various forms of energy — particularly oil and coal — were not all that abundant considering the growing demand for them. It was clear too, that a limited amount of individual material deprivation could result from psychological problems of various kinds which no amount of abundance on a national scale would in itself overcome. Nevertheless, in Britain or America in the 1950s and 1960s most people assumed that if you wanted oranges or ice-cream or beef or a car or a summer holiday you could have them. Not all of them perhaps, and not precisely at the time and of the style preferred. But, within reason, what you wanted you assumed you would and could get. And if the beef or the holiday were not exactly what you wanted, you would complain, feel cheated, and expect that you could get this commodity elsewhere next time. Material abundance, that is, had been elevated to the status of something to which everyone in the society might reasonably expect to have access. 'Today', exlaimed Roderic Gorney in *The Human Agenda*,[8] 'we are leaving the old era of scarcity for a new era of abundance, which can terminate two million years of submission to the cruelties imposed by seemingly uncontrollable fate.' This, he writes, is 'the most marvellous moment of man in which to be alive'.

As the distribution (and superseding) of technological innovation appeared to be happening at an ever-faster rate, various problems arose. Logically, the adjustment would have had to be made to the eventual possibility that the time curve between invention and obsolescence would approach zero as a limit. If this year's top of the pops is adored and then forgotten in half the time that it took last year, and next year's sequence of events will halve this year's rate, the time cannot be far off when a disc must become the current rave and then be discarded all within a fraction of a second. 'That's how fast pop is,' says Nik Cohn; 'the anarchists of one year are the boring old farts of the next.'[9] The graph of ever-faster change can lead in other strange directions. Hilary and Steven Rose wrote, tongue in cheek, that 'it has been calculated that if the increase in scientific manpower goes on at the present rate, by the middle of the next century, every man, women and child on earth will have to be a scientist.'[10]

How do you adjust to apparently exponential rates of change like these? If things were likely to change virtually as soon as their existence was established, what sort of relationship could you establish with novelty? One form of adjustment was that in various respects people would tend to 'telescope' their sense of time. It is instructive to listen to an old radio programme, a replay of an entire episode of *ITMA* or *Journey into Space* or a war-time news report. The most dated aspect of those programmes is their uninterruptedness. Any specific speech or scene sounds slow, even repetitious. The attention span that the producers required, and thought they were servicing, was longer than almost anything on radio or television or movie screen in the 1970s. If one then thinks of the speed of the cross-fading from scene to scene or voice to voice in *The Laugh-In* or *Monty Python's Flying Circus,* or in modern news-magazine shows, one is struck by an apparently diminishing sense of the continuity and duration of time.[11]

A society believing itself beset by the ravages of the ever-faster diffusion of technological change is likely to develop a somewhat contracted historical perspective. 'Yesterday is gone, and tomorrow never comes!' the Reverend Ike would tell the audiences at his televised religious revival meetings. 'Life is NOW, God is NOW, Goodness is NOW', he and they would exclaim together. Or even, after a little homily about the uselessness of praying for pie in the sky, 'I want my pie NOW — with ice-cream on top!'

In a more contemplative vein, the historian Daniel J. Boorstin wrote in *Newsweek* (6 July 1970):

> We talk about the War in Vietnam as if it were the first war . . . to which many Americans were opposed . . . we flagellate ourselves as 'poverty ridden' — by comparison only with some mythical time when there was no bottom 20 per cent in the economic scale . . . we compare our smoggy air not with the odor of horsedung and the plague of flies and the smells of garbage and human excrement which filled cities in the past, but with the honeysuckle perfumes of some non-existent City Beautiful.

Boorstin pointed out that, however polluted drinking water was nowadays, it was once undrinkable, and he summed up what he saw as a 'national hypochondria' by writing: 'We become so obsessed by where we are that we forget where we came from and how we got here.'[12]

British culture probably continued to put more emphasis on the heritage of the past than did American. This, at least, was an impression often reiterated by visiting Americans.

'I like all the old buildings in London', said an American child, in London for the first time, on a BBC radio programme in 1970.

'What do you think about when you look at an old building?' he was asked.

'The old times.'

'What old times? What are they about?'

'Well, when Julius Caesar used to live and all this sort of stuff.'

When his father (who had admiringly compared London with Bertrand Russell, 'aged . . . but distinguished, and its age written well into its façade') banteringly told his taxi driver that the fastest race-horses were in America, he was impressed by the cool retort: 'I can only suggest that you look at the book and you'll find out that the greatest horse that ever ran in any race was The Tetrarch, which was in the seventeenth century!'

But the British were not always as conscious of the durability and continuity of their past as visitors from the USA and elsewhere sometimes liked to think. Richard Hoggart[13] wrote of the temptation to live 'in a constant present' and talked of people in Britain whose minds 'rarely go back beyond the times of their own grandparents'. He went on:

> Since the world is assumed to be one of incessant change, in which the future automatically supersedes and is preferable to all in the past, the past becomes laughable and odd. To be 'old-fashioned' is to be condemned.

In a society with a contracted sense of time, the future no less than the past can also seem telescoped.[14] 'Eat, drink and be merry, for tomorrow ye may die' was an old theme the modern variations of which often counterpointed the warnings of those concerned about the dangers of nuclear annihilation or ecological disaster.[15] This tendency to upgrade the importance of the present at the expense of the future represented a significant shift of emphasis. In American culture, in particular, 'present-orientation' conflicted with the traditional 'Puritan ethic' which maintained that a person should work now and receive gratification later. America, furthermore, had long been characterized by an optimistic assumption that things were bound to be all right in the future and that one could, therefore, make long-term plans. However, with the constantly accelerating rate of change, this traditional optimism and future-orientation became more difficult to sustain.

As the curve of innovation–diffusion–obsolescence seemed to climb relentlessly, many people felt themselves to be increasingly at its mercy. The psychological pressures built up accordingly.

We are equipped with highly adaptable minds but they have their limits. As we grow older, we tend to take refuge increasingly in beliefs and values acquired during our formative years and this is part of what we mean when we talk about maturity, the tranquillity of old age, the conservatism of older people, or psychological adjustment. It has usually been easy enough for older people to make this adjustment, and to make slightly supercilious comments about their youngsters who, in their turn, are going through the painful process of adjudicating between a host of apparently inconsistent experiences and received doctrines. In other words, there has always been some sort of psychologically health generation gap.

Things are not so simple, however, during a period of apparently exponential change. If goods and services and relationships were expected to be altered or renewed with increasing rapidity, it was clearly of growing importance to the individual to know personally how to guard against being regarded as obsolete. It was no longer possible to remain committed to a fixed life-style or set of beliefs or practices; indeed, any firm commitment—except perhaps to change itself—entailed the risk of being outmoded. But every adaptive tactic involved risks too. You could pretend that this or that novelty was just not important, or that it was important but deserved unqualified condemnation. Or, like the fifty-year-old woman in the mini-skirt, you could shower it with praise in a simple-minded effort to show that you, at least, could absorb change and adapt to it.

The psychological response to change sometimes took social forms. One common tactic was for the individual so to immerse his identity in that of the group of which he was part that he felt himself relatively immured against having to deal personally with the less manageable ravages of change. 'By moving in a crowd', wrote David Riesman,[16] 'we seek to deny the accidental and chancy nature of our . . .life.' By the 1960s, indeed, there was a movement, particularly in parts of the American suburban south-west, to establish living communities for a single age-group—'adult' apartment blocks for the young unmarrieds and, for the elderly, pre-planned communities such as Mission Viejo or the Rossmore Leisure World in California and Del Webb's Sun City in Arizona. This was merely a logical extension of a tendency for people to move increasingly among those not only with their own interests and backgrounds but also of roughly their own age.

The social experiences and values of the old and the young have always been in conflict; if younger people did not question the advice and beliefs of their parents, little change or 'progress' would ever occur. But with the apparently accelerating speed of change in modern times, the conflicts between members of different generations, or between those people anxious to adjust to change and those less inclined to do so, were in danger of becoming more disruptive than beneficial. Furthermore, the very phrase by which these conflicts are described, the 'generation gap', was becoming out of date. In earlier times, society could usually adjust to the major social and technological changes that occurred by the natural processes of birth and death. But when the pace of change seemed almost exponential, the process of adjustment could no longer take thirty or sixty years. By the 1960s, it was commonly felt that there was a substantial difference between the ways in which a teenager, a twenty-year-old, a thirty-year-old and a forty-year-old experienced the world. There was no longer a 'generation gap'; there were whole series of decennial or quinquennial gaps.[17]

Just when the processes of personal adaptation to change were being stretched to their limits, medical science was enabling people to live longer than ever before. The proportion of people aged sixty-five and over was (in Britain) about 5 per cent at the beginning of the twentieth century; by the 1960s it was between about 11 per cent and 12 per cent. As for the average expectation of life, this rose (in America) from about fifty-four in 1920 to over seventy by 1970. As the percentage of elderly people in the British and American populations grew, so did that of young people. In 1940, a quarter of the American population was under fourteen; by 1970, it was over one-third. Thus, one of the underlying reasons for the generational antagonisms of the 1960s might simply have been that in both societies there were proportionately fewer people in the working-age groups than before; these people had to support a proportionately larger older generation *and* a larger younger generation than had existed when they themselves were young—a fairly sure formula, as many individual families could ruefully testify, for creating resentments all round. Thus both demographic and economic factors played their part in creating a number of coexistent 'generation' gaps.

These general remarks apply to both the United States and Britain and, indeed, to any society undergoing rapid technological change. It is arguable that people in the developing societies of the Third World were, in fact, undergoing even greater change even faster and experiencing in an even more acute form the psychological and social dilemmas discussed above than were the nations of the West. But the Western societies were in the van of technological change and had to cope first with the problems that it brought. It was there that the problems associated with the adaptation to change were most acutely felt and most pressingly in need of solution, and it was there, accordingly, that decisions could least easily be postponed or avoided.

The psychological and social ripples set up by the increasingly rapid diffusion of technological innovation were considerable. But the repercussions were particularly striking in the realm of electronic innovation. In a way, television and computers are merely technological innovations which, like tea bags, non-stick frying pans, and parking meters, were invented and marketed (and will probably be outmoded) with remarkable speed.

But they were also more than that. For these and other electronic developments made possible the collection, storage, reproduction, recall and dissemination—often within a time-span approaching zero—of vast quantities of information. This could be done with visual information, with sounds and with medical and biographical data. Millions of people can, at will, listen to the long-dead voices of Enrico Caruso or Al Jolson; or can see and hear James Callaghan or Gerald Ford talking to them at precisely the moment that he is really talking to them hundreds or even thousands of miles away. Pictures and sounds can, of course, be reproduced without electronic help (though if only Caruso had lived a few more years we might have heard that incomparable voice recorded on electric equipment); but the simultaneous transmission of visual or aural signals to millions of receivers can be done only electronically. Similarly, information can obviously be stored on bookshelves and in our heads, but gigantic, reliable, and almost instantaneous calculations and cross-references can only be done by electronically-charged machines.

Furthermore, only with the development of electronics could people begin to discover ways of storing and communicating a number of different (but related) messages all at the same time. With the development of the computer, social scientists were able to start trying to think comprehensively about entire political or social 'systems'; with the invention of film and then talkies and eventually television, it became possible for imaginative people to try to communicate an artistic concept through the transmission of several sight and sound messages at once. Kinetic (and even tactile) poetry shaped by computer became common; so did music dependent for its structure on electro-magnetic tape and the electronic synthesizer. Town planners and creative artists thought increasingly of trying to create a 'total environment'.

There are then, three characteristics of electronics that justify talk of an electronics revolution. The first is that radio and telecommunications, computers, xerox machines, condenser microphones, transistors and the rest made possible communications of greater speed and efficiency than before. Second, they enabled messages to be transmitted to unprecedented numbers of people (potentially the entire human race). And third, it became feasible to communicate complex and causally interrelated multi-level messages on a scale and with a range of means of expression never before envisaged.

The speed and efficiency with which messages could be transmitted in the electronic age were breathtaking. By the 1970s, it was possible for five hundred million people, simultaneously, to watch a football match being played in Mexico, a royal wedding in London, or even the antics of a couple of men 250,000 miles away on the moon. Whenever any important event occurred, the electronic media were expected to be able to tell people about it in detail, immediately. At a general election, for example, listeners and viewers would expect the computers at their radio and television stations to be able to tell them, on the basis of the earliest and most flimsy returns, what the nationwide trend was likely to be. Was there a cyclone in Darwin, an assassination attempt in Manila, an immolation in Hue, an earthquake in Nicaragua? People expected accurate pictures and sounds in their homes that very evening.

Speed and efficiency were qualities that people began to expect not only from the electronic media in their homes but from other sources as well. At their place of work they would expect to be able to find out on demand how much tax had been withheld at any given moment in the tax year, they would get impatient with a slow photo-copying machine or with an international telephone call that took a while to come through correctly.

Impatience permeated many strands of our lives. Not only did people expect an almost immediate response from electronically controlled phenomena, but this expectation was applied to the non-electronic as well. If a president or a prime minister made an important speech, or an author published a major new work, pundits were expected to be able to give an immediate analysis, explanation, and assessment. 'Freedom NOW' chanted the American blacks whose most revered leader, Martin Luther King, published a book called *Why We Can't Wait*. In something of the same spirit, the first major movement for women's liberation, started by Betty Friedan, was called the National Organization for Women—a title carefully chosen with an eye to its obvious initials. 'Give us *something* or we'll just start taking!' sings the chorus in Leonard Bernstein's *Mass*. They go on:

> We're fed up with your heavenly silence,
> And we only get action with violence,
> So if we can't have the world we desire,
> Lord, we'll have to set this one on fire!

As part cause and part effect of the impatience of modern life, there were many devices, some electronic, some not, designed to reduce (or 'save') labour and thereby time:

dishwashers, blenders, hair dryers, frozen pre-cooked fish
fingers, 'instant' coffee, 'instant' rice, 'instant' shampoo
('Spray, brush—go!'), college outline textbooks complete with
'test yourself' supplements, TV remote control channel
changers, electric toothbrushes and electric shavers. . . . The
list is endless. It is doubtful whether the people who enjoyed
all these things—who also had to earn enough to pay for them,
and have the time to get them serviced whenever any of them
broke down—necessarily had a more leisured or relaxed
existence as a result. On the contrary, the evidence seems to
suggest a sort of latter-day Newtonian law: a person's expectations of speed and efficiency are always one step ahead of the
capacities of the available technology.[18] We are no longer
impressed by the telephone or the TV. When they work, as
they generally do, we take them for granted. But when the
very latest things—the TV election computer, international
direct telephone dialling, 'live' pictures from the moon—
temporarily fail, we become exasperated.

This impatience is probably one reason why some people
found it difficult to enjoy the increased leisure time that
was ostensibly produced by the age of affluence. As a matter of
statistical fact, the number of leisure hours actually enjoyed
per week by members of the working population was not all
that greater at the end of our period than at the beginning[19]
while labour- and time-saving devices were sometimes
capable of demanding almost as much time and labour as
they saved. Nevertheless, the proportion of the population
too old or too young to work increased and the growing
strength of trade unions ensured that in many industries the
official working week was reduced and the length and frequency of holidays increased. Furthermore, more and more
people entered middle-class professions in which they were
able to exercise some control over the details of their daily
working schedule.[20] However, leisure began to be a major
problem for many people. This was not primarily because
there was so much of it to dispose of but because there was
only the flimsiest tradition of enjoying an activity from
which no immediate and useful product emerged. Leisure
activities, like work, had to be rendered as efficient as possible,
with rewards that came quickly and could be quantified. If a

football team lost a series of games, you gave up supporting them; if a TV programme was no good, you switched to another channel. Some people enjoyed spending their spare time driving a sports car primarily because of the sort of speed it could achieve, even though (or maybe in part because) it would be dramatically in excess of the legal speed limit. And they would get impatient at the check-out counter of their supermarket if there was a long line, and the time devoted to paying for a weeks' provisions went up by an extra five minutes or so.

This impatience and dissatisfaction, this insistence on having the 'best' and having it 'right now', was a tendency greatly strengthened by the speed and efficiency to which the electronics revolution accustomed people. Once they were used to almost instant news reports from far away trouble spots, or to the speed with which a complex computer print-out could be available, or to the idea that men could talk to them from the moon a week after being here on earth—it became harder to settle for anything slower or less efficient.

The second important quality of the electronic media was that they made possible communication on a massive scale. Prior to the twentieth century, it would have been the sheerest fantasy to imagine that a single person could communicate, with no time delay, to literally millions of people at once. Radio and then television (aided by electronic and electromagnetic recording, photo-copying, the telephone, the transistor, and the computer) brought this fantasy into the realm of everyday experience. The audiences for successful family dramas — *Coronation Street* or *Steptoe and Son* in Britain, *That Girl* or *All In The Family* in America—were enormous and loyal, twenty million people in Britain and twice that number in the States sitting in front of their television screens watching the same actors doing and saying the same things at the same time. By about 1970, the average television set in the USA was on for over five and a half hours a day and each individual viewer spent just under three hours a day in front of the set.[21] At certain moments, more people than were ever alive at one time until the twentieth century would be sitting in front of a television set.

Like the pictures and sounds that were brought into their

homes by modern electronics, people, too, were carried over great distances in huge numbers at record speeds. In 1952, the British owned about $2\frac{1}{2}$ million private cars and vans, a figure that had gone up to $12\frac{3}{4}$ million by 1972.[22] In the USA, 17 million passengers were carried by air on domestic flights (average speed: 180 mph) in 1950; twenty years later, 156 million passengers were carried (average speed: 350 mph).[23] This rapid growth in mass transportation complemented the rise of television in enabling almost everybody to have first- and second-hand knowledge and experience of other styles of life, other places, other people.

The implications were considerable. Take, for instance, the world of politics. In 1876 it had been possible for the British Prime Minister (Disraeli) to dismiss as 'to a large extent inventions' the first reports of the Bulgarian massacres. In the age of television and jet travel he would probably have seen filmed reports within days of the first rumours and the government (not to mention the television programme organizers) would probably have been able to call on the advice of people recently in the area. In the pre-television and pre-jet age, dubious policies could be pursued with relative impunity. Nobody except those at the front would know whether the Crimean war or Spanish-American war or world war I incurred unnecessary loss of life. Even the press reports of a William Russell or the photographs of the trenches at Verdun took a while for their impact to filter down into the consciousness of the folks at home. In the age of instant mass communication—of people, voices, pictures and ideas—the world's political leaders were probably no wiser or more humane than their predecessors (though the existence of the atomic bomb was assumed by some observers to have made some of them a little more cautious). But the modern media probably helped to give them and the people they led a greater sense that they were engaged in a joint enterprise. Political leaders would resort to the radio and the television screen and direct a 'man-to-man' appeal in the first person plural to their scattered audience — just as though they were Sam Adams addressing an eighteenth-century Town Meeting or Gladstone during the Midlothian campaign. One of the earliest and most skilful exponents of this style was

Franklin D. Roosevelt, whose radio 'Fireside Chats' were full of the confident and confidential phraseology of 'You and I . . .' A later American politician, Richard M. Nixon, probably saved his political career in 1952 when the sniff of scandal almost resulted in his being dropped from the Republican ticket as Vice-Presidential candidate by making a strong and excruciatingly 'confidential' television speech about his financial integrity — a speech most memorable for Nixon's reference to the little dog, Checkers, given to his children by a Texan well-wisher. People got to know and talk about the vocal peculiarities and facial features of their favourite and un-favourite politicians. And they would talk with apparent authority and sometimes considerable passion about political and other occurrences in places which they had never visited and which were half a world away.

Electronic communication, in short, helped to create the sense of a participatory democracy, a democracy in which not only politics but all aspects of the culture were open to the cut and thrust of popular participation. Since John Kennedy, Harold Macmillan, Jack Paar, Eamonn Andrews or David Frost was in your house talking directly to you, you felt that you knew them; you could and would talk back to them personally if you had the chance, and they would listen to you as you listened to them. Many well-known personalities found that wherever they went people would call them, often by their first names, as though they were old friends on terms of intimacy and equality. What you did on radio or television was less important than the apparent accessibility provided by the fact that you performed on radio or television.[24]

There was an almost salacious ambivalence towards the electronic media and their celebrities. On the one hand, like the ice princess, the media celebrities were all-knowing, all-powerful, remote. But, on the other hand, since the princess made incessant personal appearances, friendly and informal, in your own home, if also seemed as though the electronic performers were inviting uninhibited and un-limited feedback from their audiences.

Radio and television encouraged this ambivalence. Pro-grammes were often filled with 'ordinary' people: the audience for *Ready, Steady, Go* or *That Was The Week That Was* or the late-night talk shows or, indeed, the 'ordinary participants in programmes of a 'talk-back' or 'access' nature. TV, like radio, developed the formula whereby members of the audience could phone in and take part then and there in 'live' programmes. Politicians running for office would allow themselves to be interviewed by Jack Paar, Dick Cavett, David Frost or Robin Day, or would participate in debates with their opponents or even subject themselves to 'telethons'—devices whereby they, like other performers, could appear to be both 'celebrities' and, at the same time, accessible and human.

This accessibility was partly spurious. Radio and television may have helped to create an atmosphere of participatory democracy, but it was an illusory atmosphere. In a literal and rational sense, people recognized it as illusory; few seriously thought that they could expect direct contact with somebody just because they had seen him on television, nor did the person who liked to direct ugly faces or uglier comments at the statesman or comedian on the screen generally behave in this way if he ever came face to face with the unknowing victim of his fantasized scorn. But, if the accessibility was in one direction only, electronics saw to it that those on the receiving end could be numbered in their millions.

The third implication of the electronic revolution was that it became possible to communicate complex and causally-interrelated multi-level messages on a scale and with a range of means of expression never before envisaged. It was possible to begin to think of transmitting messages in their totality rather than in the fragmented and single-medium way that had usually been thought necessary in the past.

For several centuries, Western thinkers had taken for granted an inductive, logical, sequential and analytical way of thinking. To all demonstrable effects there were supposedly prior causes and from all causes there would be subsequent effects. This way of thinking spread into those aspects of experience that were not causal but predictive. Just as all dropped apples in the past have fallen downwards and just as the sun has always set in the west, people would argue, all dropped apples in the future will drop downwards and the sun will continue to set nightly in the west. As for the analytical way of thinking, that had proved so useful when applied to the so-called natural sciences, they tended to transfer it indiscriminately to personal and social experience. Anything—a rock, a gas, a person, a society — could be identified by an appeal to certain mutually exclusive qualities; if it was big it could not be small, if here not there, if quick not slow, if rough not smooth.

This model was undermined in the twentieth century by a number of different but more or less convergent developments. The insights of Freudian psychology and the insistence on the importance of the subconscious challenged the belief that all thought processes were normally sequential and analytical. Einstein's relativity theory established the inter-relatedness of such concepts as mass, time and space — concepts hitherto assumed to have mutually independent existences. Heisenberg even showed, in his uncertainty principle, how the very process of trying to assess the qualities of an electron had the effect of altering its position so that the most you could do was to measure its movement; the process of observation altered the thing observed.

In addition to these conceptual developments that challenged the faith in the virtues of ordered sequential thought, the mechanized horrors of twentieth-century warfare — particularly the death camps of Hitler and the demonstration of atomic fire-power over Hiroshima — brought to a shuddering end the long-standing assumption that man was necessarily harnessing his growing body of scientific knowledge and his delicately structured analytical intelligence to the process of improving life on this planet.

In a world affected by developments such as these, it was not always easy to maintain one's devotion to the power of inductive, logical, analytical and sequential thought. How could the traditional processes of thinking adequately explain the causes and effects of something so totally unfaceable as Auschwitz? How could we be certain, in the age that succeeded the discoveries of Freud, Einstein and Heisenberg, of the 'real' relationship between what we perceive and what we believe to be 'there'? These doubts and questions plagued intellectuals from the early years of the twentieth century. But it took more than the ingenious theories of scientists and the horrors of the concentration camps for these fundamental questions to filter down to that abstraction whom we bless with the inelegant name· of 'the man in the street'. He had not read Freud, much less Einstein. He knew little of Dostoievsky, Kafka or Mann. He probably dismissed the horrors of the death camps or Hiroshima from his mind (with more or less appropriate expressions of shock or horror). But he *did* have electricity.

Electricity was discovered in the nineteenth century but was only widely diffused in America and Britain during the second quarter of the twentieth.[25] Once it was possible to click a switch at one spot and instantaneously to flood a room or a Christmas tree or an auditorium or a whole street or city with light, it became that much harder to think of separate component parts acting in a logical progression of cause and effect. With television and the more or less instantaneous projection and reception of sound and light waves, it was no longer possible to think comfortably in terms of a sequence of single isolated cause to single isolated effect, or of a single communication between A and B. It began to be necessary to try to take in total interrelationships of meaning. In the age of electronics, effects were (or sometimes seemed) unrelated or interrelated — and, in either case, simultaneous with — causes.

In many cultures, the idea of affluence was associated with the big city. In the folklore of most modern Western societies the city was not only the place where opportunities existed for both society and sin but was also the magnet that attracted all who would partake of the available material luxuries. Whether you were Dick Whittington, the Artful Dodger or Jay Gatsby, the road to wealth was the road to the big city.

There was a counterpart to this myth or course — the idea that the city was a place where you might not only make a fortune but also lose one. If extreme affluence could come to some city-dwellers, extreme poverty and degradation could easily visit others. Indeed, in both British and American

culture, there was a tradition to the effect that you would
do better to stay away from urban life altogether. On the
English farm or the American frontier you were not likely
to become wealthy, but you might benefit from all sorts of
spiritual and psychological advantages. However, with the
rapid and massive urbanization of the nineteenth and twentieth centuries the various British and American versions
of the rural idyll came increasingly to represent a nostalgic
image rather than a viable alternative.[26] If you wanted to
become wealthy, you had to operate in one of the massive
modern metropolitan areas.

The cities of modern Britain and America, like those of
the twelfth century, developed in response to the variegated
needs of a rapidly expanding economy. They were industrial
centres, route centres, distribution and commercial centres.
They were repositories of abundant capital and abundant
labour. They were able to sustain, as rural areas could not,
a bank of professional and cultural services, and they could
always be guaranteed to supply an endless pool of ambitious
and more or less competent politicians and public servants.
To the economically ambitious, in particular, the modern
metropolis offered an almost irresistible lure.

If the private fortunes of the few would often be improved by the amenities of the city, so would the general
living standard of the many. Despite pockets of appalling
urban poverty in Britain and America, the growth of cities
coincided with a rise in the general standards of food,
hygiene, and education. Grinding poverty, illiteracy and
incapacitating disease were increasingly considered exceptional aberrations that required special attention. Infant
mortality rates dropped as did instances of serious malnutrition. Some diseases such as diphtheria, scarlet fever and,
by the later years of our period, poliomyelitis, almost
disappeared. Even during the Depression, there were hardly
ever instances of severe hunger on a par with those of
Weimar Germany or modern Calcutta.

As the general standard of living altered, so did popular
expectations and assumptions about the tangible fruits
of affluence. In the early years of the twentieth century
if was common for people to cherish individual luxury

items; a house or a little car was sometimes given an affectionate name and afforded something of the intimate attention and even affection more commonly lavished on pets and people. Just as a newly-married couple acquiring an expensive dinner service for the first time might swear that it would last them a lifetime, so the early possessor of a car, telephone, gramophone or 'wireless' would sometimes be so entranced by the new acquisition as to treat it as an irreplaceable object of special devotion. Even goods that would be consumed by use — a specially tailored suit of clothes or a gastronomical delicacy — were enjoyed somewhat gingerly, acknowledgement being given to the rarity value of the item concerned. And at times of material hardship and deprivation, otherwise common items like eggs, chocolate, butter, or fresh citrus fruits could become luxuries to be relished but rarely, particularly in the more isolated parts of the USA and Britain.

The post-war years saw an increasing tendency for people in America and Britain to assume that there was a superabundance of these and similar goods. Indeed, the belief in abundance was one of the most salient characteristics of Britain and America in the 1950s and 1960s. Evidence for this belief was not hard to find. The stores, for instance, were overflowing with goods of all kinds; by the early 1970s, the American supermarket visitor would regularly confront an average of 6,500 grocery products.[27] The economic statistics told a similar story: there was, for example, the rise in the American Gross National Product (\$284 billion in 1950 to \$974 billion in 1970) and the drop in the proportion of British consumer spending that went on that prime essential, food, from 30 per cent in the 1940s and early 1950s to 22 per cent by the late 1960s.[28]

Not only was there a lot of everything; there was also the expectation, fanned by those who produced the goods that had to be sold for the economy to continue to expand, that there would and should be more.[29] Shoppers were induced to buy in bulk. Two for the price of one, ten for the price of eight. This store held 'The Big Sale'; that TV station ran 'The Big News'. Automobiles and detergents were 'new' and 'improved' and 'more for the same price'.

Green, Pink and Blue Chip stamps were devised to induce shoppers to take greater advantage of the luxuries of modern shopping: you bought all the more (so went the trading stamp theory) in order to obtain more stamps — in order to obtain, in exchange for them, some further 'free' goods. More for more for more. The economy, the advertising pitch, and millions of individual psyches were all devoted, in a symbiotic embrace, to the idea that one was living in an age of unlimited abundance. Abundance was not only 'there', it was always almost as available as one wanted it to be. You could never have quite as much as you might have wanted, but new manifestations of abundance were never far from your grasp. Abundance, like a slightly better game of tennis, was assumed to be there for the taking if only you would devote a little time and effort to it.

What effects would this attitude have on the broader social culture? If people are accustomed to the idea that material desires can usually be satisfied without much difficulty, they might develop a culture in which forms of passivity and receptivity are somewhat elevated at the expense of more active and outgoing qualities, an inclination towards being rather than doing, receiving rather than giving. There can be no certainty of this and, in any case, in no previous era had any but a small and privileged group had easy access to material abundance so no earlier historical analogies are available. But the suggestion has some evidence to support it,[30] and was frequantly reiterated, in one form or another, at the height of the age of abundance in the later 1950s and the 1960s. There was, for instance, the oft-repeated complaint that people no longer knew how to entertain themselves: gone, it seemed, were musical soirées and vigorous domestic conversation — their place was usurped by the television set. Instead of talking and singing — the TV dinner and the beer can.

Eating and drinking were an obvious symbol of receptivity and passivity. Through the mouth, as babies, we were first able to enjoy the pleasures of abundance and take in the warm sustenance of life; and ever since infancy the mouth is normally associated with the frequent and regular intake of gratifying sensations. In the age of abundance, there seemed to recur something of the oral abandon of babyhood. The post-war years saw a growth in the popularity of exotic and tasty foods, an increase in the consumption of alcohol, tobacco, candies and gums, and a spectacular rise in the taking of various kinds of pills.[31] Eating, swallowing, sucking and licking even became special focuses of sexual attention. 'Bite the One you Love' said a food advertisement in America; 'Take Home America's Tastiest Bird' said one in Britain. The dinner scene in *Tom Jones* achieved legendary status as one of the most sexually evocative ever screened, while the reputation of Philip Roth's *Portnoy's Complaint* was initially spread in no small part because of its scenes of oral sex.[32] Oral-genital contact, indeed, rare in even the erotic and pornographic literature of earlier eras, became something of a commonplace in serious writing by the early 1970s, a *sine qua non* of the pornographic journal or the 'adult' movie, and was the central focus of the most popular pornographic movie ever made, *Deep Throat*. As for sexual contact between mouths — not just lips but mouths — this was treated in both the 'serious' and 'popular' arts more directly and matter-of-factly than the mores of times gone by would ever have thought seemly.

Since the culture of affluence partly represented and re-enacted on a society-wide scale that first experience of abundance, the unimpeded availability to the infant of the mother's milk, it is not surprising to note its emphasis on the female breast. To the infant, in a world full of shocks and surprises, fears and fulfilments, the breast is something essentially warm, soft, comforting, and, above all, giving of sustenance through the mouth. To the adult, in a world characterized not only by social and psychological tensions but also by material abundance, that maternal giver of warmth, softness, comfort, and mouthly sustenance returned to play an important symbolic role. The erotic attitude of the male adult or the erotic-nutrient attitude of the female adult towards the female breast may have been different from that of the sucking infant. But not perhaps, totally unrelated. John Updike's Henry Bech spends some of his nights with Bea — competing with Bea's baby son for the warmth and affection of her curved body. Bea, he feels, is a little like 'the giant milk dispenser in a luncheonette'.[33]

In most cultures, the breast may have had an erotic role, but its primary function was the practical one of providing sustenance for infants. As such, its importance to the baby was obviously paramount and its significance to the adult much less central.[34] In modern, affluent, Western, technological societies, however, the breast — and, in particular, that central nutrient source, the nipple — was a major focus of adult erotic attention. In the post-war years, the most popular female American film stars were not flat-chested beauties like Greta Garbo or sultry seducers like Theda Bara but pneumatic ladies such as Jane Russell, Marilyn Monroe and other lesser 'sweater girls'. Jayne Mansfield made a big name and fortune for herself largely on the strength (or size) of her bust. In Britain, minor talents such as Diana Dors and Sabrina did much the same. In time, the breast, and even the nipple, became at least visually accessible in some ordinary bars and cinemas and the widespread erotic obsession with it may have subsided. But the 'Jane Russell principle' showed remarkable resilience in the society of affluence: there continued to be something tantalizing about the fact that the object of often almost compulsive attention was constantly on display — but covered. There, but forbidden. Hugh Hefner's 'Playboy' empire was based on a symbol formed in accordance with this principle. The Playboy Bunny, a girl dressed up as a playful rabbit, had a large but tightly-packed bust with her nipples definitely (but only just) covered — and she was not to be touched by the clientèle.

The Playboy Bunny exemplified a further aspect of the age of affluence. While her untouchability and the unviewability of her nipples probably helped to make her an acquiescent and even provocative object of sexual fantasy, these factors also ensured that she was in no way likely to become a 'real' sex partner and thereby introduce the responsibilities inherent in a relationship between real people. The Playboy clubster was thus able (so to speak) to have his cake and eat it too. This avoidance of responsibility or commitment was characteristic of the culture of abundance.

It was not a new mode of behaviour. History is full of people who would not or could not make up their minds, or whose sense of commitment or responsibility was less than total; generations of English schoolchildren were brought up to admire the legendary feat of Queen Elizabeth I who is supposed to have played off one European prince against another and, over the course of several decades, maintained the inviolability of both her nation and her person. But a stance of non-commitment came close to being a guiding philosophy of life for many people in modern times.

Why should this have been so? In order to answer this question, imagine, as both archetype and metaphor, one of the most characteristic experiences of the age of abundance, a visit to a help-yourself store or a supermarket.[35]

You enter, often through a self-opening door, take a trolley or basket, adjust to the gentle music and the pleasant air temperature — and you're off into a world of magically seductive goods. Maybe you have a written shopping list, maybe only a mental list: fresh and frozen vegetables, cereals, cheese, shampoo, toothpaste, toilet tissue, meat, cat food, and the rest. . . . Whatever your particular shopping method, you are likely (a) to spend longer in the store than the mere purchase of those listed items would necessitate, and (b) to buy more items than you thought you needed when you entered the store. What happens inside the store, in that fairyland of soft music and bright colours? In essence, a great many hesitations, retracings of steps, impulse decisions, mind-changing. As you wander from one counter or stand or aisle to another, you are constantly faced with a barrage of new goods of both a type and a multiplicity of brands that you had not consciously anticipated. Even if you think you need meat or headache tablets or toothpaste, what sort do you get? The toothpaste containing MFP or the one with KL-37 or perhaps the one with Gardol? The one with the pink stripes? Or how about the brand which offers two for the price of one and a half? Or maybe a brand that is advertised as giving you whiter teeth, or stronger gums, or more sex-appeal. . . . And what of that other brand, the one not advertised at all, but with a label that explains, in undramatic prose, why it really is better for you than all those gimmicky 'name' brands? And then there are all those other less obvious pressures before you can make your final choice: the brand that you are used to, the one in a box painted your favourite colour, the one with a name that has attractive associations, the one on the eye-level shelf, the one that's at the end of the toothpastes and adjacent to the next shelf that you plan to scrutinize...

Factors such as these can cause hesitation and confusion when it comes to purchasing something you firmly intend to buy and even greater confusion when you are confronted by something you did not intend to purchase but find unexpectedly tempting. You didn't plan to buy any canned fruit, but those cherries look so tempting. But then, so does the tinned pineapple . . . lychees! Now there's an idea! The big can, the middle-sized or the small? Is there anyone in the family who won't like them? Will they keep once opened?

And so the debate goes on and on. The time in the store can mount and so can the eventual bill. In some ways this experience is not all that new. There have always been people who enjoy spending a lot of time at the store— at the local 'all-purpose' corner shop or at specialist stores no less than at today's supermarket. But there is a difference between the general shopping style of the abundance era and the period that preceded it. The delays that took place in the corner shop or at the butcher's or baker's or candlestick-maker's were essentially social delays; the shopper enjoyed talking to the assistant or to the other shoppers and indeed would often go shopping largely in the hope of being able to meet someone to talk to. The actual commodities from which he or she would be able to choose would generally be rather limited, so it was not the process of purchasing that took up the time. The delays of the abundance era, however, were largely those imposed by the dazzling range of apparent choices presented by the fact of abundance itself. The time was not spent talking to other customers so much as weighing over with oneself the alternative goods and brands with which one was confronted.

The supermarket experience was one of the typical experiences of modern times, the most common head-on confrontation between the individual and the fruits of the age of abundance. Its characteristic mood was one of hesitation and confusion in the face of an *embarras de richesse*. Choice — or the illusion of choice — was so great that it would impede the capacity to make decisions, to make irrevocable commitments to this rather than that. In life, as in the supermarket, there were so many choices, or apparent choices. Some were big ones which not everybody was faced with: where to go for one's holidays, what sort of car or job to try and get, where to live, whom to live with, whether and when to have a family. Most were less important: what food and drink to obtain and consume, whether to spend Saturday visiting the in-laws or the football match, whether or not to buy a particular shirt or jacket or dress or belt or bag. Every one of these decisions had to be made in the wide-open context of a host of other as yet unpre-empted decisions. If you bought the bag, what would it go with? If you tried to get this job rather than that, where would you need to live? In most previous societies, these choices — the big ones no less than the small — were either non-existent or foreclosed by others. A youth, wrote Kenneth Keniston,[36]

> could choose to be a farmer, peasant, merchant, soldier, or seaman, and by this single decision resolve a variety of other questions: the kind of woman he must marry, the place he must live, the things he must believe, the style and shape of his adult life.

But in the age of abundance, uncertainties and confusions, like those of the supermarket, accompanied what were often an almost unmanageable range of discrete choices.

Many of these choices were probably more apparent than real. The difference between a semi-detached home in a neat suburb and another semi-detached home in another neat suburb may not have been as substantial a choice as all that. A Morris or Austin 1100 or a little VW or Datsun — the basis for choice often lay more in the advertisements and the accessories than in the different performances displayed by the cars.[37] Manufacturers of cosmetics for women would invent supposedly evocative names as a way of enabling the buyer to distinguish between them: Softique, Feminique, Tender Touch, Sweet Earth, Natural Honey. It was the same story with detergents. The assiduous shopper could 'choose' between Tide, Cheer, Bold, Dash and Gain (all Procter and Gamble products), and between a big packet or small, blue detergent or white, lumpy or powdery, and so on. As for competing airlines, one would emphasize leg space for passengers and another its exotic menus; National invited you to fly not their planes but their stewardesses. But in all essentials, one airline gave exactly the same service as another. Times and fares were similar; the planes themselves, including all mechanical and safety devices, were identical regardless of airline; so were the professional skills performed by and expected of crews, and even, it often seemed, the plastic on the walls, the quality of the air blowing down on you, and the intonation of the stewardesses telling you about the safety precautions or delivering the 'We will shortly be landing. . .' message.

In all these fields, in cars and cosmetics, detergents and airlines, the 'choices' available to the consumer were generally between this and that peripheral characteristic of a series of functionally more or less indistinguishable products. There is nothing sinister about this. The demands on a car or a plane or even on detergents or perfumes were such that very little margin or variation of performance would have been acceptable. Some cars had rotary engines instead of piston engines; some detergents contained enzymes while most later ones did not. But the choices between one product and another were often, perforce, the icing on an otherwise standardized cake.

There was a more fundamental sense too, in which these choices may have been more apparent than real. Even if you could choose between this or that product, you were often choosing in accordance with a more or less fixed orientation towards the new abundance. The choice between this or that type of television set or airline—or even the choice between *either* an air trip *or* a TV set—was still a choice within a psychological framework to which both television and air travel

were important. If you were on the conveyor belt (or tread-
mill) of what came to be known as 'consumerism', you had
a more or less fixed and comprehensible context in which to
make your choices. Thus, while the pseudo-choice between
this or that detergent or airline could be a difficult and expensive and even a momentarily paralysing one, the real
choice—whether or not to avoid the sort of life that necessitated so many paralysing pseudo-choices—was the hardest
of all to make and one, indeed, of which many people were
probably hardly even aware.

The seductive opportunities for choice and pseudo-choice
presented themselves in many forms. The emphasis here
has been on those of the material world: on the dazzling array
of toothpastes, detergents, and ice-creams, and on the range
of cars to drive, airlines to fly, and locations in which to live
or spend one's holidays. It has also been suggested that many
of these choices tended to conceal an essential lack of choice;
people were probably hooked into the patterns of consumerism because, quite simply, it was easier to vacillate over the
almost irresistible appeals of alternative material products
of a more or less luxurious nature than it was to withstand
all but the most essential of those appeals. But it was not to
the material world alone that these comments applied. When
you decided on your cigarette or your shirt, your car or your
house, you were also likely to be making a decision concerning the way in which you wished your personality to be
perceived both by yourself and by others.[38] The choice
between material objects, in fact, could be a metaphor for
the choice between life-styles. Where you a Marlboro Man
or perhaps a Virginia Slims Girl? A semi-detached/lace
curtains couple or a town apartment couple? Did you go in
for sweaters or flowery shirts or for collar and tie, convertible
or sedan?

In the age of abundance, you could effect substantial
identity adaptations at a relatively low financial or psychic
cost. On a whim, or because she was feeling a little depressed,
a woman might have her face radically altered by lipstick,
rouge, eye make-up or even 'cosmetic surgery', and her hair
dyed, cut, or covered by a wig. She might experiment with
very short dresses or 'hot pants', denim shirts or faded jeans.

Billy Pilgrim's mother, in Kurt Vonnegut's *Slaughterhouse Five,* is described as 'trying to construct a life that made sense from things she found in gift shops'. A man, too, might try on all sorts of off-the-shop-window identities; the homely tweeds and pipe, the sportscoat and the MG convertible, the long hair and studied casualness of the counter-culture, the button-down shirts and slim ties—or later, the flowered shirts and wide ties—of the bright man of business.[39] And one was able to reject what one did not like, choose to change back again, choose to change some aspects of one's apparent identity and not others.

It was this that distinguished the age of abundance from the previous ages of scarcity. The adolescent may, in most times and places, make various identity-changing experiments and search for and eventually settle on a new, independent self-image. But in Britain and America in the age of abundance, almost everybody felt able to do this to some extent—felt encouraged to do it, even.[40] As the opportunity of experimenting with off-the-peg identity-kits came within the reach of almost everybody, the depth of a person's 'new' identity-commitment tended to be less profound. The apparel, proclaimed Polonius, oft proclaims the man. But in the age of abundance, when there was a constant stream of varied and new—and soon to be old-fashioned—apparel from which to choose, it became harder for the inner person to be truly identified by the outer clothes. Furthermore, as everything from tough and faded denims and jeans to smartly tailored suits and synthetic-but-looks-like-real fur coats became economically available and psychologically acceptable to many different strata of society, the lines separating the different social strata themselves became somewhat blurred and harder to distinguish.[41]

There were then, a number of intertwined implications of the widespread assumption that the modern age in Britain and America was one of abundance. First, there appear to have been a number of psychological correlates of this assumption: a certain 'passivity' and 'receptivity' and the importance of such symbols of abundance as the mouth and the breast. Second, the culture of affluence would in some ways make it hard for people to make real choices and commitments; the supermarket life offered an enormous range of choices—except that of opting out of the ethic of consumerism. Third, people were increasingly inclined and persuaded to consider their material choices as life-style choices—and neither type of choice was as permanent as in the past. In both the social and the psychological choices that one felt increasingly able to make, one choice did not necessarily foreclose others: your social and psychological options were like a 'smorgasbord' of the mind—a little of this, a little of that, none of the other. Long hair and blue jeans for a bit, but a 'good' job and an expensive car; no furniture worth speaking about, not even a car—but an expensive international holiday at the end of two years; suit and tie and suburbia maybe, but also a taste for hot Indian curries or the exquisite refinement of the Japanese cuisine and the ladies who brought it to you. The variations were infinite but the theme the same. Many of the choices, in the age of putative abundance, may have been more apparent than real. But the fact that they were assumed to exist and that people relished the opportunity of facing them and making decisions in their role as consumers gave modern Britain and America a quality unique in history.

6   The 'new' values

INTRODUCTION

It was argued in Part I that America and Britain in the post-war years proved to be among the most stable of modern societies and, in particular, that the dominant values of each had roots in the long-distant past. Nevertheless, there are certain characteristics of the modern age that have set it apart from all previous history and among those characteristics are the astonishing rate at which modern technology has developed and been diffused, the particularly influential revolution in electronics, and the evident availability of widespread abundance.

As a result of these factors, it seemed to some by the 1950s and 1960s as though, for the first time in history, most vital problems of a material and quantitative nature were close to solution, at least for the majority of those living in modern Western societies. Furthermore, it was commonly felt that as material comforts filtered through society and eventually reached everybody, people would thereby be able to deal more successfully with life's spiritual and qualitative problems. In retrospect, it is clear that this type of outlook was wide of the mark, but it was none the less widely shared.

As the new forces of technology, electronics, and abundance cast their apparently benevolent spell upon America and Britain, there seems to have been a subtle shift in the relative salience of various social values. In any society, of course, there are many sets of values jostling alongside one another, and the traditional values of British or American culture were by no means entirely displaced in the 1950s and 1960s. During that period, however, many people seemed drawn to certain hitherto relatively quiescent values while the dominant values of yesteryear appeared to be at least partially eclipsed.[1] It is to some of these 'new' values, their roots doubtless watered by centuries of history, that we now turn.

185

TECHNIQUE INFATUATION

Don't look for content beneath the style;
Sit back and smile. Blues singer from Leonard Bernstein's
Mass

[*Teddy boys*] *had no concern with morals, politics, philosophies of any kind — style was their only value and, about that, they were fanatic.* Nik Cohn: *Today There Are No Gentlemen*

One of the curious by-products of the view that quantitative and material problems were on the verge of solution was that substantive matters often did not get as much attention as they would in less well-provisioned societies. Once people think that there is enough bread and cake for everybody, they are more likely to take the product itself for granted and become connoisseurs of the differences between the way the bread and cake are wrapped or sliced, or the different advertising slogans used by the manufacturers. At any rate, there developed in modern Britain and America a preoccupation with technique, with form, style, packaging, presentation, often at the relative expense of substance and content. An interest in gimmickry and gadgetry and short-cuts, an interest, even, in appearance (or what came to be called, in a concept appropriate to the television age, 'image') as though it were part of reality. The practical means by which problems were solved took on greater significance than the theoretical ends to which the solutions were supposedly leading.[2]

There is nothing entirely new about any of this, particularly in America where, according to Tocqueville, 'the purely practical part of science is admirable understood, and careful attention is paid to the theoretical portion which is immediately requisite to application.'[3] Some of the greatest heroes in the American political pantheon, such as Franklin and Jefferson, were resourceful inventors, and the quintessential representatives of the American genius were people like Thomas Alva Edison and Henry Ford. Nor was a fascination with technique new to the British, who had, after all, pioneered the Industrial Revolution.

But the *technique infatuation* of modern times was not a mere fascination with the ways and means of dealing with practical problems. It was the subordination of substance to

style, of content to form. In the words of Roderic Gorney,[4]
it

> signifies the general tendency to be interested more in
> technological method than human purpose. Its hallmark
> is a chilling preoccupation with *measurements*, whether
> they be the auto's stroke, bore, and compression ratio,
> the hi-fi's impedence, resistance, and wattage, the baseball
> player's lifetime home-run record, batting average, and
> stolen-bases tally, the Army's reconnaissance range, fire-
> power, and kill ratio, or the beauty contestant's 38, 24, 37.
> One can't escape at least a dim awareness when treated to
> such admirable precision that somehow it misses the main
> point, the *use* to which these resources are put.

Manifestations of this subordination of human ends to
technical means are not hard to find on both sides of the
Atlantic. Some would say that most modern advertising was
susceptible to this accusation; it was, after all, primarily concerned with the technique of persuading people to part with
their money, and not with whether they would benefit in any
way by drinking more beer, driving a faster car, or smoking
more cigarettes. For every advertisement with a predominantly social or humanitarian purpose (warning children
to be careful when crossing the road, for instance, or inform-
ing the indigent about rate rebates), there must have been
hundreds recommending luxury items that were actually
injurious to lungs, liver, or teeth.

One does not, however, have to take so radical a view of
advertising in order to illustrate the preoccupation with
technique. Indeed, some advertisements were selling technique itself. There were, for example, the advertisements
for Dale Carnegie courses. 'Improve your Speaking Skills,
Memory, Human Relations, Self-Confidence, Personality',
said the advertisements in the London tube trains, showing
a smart young man looking intently at a graph, and concluded: 'How to Maximise Your Potential'. But for what? They
would never say.

'Do You "Get On" With People?' asked a headline over
an article in a British newspaper advertising 'Conversation
Studies'. The article, by 'an Expert in Human Relations',
began:

I think most people will agree that success in any sphere
of activity—business or social—is largely dependent on
how you 'get on' with others. But take it from me—you
will never make headway in this direction unless you become a good conversationalist. . .

Television advertisements for home sports gave out a similar
message. Here is part of the text of a commercial from American television for NFL Electric Football:

. . . total team control. Now you can control every player
and run authentic football plays. Slant right? You wanted
it. Slant left? You called it. You pre-set the players, and
the vibrating field makes them go.

This concern with technical control, with style covered the
gamut of human concerns. How to improve your business
acumen, your income, your tennis, your love-making; what
was important was not so much why you did these things
as that you did them well. Killing was a technique, and the
soldier in Vietnam prided himself if he did it competently.[5]
Loving was a technique—for every book about love there
must have been a hundred on sexual technique.[6] 'A gun',
said Shane, was 'as good or bad as the man who uses it.' Much
the same was said about radio and television and atomic
research.[7] The sheer availability of a new technique was
generally enough to guarantee that it would be used and
that any earlier technique would be superseded. When, in
1972, I told a young neighbour in California that I was going
to spend the day sitting in the garden typing, he asked me
quizzically where I was going to plug in the typewriter. He
had no idea what I was writing, but did not think it could be
much good if bashed out on a pre-electric machine.

One of the major repositories and generators of this concern with technique and style was the mass media. Within
media organizations, technical criteria would often be applied more rigorously than substantive ones to the finished
product. A television film was admired if it was cleanly shot
and edited and if its colour quality was well printed. A newspaper edition was praised if there was a balance between
light and heavy stories or if each page had the right proportion of print to picture. A TV commercial was 'good' if it

reached its punch-line the requisite number of seconds from
the end. Questions of content would often be largely sub-
sumed under questions of style. The medium, as Marshall
McLuhan said, is the message.

A concern with style and technique can easily be allied to
a preoccupation with replication, for once a technique is
established, the temptation will be to use it again and again.
Here too, the mass media provide examples. One thinks,
for instance, of the development by the Sunday newspapers
of weekly instalment projects; of the series of advertisements
in the London Tube trains for wool (in the 1950s), or Brook
Street Bureau (1960s and 1970s); or of the rigidly repetitive
scheduling of radio and television programmes on both
sides of the Atlantic. Nothing should of course, appear to be
an exact repetition of an earlier article or programme or of
an advertisement that had had an earlier run. But the preoccupation with replication dictated that the formula of
earlier successes could and should be repeated, with slight
variations, indefinitely.

Respect for the idea of replication took many forms. An
advertisement in a British paper carried the caption NOW
ANYONE CAN DRAW LIKE A REAL ARTIST WITHOUT
TALENT OR TRAINING. The text went on: 'This amazing art reproducer enables anyone to copy models, photos,
pictures, plans, etcetera, from a reflected image, just like a
commercial artist.' An endless succession of xerox,[8] itec,
mimeograph, Gestetner and other machines enabled people
to copy and recopy documents and, as though in response
to the new technology of replication, letters and forms, by
the 1960s, often had to be submitted in triplicate.

There were the more or less identical chain-stores and
eating places that dotted the two countries, so that one could
be shopping in Mississippi or Somerset and imagine oneself in Maine or Suffolk, have a meal in Nebraska or North-
umberland and believe oneself to be eating home cooking
from some place back in Wales or Wyoming. In California,
the Holiday Inn chain of motels built three absolutely identical tower buildings alongside the San Diego Freeway — but
in three startlingly different locations separated by some
150 miles.

Everything, it seemed, could be or should be or had been
or would be reproduced. There was, for instance, Independence Hall—at Knott's Berry Farm in California. At Knott's,
not only did they build an exact replica of the building in
Philadelphia where the USA was conceived and born, but
in some ways they 'improved' on the original. For example,
in the high hall that contained the Liberty Bell (forged to
within five pounds of the weight of the original—complete
with crack), the walls were painted the same colour as were
the originals in 1776; and Walter Knott's workmen had had
to work their way through forty-odd layers of paint at Philadelphia to discover what the original paint was. Another
lavish American illustration of the passion for replicability
was colonial Williamsburg, an entire city restored with loving
care to its eighteenth-century condition. Williamsburg became not only a magnificent historical museum and, indeed,
a work of art; it was also an imaginative monument to the
ability of twentieth-century technology to reproduce exactly
something that existed at another time and place. At a less
spectacular level, this desire for replicability took such
diverse forms as the vogue for the camera, the record-player,
the cassette, and even artificial grass and shrubbery (which
kept its colour and didn't need watering). And think of the
frequent use to which television producers put that marvellous gimmick, the instant, slow-motion action replay.[9]

Replication was an essential ingredient of the theory
underlying the development of technology and even more
so, the development of electronics. With growing industrialization came the capacity and then the desire to apply abstract
theories to particular cases and to produce prototypes from
which identical copies could be made. Until the Industrial
Revolution, every article of clothing was separately and
specially made; most shoes were made loose and 'straight'
so as to fit either a left or a right foot. With industrialization
came standardization, ready-made clothing to fit pre-deter-
mined sizes, and precisely manufactured left- and right-
foot shoes.[10]

British and American societies were launched into the
irreversible throes of the revolutions of technology and
electronics very early compared with most other societies,

so their modern concern with technique and with replicability can by no stretch of the imagination be termed completely new. However, the flowering of the values of technique infatuation and replication was held back by the pall of war and depression, for at times of relative hardship matters of substance will necessarily take priority over matters of form; the assembly-line achievements of Henry Kaiser and Lord Beaverbrook would not have been mythologized if their ships and planes had not won the war. It was only with the onset of the economic safety net of the affluence of the 1950s and 1960s that these values finally came into their own.

PARTICIPATORINESS

His parents were dismayed as Jonathan spent whole days alone. . . 'Why, Jon, why?' his mother asked. 'Why is it so hard to be like the rest of the flock, Jon?' Richard Bach: *Jonathan Livingston Seagull*

The preoccupation with technique in post-war Britain and America was in many ways a positive adaptation to the widely-diffused technology, the electronics, and the abundance of the period, a product of them and a way of accommodating to them. However, some of the 'new' values seem to have represented more ambivalent reactions to these forces. Such was the case with *participatoriness*. This was not the same as participation. Participation means that people join in and do things together; participatoriness means that people believe that barriers between them should be withdrawn so that they can join in and do things together. It stood for inclusiveness rather than exclusiveness, bridges rather than moats, an emphasis on accessibility, consultation, communality and communication. Participatoriness, like technique infatuation, was a social value; just as something would gain approval if technically proficient, approval also tended to be given to people, institutions, or activities that induced people to participate in things together.

In the discussion about electronic innovation, it was noted that one of the effects of television was to create the illusion of a participatory democracy. Although communication across the screen was clearly in one direction only, there was a sense in which television enabled people to feel directly in touch with those who made the decisions by which they would be affected. Television, wrote Anthony Sampson,[11] 'broke through the high walls which separate British institutions from each other, and dragged almost everyone into its studios.' The hierarchical barriers appeared to have been breached; no longer, it seemed, could 'they' make decisions unscrutinized by 'us'. And yet the very fact that members of the social and political elite constantly appeared in one's living room was a regular reminder of how illusory was their apparent accessibility and how far the electronic revolution was from creating a real, participatory democracy. One could not easily talk back to the people on the TV screen or join them and appear before the millions. In this sense, the mass media of communication created a new elite and a new proletariat, a new 'them' and 'us'.

The value of participatoriness developed in the post-war years partly as a reaction to this frustration. If you could not have real access to the people who had access to you, perhaps there were other, more genuine, two-way lines of communication that could be unblocked, new ways of enabling people hitherto cut off from one another to do things together.

There was a further sense too, in which the electronic media, while failing to satisfy the appetite for participatoriness, nevertheless did a great deal to whet it. By broadening everybody's experience of other places, people, and styles of life, they were instrumental in helping to reveal cultural discrepancies hitherto less widely appreciated. You may not have felt that you could do much about the plight of the Florida fruit-pickers or the homeless in Clapham; or you might have sighed longingly at the Cadillac advertisements, or at the material comfort in which Lucille Ball and her family carried on their weekly capers. But at least television brought clearly into every living room something of the range of experience possible in modern Britain and America. This kind of revelation made it harder for the wealthy to remain ignorant of what life was like for the less privileged, and harder still for the deprived to accept with equanimity that they were not able to participate in the abundance that they knew to be all around them.

Thus while the electronic media might have rigidified certain lines of communication and created a new elite, they also tended to strip existing beliefs and social arrangements of some of their mystique and enable them to be subjected to closer scrutiny than before. And not far behind the opportunity for scrutiny would often be heard a cry for participation.

If the value of participatoriness was partly generated by the mass media, it was also embodied by them. One sees this, for instance, in their organizational structure.

Journalists, broadcasters, studio and print-room staff began to demand the right to take a greater part in making some of the policy decisions hitherto almost exclusively reserved to the people who employed them. Labour-management disputes hit the media and on a few occasions management's public expression of its viewpoint through editorials or cartoons was impeded by industrial action. Generally, however, the impulse towards participatoriness within the media expressed itself through common aims and philosophies shared by most of the practitioners.

One such aim was that their product should reach and be appreciated by as wide an audience as possible — a consideration that happened to coincide in the commercial media with economic exigencies. The founding fathers of modern journalism, the Harmsworths in England, Hearst and Pulitzer in America, had had this very much in mind when aiming to make their papers as widely and easily accessible as possible. They encouraged new, fast techniques of printing and distributing and were also interested in innovations, such as the Miss Lonelyhearts column, the quizzes-with-prizes, and the emphasis on local 'celebrities', designed to encourage people to feel that this or that was their personal newspaper, the one that was interested in hearing from them. This tradition was strengthened in more recent times as street interviews and informal polls of readers were added to the staple news fare. Radio and television too, embodied the virtues of participatoriness as programmes began to include *vox pop*, studio audience and phone-in features and were given titles like 'It's Your Line' and 'Talk Back'.

A further respect in which the value of participatoriness

was engendered and reflected by the media was the extent to which media products were 'personalized'. The post-war decades saw the final withering away of the anonymous contribution in almost all British and American journals, so that readers of, for instance, *The Times* in Britain were at last able to know that a story from Washington was penned not merely by 'Our Washington Correspondent' but by Louis Heren or Fred Emery. BBC newsreaders, similarly, were permitted to identify themselves, a practice that had generally been frowned upon in the past, except during the war. In America, millions of viewers, loyal to CBS, would tune in to 'The Nightly News With Walter Cronkite' — even if it was presented by Roger Mudd. A similar trend can be seen in advertising. 'Hi!' said the cheerful voice endorsing a product across the air-waves in the USA, 'I'm Doris Day.' The media would try to personalize not only the remote presenter but also the anonymous recipient. '*Time* Magazine', said a radio voice, 'makes everything more interesting — including you . . .'[12]

There was considerable irony in this. Until the development of the telephone, people never normally talked to each other without being able to see each other. In the modern age, one person was able to write or talk directly to millions of others at once while remaining unable to see or hear them. So, as the field to which a person could communicate widened, the genuinely personal contact with which communication was accompanied tended to diminish. No communication could be more impersonal than a message transmitted across the pages or air-waves of the mass media. As though to compensate for this chasm between those who projected messages and those who received them, the media tended to elevate to major importance any mechanism that could contribute towards a greater appearance of participatoriness; hence the 'personalization' of impersonal messages.

Finally, there was a sense in which people looked to the electronic media to enable them to feel a sense of personal participation in the world's problems. The fact that the media brought them into your living room could be curiously comforting; the problems might be awful, but at least you were not being passed by. There was also the opportunity for moral catharsis. You could share the general feeling of outrage at what was going on in Biafra or Bangladesh or Belfast and yet, at one and the same time, reassure yourself that this very sense of outrage, induced by your voluntary exposure to the media, had absolved you from the responsibility of doing anything about it. In the same way, the common assumption, enforced by law to some extent in both Britain and America, that 'fairness' was of the essence in the reporting of news and current affairs on radio and television often meant that a viewer or listener was offered two roughly equal statements representing opposing views and that a moderator or editor would be in charge of the ring. The ultimate authority, in other words, was not with either of the protagonists but with the person who got them to participate in the programme and talk to each other, the neutral ring-holder. Here, too, the ultimate effect was often not so much to expose the media recipient to real and bitter debate about major issues as to reassure him that, simply by being a responsive recipient of the media fare, he had joined in and played his part in doing all that the ultimate authority — the moderator or editor — could require of him.

This attempt to bridge the gap between producer and consumer — to merge the activities of the elite with those of the people to whom they ministered — can be seen in many other social and cultural institutions in Britain and America in the 1950s and 1960s. In the theatre, for instance, some imaginative directors would try to create greater contact between actors and audience. New theatres, such as those at Chichester in England or Minneapolis in the USA, were built 'in the round' with no proscenium arch or curtain, and actors would often come on stage through the auditorium. Some of the more avant-garde companies, such as New York's La Mama or the peripatetic Living Theater, would engage in partly unscripted dialogue and perhaps draw members of the audience into the action. The theatrical experience was not at its most valuable, it seemed, unless it could be shared by performers and audience alike. 'I'm interested in making contact with audiences', said Gordon Davidson of Los Angeles' Mark Taper Forum during a TV interview, 'and

sharing a common experience . . . together investigating
the nature of our lives in contemporary society through the
medium of the theater.'[13] And Peter Brook emphasized how
a play like Genet's *The Blacks* can take on its full meaning

> when there is a powerful shifting relationship between
> actors and public. In . . . London, where no audience could
> be found who cared about either French literature or
> Negroes, the play was meaningless; in New York . . . it was
> electric and vibrant. I am told the vibrations changed from
> night to night depending on the proportions of blacks to
> whites in the house.[14]

Another artistic gap that was somewhat bridged in the
1950s and 1960s was that between 'high' and 'popular' art. In
the early post-war years there had been no question that
Frank Sinatra or Vera Lynn were 'popular', while the poems
of Robert Frost or the sculptures of Henry Moore were 'high'
or 'serious' art. When the great operatic bass Ezio Pinza decided to join the cast of *South Pacific* in the late 1940s, the 'serious'
music world was scandalized. By the 1960s however, it was
acceptable and even fashionable for the traditional connoisseurs of 'serious' music to incorporate popular singing groups
like the Beatles into their own critical system.[15] Imaginative
creators in the visual arts such as Jasper Johns, David
Hockney and Andy Warhol deliberately set out to encompass in their work the values of the 'pop' world. Indeed, the
very distinction between 'art' and 'life' became blurred. There
were soup cans in the art galleries, people made love on the
cinema screen in 'art' movies, and the aesthetic values of the
designer burrowed their way into such commodities as mass-
produced clothes or domestic furniture. 'Pop culture', wrote
George Melly,[16] 'has not only introduced contemporary
life to art but also kicked art out into the streets to fend for
itself.' There was, in effect, a democratization of culture, an
application of the value of participatoriness to the world of
aesthetics.

Traditional distinctions were challenged too, in the natural
and social sciences. For three hundred years or more, the assumptions of post-Renaissance physics had reigned supreme.
In particular, it had been widely accepted that all problems
were susceptible to intellectually objective and verifiable

solutions. If the investigator was a model of rational objectivity, his results would be likewise. The observer and the phenomenon observed were discrete categories, the former investigating and throwing light upon the latter.

The post-war generation of physicists, chemists, economists and sociologists was still trained to think of itself as practising value-free, 'objective' science by means of making replicable experiments in controlled environments and then drawing logical inferences. This model still prevails, but some of its hard and fast principles came under attack in modern times. In particular, scientists increasingly recognized that they themselves might be a variable in the subject that they were studying. During the generation after Belsen and Hiroshima, many found it difficult to claim that they were furthering their studies in a morally watertight shell. Chemists or physicists sometimes found themselves forced to grapple with the knottiest social and ethical problems. Linus Pauling, the American biochemist and double Nobel laureate, became an expert on radiation and an indefatigable campaigner for the cessation of nuclear tests. 'As scientists', he wrote (in a statement signed by 2,000 eminent colleagues and addressed 'to the Governments and to the people of the world' in 1957), 'we have knowledge of the dangers involved and therefore a special responsibility to make these dangers known.' Similarly, social scientists interested in, say, family structure or race relations increasingly recognized that the investigator was part of the total subject under investigation and that it was moral cowardice and intellectual myopia, not objective dedication to science, to pretend otherwise. 'To detach oneself and treat others like so many objects', wrote Charles Hampden-Turner,[17] 'is not to be value-free but to choose to devalue others.' The anthropologist Edmund Leach said in his Reith Lectures on BBC radio in 1967:

> Scientists do not just discover the truth once and for all; their discoveries have consequences which alter the state of the world, and the truth is then no longer what it was. Whether he likes it or not, the observer is always bound to get mixed up with his subject matter.

No longer could you insulate yourself and your work from

the wider world or expect the wider world to defer to your predilection for ivory tower isolation. As a scientist, you knew that you were part of the subject you studied; as a product of the technological and electronic age, you were increasingly likely to believe that there should be open lines of communication between your specialized work and the wider public of which you were but part.

If some of the barriers between the 'elite' and the 'rest' were being removed in mass media, the arts, and the sciences, something not dissimilar was happening too, in the world of education. In 1969, a survey of American schools asked teachers, parents, and students how important they considered the participation of students in the making of school policy. 25 per cent of teachers thought this issue 'very important' — as did 30 per cent of parents and no less than 54 per cent of students. The survey asked whether there should be more student participation than at present in school policy making, a question to which 20 per cent of the teachers, 34 per cent of the parents, and 58 per cent of the students gave an affirmative answer.[18] Any school head or college president who insisted on maintaining a rigid distinction between the functions of teacher, administrator, and student did so at his peril. A similar dissolution of traditional barriers sometimes found its way into the curriculum itself. Exponents of the older academic disciplines would find themselves rubbing shoulders with people studying or teaching motor-car maintenance or the social effects of television. Some colleges and schools experimented with interdisciplinary courses in which some acquaintance was required with a number of hitherto separate fields of study.

The erosion of previously firm and exclusive conceptual boundaries even found its way into organized religion, generally a more traditional and hierarchical world than most. Some churchmen invited pop groups to perform inside the holy portals, and women were, in a few instances, allowed to preach. Successive Popes were increasingly pressed by many of their adherents, particularly in north-west Europe and North America, to decentralize Vatican decision-making and to permit the local bishop to take a greater part in making policies that affected his own diocese. Above all, most of the branches of the Christian Church eagerly espoused that greatest dissolver of barriers, the ecumenical movement.

The ecumenical spirit pervaded many aspects of life in the 1950s and 1960s. The very structures and hierarchies of society itself were not left unaffected. In particular, the channels of mobility enabling a person to move from one social group to another became somewhat better lubricated. This change should not be exaggerated. Many of those channels — particularly in Britain — continued to flourish in their traditional forms throughout the post-war years; a young Englishman aspiring to a career in the Administrative branch of the Civil Service continued to benefit if he was the product of a public school and an Oxbridge education, while few of the top jobs in industry or the diplomatic service in America were opened to non-WASPs. Nevertheless, during those years the ways of making (and losing) money, prestige and power in both societies were considerably augmented, and the old assumptions about the sort of life-style towards which a given social background necessarily propelled you were often modified.

The new mobility paths that appeared during those years did not seem to settle down into a set of recognizable and accepted patterns about which one could easily generalize. Deference patterns, similarly, became indistinct but did not seem to be systematically replaced by new ones. It could no longer be assumed that the young man in Britain (particularly the middle-class southerner) would necessarily 'respect' his teacher or his father, or that black or brown or yellow or red Americans would acquiesce in the dictates of the local white power structure. The old-style authority figure might be treated in a traditionally deferential way; but he could just as easily find himself ignored, treated as an equal, or (like Bellow's Mr Sammler who is invited to talk at Columbia University and gets shouted down in mid-lecture) openly scorned by those towards whom his authority has traditionally been exercized.

Although there were important differences between the social patterns of post-war Britain and the USA, there was in both societies a blurring of the distinctions between the various class and status groups and of the traditional routes from one such group to another. With the mass production and mass availability of cheap, strong clothes, it was becoming harder to tell whether the man in the faded jeans was a casual millionaire or an impecunious worker; whether the girl in the smart coat was wearing real or imitation fur. Even if you had a great deal of money or in the British case, an inherited title, you would not necessarily be afforded the deference and the status that had formerly been more or less guaranteed. Those with the traditional trappings of status were being increasingly challenged by those equipped with such newly-elevated criteria as a good university education. The educational elite had status ladders of its own, of course, and someone with an excellent record from the University of Southampton or Missouri would often be made to suffer in competition with someone, possibly less bright, from Oxford or Harvard. But, with all its imperfections, the enormous burgeoning of higher education in modern times and the new status associations that developed with it helped to make it clear that the traditional categories of class and status could not any more be taken for granted.

The blurring of traditional social demarcations had its dangers and not only to those whose direct vested interests were threatened. In particular, if the new participatoriness suggested that almost everybody should be able to have access to almost anything, the result could be a flat and uniform culture. Some people worried that aesthetic and moral judgements would lose their cutting edge and become dependent upon the somewhat volatile predispositions of popular taste and that individual eccentricity and excellence might be subordinated to what Tocqueville called the 'tyranny of the majority'. The hallmark of a culture thus indiscriminately democratized could easily be a dull conformism and this was a fear frequently expressed in the post-war years.

Worries about conformism had recurred throughout American history in one form or another. In particular, whenever 'liberty' and 'equality' were interpreted as representing the requirements of, respectively, individual self-expression and social justice, some feared that the exigencies of the latter might snuff out the flame of the former. In British culture, concern about the danger of conformism was generally less pronounced. Britain was a more rigidly stratified society than America and people were less likely to see disadvantages in conforming to the norms of their own social group. The elite institutions of British society, consequently, were possibly more tolerant of (if only because less threatened by) occasional instances of individual eccentricity.

In the post-war years, worries about conformism continued to plague the Americans more than the British, but on both sides of the Atlantic this concern found more urgent expression than for some time past. Its distinguishing mark was an inclination to seek out the origins of conformism not only in the city hall, the boardroom, the press office or the club, but also in the nursery. Those who feared the erosion of individualism had always been aware of political, economic, and social pressures towards conformism. But this was also the age of child psychology.

The Bible of most post-war mothers was Dr Benjamin Spock's *Baby and Child Care*. Spock appeared to be saying that, within limits, whatever your youngster was doing was normal enough and your instinctive reactions to your child's behaviour were often the most beneficial. This sort of message was enthusiastically received by a generation just emerging from the disciplines imposed by depression and war, and helped to bring about a return to more permissive child-rearing attitudes.[19] Many post-war children were nursed, weaned, toilet-trained and taught to walk, talk and grow up generally as and when their own natural development seemed to dictate. And the permissiveness of the home was often extended to the kindergarten and the school.

The attractions and hoped-for advantages of permissive child-rearing attitudes and techniques were obvious. The relationship between children and parents (and teachers) could become one of love and mutual trust, free of repression and guilt. Modern-minded parents and teachers could not easily act out on their children their own frustrated authority needs or push youngsters into premature adulthood. Children would grow up in such a way as to be able to maximize their potential abilities in whatever directions most appealed to them.

But there were also disadvantages. For one thing, the belief in permissiveness was inconsistent with, for example, the traditional 'Puritan' values of America or the British attachment to such values as deference and self-restraint, and the conflict that this represented to many parents was bound to be transmitted to their children. If parents and teachers were reluctant to guide their children towards specific standards of behaviour and judgement, the tender ego of the youngster could suffer from a sense of social and psychological rootlessness or *anomie*. Every child needs a framework of values in order to develop a mature and adjusted personality — if only to have something to consider and reject later on. But if indications of approval and disapproval, reward and punishment are not clearly forthcoming from adults, the child will look to his or her own peers for them — a lead which many adults, no longer certain of the tenability of their own early beliefs, would often follow.

Thus, the permissive child-rearing attitudes of the post-war years, in conjunction with other factors, tended to encourage what David Riesman called 'other-directedness'.[20] This phrase gave a simple and memorable name to a widespread and nagging feeling in the years after the war, particularly in America, that people were no longer thinking and making decisions for themselves but were taking the soft option of conforming to the tastes and fashions of their peers.[21]

Conformism can become addictive and, like any addiction, unsatisfying. David Riesman, at the end of *The Lonely Crowd*, says of 'other-directed' people that 'they can no more assuage their loneliness in a crowd of peers than one can assuage one's thirst by drinking sea water.'[22] The traditional sea water groups continued to flourish of course — particularly in America, land of Lions and Kiwanis clubs, of flourishing church groups, of PTAs and local culture clubs. But to many, the attraction of traditional groups such as these seemed inadequate and they looked elsewhere for fulfilment.

The search took many forms. To some people, the important peer group was one with which one might learn emotional and, perhaps, tactile sensitivity. There was a flowering of ethnic groups, consciousness-raising groups, and groups advocating sexual liberation. Some groups were so large that their members could not possibly all have known of each others' existence; they were held together by commonly-shared physical or psychological characteristics or by shared values and life-styles rather than by any necessary geographical proximity or personal intimacy — what Daniel Boorstin has called 'statistical communities' and 'consumption communities'.[23]

As time passed and the disproportionately large number of immediately post-war babies became the rebellious youth of the 1960s, it looked to some as though an entire generation had amalgamated into a single social group; 'a whole generation with a new explanation', said the song. The principle of participatoriness, if seemed, had never been more fully put into practice. There was much talk of the 'Movement', the 'Youth Culture', the 'Alternative Society', and the 'Counter Culture' as though the many different strands of political protest and life-style experimentation had been melded into a single group-experience. To many of the young, the period was one of great exhilaration. But many adults felt disgruntled and even threatened. Barriers between the young might have been eliminated, they felt, but new ones were being created that made their own children less accessible to them than before. Some pointed back to 'permissiveness' and Dr. Spock as the root cause of the problem. Spock himself, although temperamentally and morally a conservative man, was active in the movement against the Vietnam war and this enabled those inclined to blame him for the supposed irresponsibility of the young to bolster their case with fresh evidence.[24]

By the later 1960s, despite the strong conformist pressures that existed in most sub-cultures in Britain and America, not least that of the almost uniformly long-haired, jeaned youth, widespread concern about the dangers of conformism had probably subsided somewhat. There was less talk now of the 'organization man' or a 'nation of sheep'[25] and rather more about 'radical solutions' and the 'politics of confrontation'. Indeed, far from being worried that everybody might succumb to a dull cultural conformism, many were fearful of the opposite danger, that of cultural polarization or fragmentation.[26]

Participatoriness thus proved a two-edged weapon. It was a virtue to which, in one form or another, most people in the USA and the UK in the 1950s and 1960s found occasion to appeal. Leaders of industry would try to give their shareholders and workers a sense of participation in the running of the industry, and union leaders would assiduously consult those on the shop floor; government offices in Washington or London would pay careful attention to the views of Des Moines or Bristol, New Orleans or Newcasttle; legistation made it illegal to exclude people from places of public accommodation on grounds of race, and there were attempts to remove sexual discrimination also; some young people experimented with 'communal' living arrangements. Consultation, communication, access, participation — these were the vogue words. On the other hand, problems could arise if these ideas were too vigorously pursued: to those who felt 'inĉluded' there was the risk that one might subordinate one's individuality to a dull conformism, while to those who felt 'excluded' there opened up new and deeper chasms of inaccessibility than before.

TRANSITORINESS

I'll never get used to anything. Anybody that does, they might as well be dead. — Holly Golightly in Breakfast at Tiffany's *by Truman Capote.*

Put action into your films. Don't stand when you can be moving — KFMB-TV, San Diego, staff memo, quoted in TV Guide, 1974.

A third value of the modern period might be called *transitoriness*. This arose out of the belief that since we seemed to be living in a world of ever more pervasive change, it was as well to be adaptable to the unanticipated novelties with which we were constantly likely to be beset.

Transitoriness, like other values discussed in this section, was by no means completely new. Many of the myths of the American past concerned the benefits that could be bestowed by recurrent change, and the British had traditionally been proud of their political adaptability and their receptivity to industrial innovation. 'All things change except the love of change' said the words of an English madrigal dating back to 1601.

What does seem to have been new, however, was the tendency to look upon change more as an end than as a means. In the past, it was generally assumed that if you moved home,[27] for example, it was probably in order to settle somewhere else where you could live a better or more fulfilling life; if you changed your diet or your style of clothes or possibly your job or even your spouse, this was normally a step from one plateau to another which it was hoped would be more rewarding. The process of change and the need to adapt might occur many times, but it was usually with a more or less achievable end in view. In the modern world, however, there was an increasingly pervasive expectation that nothing would or could or even should remain unchanged for long. The 'latest' was often automatically thought to be the best, while words like 'old-fashioned' and 'out of date' were the new terms of abuse. Stability began to suggest obsolescence whereas that which was most valued was that which, like the new disposable paper plates or towels or handkerchiefs, was essentially transitory.[28]

Thus the capacity to adapt to novelty became an important skill to cultivate, and it was emotionally useful to avoid commitment to objects and experiences that would inevitably prove to be transitory.[29] Don't get too attached to your floating coal-tar soap, your dial phone, your aerosol spray, your enzyme detergent, or the running boards and side indicators on your car because you'll miss them when they become superseded. Electronic innovations, in particular, invited this expectation of imminent obsolescence: silent movies, crystal sets, 3-D movies, 78 rpm records, black and white television sets and many other technical developments in 'entertainment' electronics went through the inexorable process from novelty to eventual obsolescence.

This was true of the content of films and television programmes too, and of those who appeared in them. Nothing, they used to say, was so stale as yesterday's news. But in the age of television, nothing was so stale as the news of an hour ago, a commercial that they stopped showing, the re-screening of a sports event that had already been shown 'live', a

joke that had already been told on an earlier show. Radio
and television, even more than the daily or weekly press,
had an extravagant appetite for news, personalities, entertainment acts, voices, and faces, and very few could withstand
its omnivorous jaws for more than a few months or years.
Certain types of formula, of course, proved 'popular' and
were therefore repeated year in and year out. For instance,
once the Huntley-Brinkley news format had been worked
out, other news networks tried the two-person style.[30] The
popular and irreverent family soap opera *Till Death Us Do
Part* originated in Britain and was successfully imitated in
America under the title *All In The Family*. And, of course, some
individually popular programmes and artists—Amos 'n
Andy, Lucille Ball and Walter Cronkite in America, the
Archers and Dales and, in various roles, Robin Day in Britain
—did stand the pace. But generally speaking, the turnover
in personnel and ideas in the electronic media was frequent
and ruthless.

Furthermore, there was a tendency over the years for
individual items on radio and television to get shorter and
for audiences to respond better to transitory images and
messages than to sustained ones. The flickering television
screen in particular seemed constantly to be labouring for
your momentary and transitory attention. Forget what you
were thinking about before, it seemed to say, and don't think
about tomorrow. But gaze into the TV screen *now* and be
momentarily captivated.[31] During the course of a single
evening, the little screen would serve up an interweaving
mosaic of say, *Double Your Money*, Roy Rogers, Eezy-Kleen,
starvation in Biafra, a government statement on prices and
incomes, Nice'n Easy Shampoo, and jokes about breasts and
bottoms. The elements in this mosaic would be all the same
size and visual intensity, and except for some louder commercials their sound quality would also be standardized. If
one set of sounds and pictures was easily dispensable, so were
they all. This morning's *Double Your Money* was a bore by
this afternoon; so was this morning's report from Biafra. If
they showed that again, you would probably be tempted to
ignore it, change channels, or with one disdainful flick of the
wrist, switch it off.

You could switch off a TV set or a light. Or you could just, in the vernacular, switch off. Either way, transitively or intransitively, the idea of switching on or off implied controlled and total engagement or disengagement. What was 'on' at one split second could be 'off' at the next; in the days of transistor radios and the 'instant start' TV mechanism, you could even switch your radio or television on without a warm-up period. And it could be switched 'off', regardless of what it was transmitting, with the same ruthless speed.

In the age of abundance, the apparent availability of virtually all material necessities tended to lead people to expect speedy gratification of their desires and to have little sense of the length of time over which people in other times and places had had to wait in order to have some of their more basic material needs satisfied. Things were speeded up, in particular, by the development of finance, of credit buying or 'hire purchase'. Once a deep freeze or a dishwasher or even a car or a house was relatively easy to 'own' — once, that is, there were more of them available and there were finance companies that helped you to have more or less the one you wanted — you were less likely to cherish it, give it a name, or think of ownership as permanent. If you could buy on credit a house or a car at twenty-five or even twenty-one, you could probably expect to buy a better one five years later. Manufacturers indeed, produced goods that were intended to become obsolete within a fairly short time span; producers, like consumers, expected, in the age of affluence, that whatever you might have possessed now, you would soon be likely to covet and then own other, 'better' things. The objects of the past, like the past itself, came to be thought of as obsolete, discrete, disconnected, and of little relevance to the present. By the same token the present was inevitably transitory and increasing attention was devoted to the speed with which the present was likely to merge with the future. Evocative new words and phrases were added to the vocabulary, such as *motel, astronaut, skylab, laundromat, autoroute, re-cycle, heliport* — words redolent of an affluent and technology-filled existence in which everything worthwhile was on the move. In

America, there were drive-in banks and movies and even your food could be 'to go'.

The transitoriness which people expected in their dealings with material objects was also expressed in their dealings with other people. Much in the same way as they expected to trade in a car after a few years or to throw away paper plates or handkerchiefs or underwear once they had been used, so people also seemed to expect their human relationships to be more superficial, more numerous, and more transient than had once been the case.[32] There were many reasons for this sort of expectation. In an age of mass communication, mass transportation and huge conurbations, one could hardly fail to be acquainted with more people than ever came the way of the medieval villager. Furthermore, as modern economies became directed less predominantly towards manufacturing and more towards service industries, you were bound to have more and more contacts of an increasingly depersonalized nature with those who took your train or bus fare or served your hamburgers or helped you with your insurance or tax forms. Economic pressures too, helped to induce everybody from ambitious young business executives to the girls on the 'temp' circuit to want to change their home or job location with some frequency. But the transitoriness of a person's relationships was primarily regarded not only as a necessary by-product of other compensating pressures but also as something approaching a social virtue. It demonstrated a person's capacity to make new friends, and that he or she successfully avoided the pitfalls of sinking into a social rut or being part of a 'clique'.[33] The frequent transitoriness of things—of objects and of human relationships—was not only a fact; it was for many people a quality to be valued.

SELF-INDULGENCE

You Must See This . . . Movie Or You'll Never Know advertisement for *Sexual Secret of Marijuana,* Los Angeles, 1973.

If you don't try Foremost candy-cane peppermint ice-cream over the holidays—you'll never know what you've missed! US radio commercial, Christmas, 1972.

I think that's what life comes down to. If you're not having fun with

your husband or wife, go have fun with somebody else. Life is too
short to have somebody oppress you. Sally Struthers (actress who
played the daughter in *All In The Family*), *1973.*
A fourth 'new' value is what one might call the ethic of *self-*
indulgence. Gratifications and rewards can and should be
immediate rather than deferred, and should correspond
not only to our basic needs but also to our more transitory
and impulsive desires.

The quest for immediate gratification was not new and is
indeed, experienced by every infant. The hungry or thirsty
child does not know about the Puritans and the work ethic, or
the idea that one should practise self-restraint. Furthermore,
British and American literature and folklore are full of variations on the theme that the streets of New York or London
are paved with gold or that there was immediate money to
be made in the hills or farmland of this or that legendary and
as yet largely untapped part of the country.

The ethic of self-indulgence implies more, however,
than a mere shortening of the time-span between want and
satisfaction; it also suggests something about the nature of
the wants themselves. Everybody 'wants' adequate food
and shelter. In temperate climates everybody 'wants' some
sort of clothing. These things are among the material prerequisites for a functioning life. At a more sophisticated
level, virtually everybody in modern Western society may
be said to 'want' access to mechanical transportation and
to artificial lighting. But the things that people said they
wanted in modern British and American society went beyond
basic material necessities and were often of a psychological
almost as much as a material nature: love, reliability, security.
In the age of abundance, these qualities were saleable and
were often sold in conjunction with the material commodities
and services in which they were said to inhere. With your
Hertz car, for example, you also got 'One less thing to worry
about'. Furthermore, many of those goods and services themselves would never normally have been 'wanted' by someone ignorant of their existence and qualities. You don't need
advertisers to tell you that when you are hungry you want
food and when you are cold you want clothing and heat. But
you are unlikely to feel that you want a colour television set

with a remote control channel changer or a package holiday three or four thousand miles away unless the purveyors of these attractions spend time and money telling you about them and encouraging you to think that they *are* commodities that you want.

There is probably a loose continuum between, at one end, those 'wants' that are universal, recurrent and unavoidable, and, at the other, those leisure/luxury 'wants' that are only experienced by people with surplus time and money who are on the receiving end of intensive advertising compaigns.[34] Those wants that fall closer to the first end of the spectrum (such as adequate food and shelter) might be called 'needs' while those that fall near the other end (like colour TV—or substantially more than adequate food and shelter) might be called 'desires'. The satisfaction of 'needs' was almost universal in Britain and America during our period; but there was also a constant spiral process consisting of the creation and subsequent satisfaction of often transitory and even impulsive 'desires' followed by the stimulating of new and greater ones.

There are two further aspects of the ethic of self-indulgence that should be discussed. The first is that, in conjunction with the constant stimulation and partial satisfaction of desires, there was a new emphasis on the value of first-hand experience for its own sake and a tendency to disregard the processes that led to it. The second is the increasing importance that was attached to experience enjoyed not by the intellect or even the emotions but through the senses.

There were many reasons why the emphasis on personal experience—of which there was a long lineage in both British and American history[35]—reached particular prominence in the decades following the second world war. For those of a philosophical predisposition, it was probably reinforced by the popularity of existentialism[36] with its stress on the obligation of the individual to develop his or her own essence as a result of freely-chosen action—a philosophy taken by many who knew something about it to be advocating almost any novel experience as preferable to routine. The only bad action was one in which nothing new was experienced, for this would leave one's essence untouched. Another popular philosophical line of thought that tended to elevate the significance of experience was that of neo-Freudian psychology. Freud had long been understood (or misunderstood) as arguing that one should clear one's emotional blockages to uninhibited self-expression. If you want to love or hate or scream or cry, said some of the post-Freudian psychologists and their popularizers, do so; it is good for you.[37] Thus, by a dubious sleight of logical hand, the conscious personal experience of hitherto hidden or repressed or even non-existent emotions was equated with being 'good for you' and even, by a small further extension, with being 'good'.

In addition to the popular philosophical trends of the post-war decades, the revolutions in technology and electronics and the new leisure and luxury of the age of abundance all helped to make a large range of new experiences more widely accessible than ever before. If you wanted to go to Morocco or Afghanistan, you could probably find ways of going; if young people from the provinces, inspired, perhaps, by what they had read in the papers or seen on television, wanted to lose themselves in the anonymity of the vast metropolis, eating Swiss cheese and Hungarian sausage and drinking French wine, this too was possible. There were drug experiences,[38] sex experiences, travel experiences, communality or loneliness experiences, clothes experiences — all, for the first time in history, available to far more than a tiny social elite. Anything new was a new experience. New was good.[39] Experience was good. The very concept of experience was widened to include almost anything that was thought to be good. 'You don't just see New York,' said Chet Huntley's authoritative voice over the television commercial for American Airlines (with their sung slogan 'To the Good Life, To Be Free'); 'You experience it.' And the Cecil Holmes people promoted a disc containing music from such movies as *Hit Man*, *Lady Sings the Blues* and *Shaft* with the words 'The Black Motion Picture Experience'.

In order to enjoy 'experience' to the full, you would probably be inclined to disregard or by-pass or short-circuit the sometimes laborious processes that made it possible. This, too, is a theme that recurs in modern British and American culture. For instance, advertisements for a complex product would often encourage you to think that 'all you have to do' is to switch it on or set it up or add water and, hey presto, it would do all manner of miraculous things for you. Maybe it contained some magic formula or, as in the case of puffed wheat, was 'shot from guns'. The important thing about the product was that it gave a guaranteeably gratifying experience. Here is a splendid example, the wording of an advertisement from American television for the Pierre Broussard Home Wine-Making Kit — 'the fastest easiest way yet to make your own wine':

> This complete kit has everything you need, even the imported grape concentrate made from the finest European grapes. Yes, here's the only kit that makes wine in just two steps, not five or six like most other kits. So you'll have six large bottles of fully-aged wine in just six weeks. But look, there's no need for bottles because you can leave the wine stored right in the box. . . . So get in on the fun and satisfaction of making your own delicious wine with the Pierre Broussard Home Wine-Making Kit.

This relative indifference towards the processes whereby experience is made possible and available were extended to experiences not just of things but also of people. Norman Mailer, in *An American Dream*, wrote of the attitude of Stephen Rojack's wife to others. She had, he said, 'an aristocratic indifference to the development of talent. One enjoyed what was in flower, one devoured it if it were good for one, but one left the planting to others.'

Attitudes like these were not uncommon. In a large and impersonal society, the life of the individual could easily become fragmented: he would mix with one (constantly shifting) group of people at work, an entirely different group away from work, and within a few years, move somewhere else and have to build up a whole new series of friends, associates, and contacts. As metropolitan areas grew in size and people became accustomed to commuting to and from work and to driving large distances for almost any social amenity, the likelihood that you would encounter people by chance whom you already knew became less frequent. It

also became less common to talk to people to whom you had
not been introduced; after all, they — unlike the members
of a village community — probably had their own network
of friends and contacts which, in all likelihood, would in no
way overlap with yours.

Under these circumstances, it was hardly surprising that,
when people did meet, there was bound to be a tendency
for them to type-cast each other according to whatever roles
they seemed currently prepared to play. 'What do you do?'
and 'Where are you from?' were the typical questions asked
of a stranger to whom one was introduced at a social gather-
ing. People would try to establish that they had the same
preference for a particular drink, movie actor, or cigarette.[40] This initial conversational sparring would, in
effect, be a way of saying to the other person: 'You and I are
bound to have come from and been through different places,
had different types of domestic and professional experiences,
and developed different tastes. But there must be a meeting
ground somewhere. . . . Let's try to find where it is.' Let us,
that is, try to get a clear picture of the characteristics of the
other person as those characteristics are presently combined
(or, to use mildly existentialist terminology, let us examine
the present state of the other person's constantly developing essence), and let us then see if there is anything in
that current picture that corresponds to anything within our current picture of ourselves. This approach can
involve a predisposition to understand the other person —
and even ourselves — almost exclusively as at present constituted, as finished objects. Experience, of people as of
things, of ourselves as of others, was of the here and
now.

For 'experience' to be *really* good, it had to be enjoyed
through the senses. The emphasis on the senses and the
accompanying vocabulary could sometimes be inchoate and
ill-defined. Generally, one is talking about the five physical
senses of touch, taste, smell, hearing, and sight (with an
optional sixth occasionally thrown in, known as extra-
sensory perception or ESP), although words like 'sensuous'
and 'sensual' were sometimes used almost interchangeably

and both would occasionally overlap sloppily with 'sensitive' and even 'sexual'.

By the 1960s, many people, reaching out for what they understood to be cultures and philosophies of oriental origin, learned how they had undervalued the capacity of their senses, particularly those of touch, smell, and taste. This realization was reinforced by the widespread availability in the age of affluence of new colours and textures for the adornment of one's home and one's body; exotic perfumes and cosmetics for both women and men, tasty new foods and drinks, scented candles, incense, and sculptured playgrounds for children. Drugs too, played their part, particularly that mildly sensitizing plant known variously as cannabis, marijuana, grass, pot, tea, the weed, acapulco gold, and (in its more refined state) hashish.[41]

We were becoming, wrote Ernest Dichter,[42] President of the Institute for Motivational Research at Croton-on-Hudson, New York, a 'tickle' society and a 'titilation' culture,

> gourmets in terms of our lives and our bodies, not just our palates. . . . I can go into hitherto forbidden areas; I can tickle myself between the toes; I can massage my hair with an electric brush; I can overheat my body and then cool it in ice-cold water after a sauna and discover a new form of exhilaration—a less dangerous one than alcohol produces. In a sauna you suddenly see another part of yourself, you discover a new part of your consciousness.

Dichter suggested that in order to encourage tourism to the USA, Americans might produce a gift-pack of typical products for sale at places like airport terminals. He lists the sort of thing that such a gift-pack might contain—goods 'that would surprise and enlighten prejudiced foreigners'—and they are almost all (except, perhaps, the small useful gadgets and soap products) goods that are appreciated directly with one or other of the senses:[43]

> fashion-smart cosmetic or toiletry items; delicious foods not usually thought of in connection with this country, such as cheeses, pastries, soups, jams and jellies, and wine (if feasible); small, useful gadgets; tobacco products; a hot shaving cream; a new laundry product; a soap or bath

product; fine candy; a new soft drink in a can; canned cocktail mix; etcetera.

No books, no pictures, no clothes, no watches or glassware; but a whole catalogue of things to stimulate, assuage, and smooth and soothe the senses.

Behind the word 'sense' was often the idea 'sex'. As well as the hot shaving cream and the sauna bath, the technology and affluence of the 1960s made available a plethora of creams and lathers, paints and powders, and objects of plastic, elastic, and rubber, all designed to increase one's sexual sensitivity. Figures were published showing that the incidence of sexual intercourse among teenagers was on the rise, that there was more admitted adultery (even elevated in some sub-cultures to an organizedly 'swinging' life-style) than ever before, and that all the traditional off-shoots of promiscuity — venereal disease, illegitimacies, abortions, divorce — were also increasing.

Whatever the shaky reliability of any statistical report on so private a topic, there can be little doubt that the members of the post-war generation in America and Britain had a less inhibited attitude towards sex and towards sensual experience in general than their parents and grandparents had done. These youngsters were brought up without first-hand experience of the deprivations of depression and war and were raised in a society of great affluence and technological sophistication which facilitated and encouraged the financial and geographical independence of children from their parents. Furthermore, the development and rapid distribution of the diaphragm, the birth-control pill, and the IUD enabled women for the first time to take responsibility for the time-table of their sexual and reproductive lives. Within such a context, it was only to be expected that there would be an increase in sexual activity, particularly among young people. Accompanying this increase in sexual activity, there was a corresponding elevation of the expression and satisfaction of sexual desire from its customary status as something to be waited for and rendered all due appreciation when its time came, to something approaching the apotheosis of the value of self-indulgence. Sex was no longer something that you would one day have the privilege of enjoying

or, indeed, something that was, overtly at any rate, confined
to partners whose relationship was sanctioned by law. By the
later years of our period, there is little doubt that, of all the
forms taken by the 'new' emphasis on experience for its own
sake and on sensual self-indulgence, the so-called sexual
revolution was at once the most conspicuous, the most provocative, and the most unavoidable.

The new emphasis on sense experience was partly stimulated and partly encapsulated by new commercial products.
There was, for instance, a huge new 'smells' industry. In
some ways, it was really an anti-smells industry. Just as the
scent of roses was once believed to keep you from smelling
(and therefore from being affected by) the plague, so the
modern deodorants, while preventing users from smelling
of one thing, ensured that they would emanate an aroma of
something else. Some had negative-sounding names, like
'Ban' and 'Arrid'; others, like 'Safeguard deodorant soap',
sounded neutral; and there were those, such as 'deodorant
Zest' (a soap that 'makes you feel cleaner than soap') or the
anti-perspirant 'Mum', that had names with more positive
connotations. The anti-smells industry included mouth-
washes ('Scope helps keep you face to face') and even baking
soda. The Arm and Hammer people had an American television advertisement suggesting that you leave an open box
of their baking soda in the refrigerator: 'It actually absorbs
food odors. . . . It'll keep your refrigerator sweeter, cleaner
and fresher-smelling. At the end of two months, put in a new
box—and pour the old box down the drain to make *it* clean-
smelling.'
     As well as the smell-reducers, there was also an avowedly
smell-giving side to the industry. 'Arden for Men suggests
Success', said the proud advertisements. 'And because its
tangy fragrance has staying power—the feeling lasts.' The
way to feel successful, it seemed, was to use any of Arden's
twenty-odd products ('for Men') and smell of Sandalwood
or Citruswood.[44] Or if you wanted to smell tough, why not
try something with 'Karate', 'Command' or 'Brut' written
on it? For a woman, particularly in the ecological late 1960s
and early 1970s, the thing to do was to smell 'natural'. Coty

came out with 'Sweet Earth' Fragrant Oils; their advertisement showed a girl in jeans walking through a beautiful
green field with a back-pack. And the caption? 'From the
quiet places of the world where you can hear things grow.'
Revlon's 'Natural Honey' Dry Skin Moisturising Lotion
would relieve dry or chapped skin in five sweet-smelling
ways, one for each of its five ingredients: Natural Honey,
Peach-Kernal Oil, Real Protein, Organic Herbs, and Sili-
cone. In one of the magazines handed out at Tube stations in
the early 1970s to girls commuting into London, Floris, 'the
well-established London Perfumers', were asked about the
meanings of some of the flowers used in their 'fragrances'.
Bluebell, it seems, stands for 'faithfulness', citron for 'ill-
natured beauty'; the chrysanthemum is the 'Golden Symbol
of Japan's Emperor', while the daffodil is the 'lily flower of
ancient days, sometimes called "The Lenten Lily" meaning
"I return your affection".'

One of the more extreme examples of the smells industry
at work comes from an advertisement for Musk Oil ('The
World's Most Exciting Perfume'). Just a drop behind the
ears, went the text,

> at the base of the throat, or at the wrist, will release its
> gentle fragrance. Suddenly, as if by magic, the fragrance
> of desire, the perfume of passion, the aroma of love—
> brings on the new YOU.

All this with a money back guarantee!

In addition to the sense of smell, that of taste too, was
commercialized on a big scale in the age of affluence. This
was hardly surprising in a period in which much attention
was devoted to pleasures drawn in by the mouth. 'What a
good time for the good taste of a Kent' said one cigarette
advertisement; 'enjoy the taste of extra coolness' purred
another. Howard Johnson's sold twenty-eight flavours of
ice-cream; Baskin-Robbins sold thirty-one. British customers of Colonel Sanders were invited to 'Take Home America's
Tastiest Bird'.

The 1950s and 1960s saw the burgeoning of restaurants
serving Indian food (in Britain) and Mexican food (in the
American south-west). This was due to many things—not

least of course, the immigration of Indians and Mexicans during the 1950s and 1960s, itself a product of the affluence of those years. But the people of London, Manchester and Glasgow, or Dallas, Tucson and Los Angeles clearly liked what the spicy food did to their taste buds or they would not have chosen to consume so much of it. It is arguable that a lot of curry or hot pepper can ruin your sense of taste rather than develop it by making it indifferent to all but the strongest stimuli. But more and more people were prepared to seek out gastronomical adventures and to think of their sense of taste as one worth cultivating. Exotic and tasty foods —not just Indian and Mexican but also Greek, Japanese, Italian, Chinese, and 'Jewish'—all became far more familiar to the general consumer. People would buy the appropriate ingredients and spices and try out their own home-made Madras curry, sukiyaki, moussaka or gefilte fish—followed, possibly, by rum-butter ice-cream or mango sherbet and then maybe by jasmin-scented tea or Turkish coffee.

Children's foods too, took off in a variety of new directions. The big cereal firms, in particular, spent vast sums appealing to young consumers who may not have had any money of their own but who were important and almost irresistible influences upon the cereal-buying proclivities of their mothers. Sometimes the cereal would have an 'adult' or 'scientific' appeal: Kellogg's 'Sugar Pops' were 'fortified with eight essential vitamins', for instance, while their Raisin Bran contained '100 per cent of the officially established minimum daily adult requirement of iron in one ounce'. There would occasionally be a touch of patriotism: 'Britons make it, it makes Britons' said Welgar Shredded Wheat, while Corn Chex was 'made of the grain that helps America grow'. This product would be 'New' while that would say 'The Best to You Each Morning'. But above all there was the appeal of taste. Count Chocula, a General Mills product, was 'Sweet Chocolate Flavor Cereal and Marshmallow Bits'; the combination of a pseudo-scary Dracula on the front and the offer of a 'Monster Towel' on the back helped to make the package all the more attractive to children. This formula —an appealing combination of tastes and consistencies with the added incentive of a laughably grotesque picture on the front and a free offer on the back—was obviously a success, and was used by General Mills in Franken Berry ('Sweet Strawberry Flavor Cereal and Marshmallow Bits'), as well as in Sir Grapefellow, Baron von Redberry, and others. Nabisco produced such goodies as 'Sweet Wheats' (Honey Cinammon, frosty bits of shredded wheat cereal) while Kellogg, the first big firm to go in for sugar-frosted and other taste-embellished cereals, continued to lead the field, and in Britain, were able to sport the royal coat of arms, along with a jovial tiger and a free offer of a gyroscope or whatever, on their packages.

The tactile sense, too, received its fair share of commercial attention. 'You cannot possibly appreciate the sheer, sensuous self-indulgence of cashmere until you try it', said the advertisements, so 'come along to Harrods and slip into a cashmere coat by Aquascutum.' A Canadian blended whisky advertisement featured a slinky blonde, clad in black, purring that 'Black Velvet Feels Good On You'—a sexy cousin, perhaps, to that perennial British underwear slogan: 'Next to Myself I Like Vedonis'. Scholl came out with a softening lotion 'that has cocoa butter softeners to help make winter-dry legs and feet soft and smooth again. . . . Makes you feel butter-soft all over!' More and more of the products that we use, wrote Ernest Dichter,[45]

> are ticklers and titillators, elements of self-stimulation. Clothing that appeals by means of its 'inner feel' may well be on the way, for example, dresses with caressing linings —or ones that tickle—or pocket linings that provide a tactile adventure.

And Tom Wolfe described the sheer sensuality experienced by a girl in the 'swinging London' of the 1960s trying on a new—and tight—pair of trousers:[46]

> She puts the trousers on and she could feel the trousers gripping her whole sacred ischial dark damp taboo wonderland of folds, flaps, integuments, tissues. . .

It was not only one's drinks, underwear, foot oils and ischial integuments that had to 'feel' right. So in a specifically tactile as well as a more general way, did other people. The Esalen Institute in California was only the most famous of many organizations in the later years of our period that encouraged people to be more sensitive towards the nonverbal communications, the body language that took place between people. It was important, said the sensitivity trainers, for you to know how to touch and be touched, to feel from another person's nose or forehead or shoulders or back— and not just from their voices and eyes and hands—what they were wishing to communicate to you. The people at Esalen and elsewhere maintained that physical contact had been so firmly reserved for the realm of the purely sexual that it had almost lost any other role in adult behaviour. But there was no reason why everybody should not be encouraged to sensitize his or her own body—particularly the fingers—to whatever messages they may encounter from other skins, bodies, and fingers.

The senses of sight and hearing had been less neglected than those of smell, taste, and touch, but they too received a boost. For example, one of the things that most struck American prisoners of war returning to the USA after years in North Vietnam was that everybody was wearing brighter colours than they used to do. The POWs were catching the legacy of the age of 'op' art and psychedelic posters.[47] And as for the heightened sense of hearing people accustomed to the hi-fi and stereo sets of the 1960s, for example, found it increasingly difficult to listen comfortably and uncritically to music reproduced on earlier radio and record-playing equipment.

The commercialization of the senses was a characteristic feature of modern culture. The commercialization of sex, on the other hand, is as old as commerce itself, and there is nothing particularly modern about the suggestion that along with a particular commodity, you might get some sex too. Nevertheless, one aspect of the use of sex in modern advertisements is worth nothing. Until the more affluent post-war years, advertisements usually tended to emphasize the legitimacy and normality of the sex that was being offered; it was either happy marital sex or a wholly acceptable surrogate. What was offered was not real, physical sex, furthermore, but something less definable such as warm and secure

companionship. In modern advertisements, things tended
to be more overtly physical and the emphasis was increasingly on you, the individual sex-seeker and -getter rather than,
as in the days gone by, on you as part of a legitimate and
stable partnership.

Often, the sexual appeal was direct and cheerful. MILK
DRINKERS MAKE BETTER LOVERS, said the bumper
stickers, while the California Pizza Houses asked 'Had A
Piece Lately?' Slumberdown continental quilts advertised
in British papers and magazines showing a pursed-lipped
girl in bed anxiously covering her bosom; their caption was
'Ever slept with a continental?' Even more unambiguous,
perhaps, was the girl on the posters in London's Tube stations
standing with her back to you, legs wide apart, wearing the
shortest of hot-pants, part of a buttock visible, and inviting
you to 'Come On In' ('to the colourful world of Elle tights',
of course. . .).

The sexual appeal was not always so inviting and so totally
free of an association with guilt. Indeed, a characteristic
theme in the advertising of later years was the emphasis on
slightly outré forms of sexual activity and the implication
that sexual insecurity or irregularity was not as uncommon
as you might have thought. 'Make Sure the Dubonnet She's
Drinking Is Yours' said the caption to the picture of the girl
being punted along the romantic river by one young man
while surreptitiously accepting a drink from another on the
bank that the boat is passing.[48] Another Dubonnet advertisement, combining the usual appeal of unadulterated sexual
acquisitiveness with an undercurrent of sexual challenge,
told television viewers in America about a mixed drink with
an enticing name. 'Some people think Dubonnet is a drink
for little old ladies,' murmured the sexy female voice, 'have
a French Wench and see.' What self-respecting American
man could refuse a French Wench after that? If you weren't
up to Dubonnet, perhaps you weren't up to other activities.
Fear of impotence made possibly its most blatant appearance
in the advertisements for Heineken beer in Britain in
1974. There was a 'Before' picture (a man with a long,
droopy moustache or nose) and an 'After' picture (the
moustache now long, upturned, and stiff) — with the mess-

age: 'Heineken. Refreshes the parts that other beers cannot reach.'

There were other types of sexual uncertainty, too. Cossack vodka, ostensibly telling you that their product did not leave a nasty taste in the mouth, featured a girl in a Lichtenstein-type drawing wondering to herself 'It's Been Wonderful, really wonderful. . . But How Will It Seem In The Cold Light Of Morn?' And, of course, there were the attractions and fears of infidelity. 'Next time you fly a 747 to New York,' said the advertisement for Air India, featuring a beautiful air hostess, 'Be Unfaithful'. It went on:

> There comes a time in every man's life when he gets a little bored with the obvious. Bored with doing the things he's always done. Simply because he's always done them. Take flying. The obvious choice to anywhere is your national airline. Until one day, for no apparent reason, you decide to break the habit. And sample the competition. Maybe an Air India hostess catches your eye in the departure lounge. . .

And the final punch line? 'We'll try to turn that little flirtation into a big affair.'

The widespread emphasis on self-indulgent sense experience in modern times had one further implication of some significance: a corresponding tendency in some circles to downgrade the importance of intellectual experience. Daniel Yankelovich,[49] a few years after the height of the university ferment, wrote of

> student mistrust of rational, conceptual, calculative, and abstract modes of thought. . . The scholarly professor of English literature begins to wonder about his own sanity after a long day's experience with the glories of the English language being reduced to a repetitive series of 'like', 'you know', 'freaked out', etcetera.

The historian, too, wrote Yankelovich, began to question the validity of his own academic subject as he spent months with students for whom only the present and the future seemed to exist. Time itself, he concluded, 'loses its ordered sequences, becoming a patternless series of quantum leaps from one sensory impression to another.'

There was nothing new about a streak of anti-intellectualism in America. Richard Hofstadter devoted a major work to the history of this tendency and showed how, at all periods of the American story, a strain of anti-intellectualism may be said to have existed.[50] In Britain too, a certain distrust of cerebration and of those who were conspicuously good at it had long been evident. In the USA, Adlai Stevenson probably lost some potential supporters as it became clear to everybody that he was what was unkindly dubbed an 'egghead'; in Britain, Iain Macleod was characterized, with not a little contempt, by one of his lordly superiors, as being 'too clever by half'. In both cultures, there was a proud pragmatism and a suspicion of anything purely theoretical.

The reasons for anti-intellectualism in Britain and America were varied. In America, it was probably related to a suspicion of foreigners and their supposedly inflexible ideologies; anti-intellectualism often tended to become stronger after periods of large-scale immigration or other (for example, military) involvement in the affairs of people in other parts of the world. In Britain, those few with highly-trained minds had traditionally affected a certain diffidence about the fact, while those without advanced formal education had rarely permitted themselves to feel deprived and had often rationalized the deprivation as being even something of an advantage.

Even among thinkers of spectacular intellectual accomplishment, the idea had often been put forward that controlled thought expressed in cogent and carefully structured language could inhibit rather than facilitate the release of certain types of concept. 'Up, up, my friend, and quit your books/ Let Nature be your Master!' wrote Wordsworth, giving vent to a powerful urge that swept the romantic movement of the early nineteenth century. The writings of the metaphysical German philosophers—Kant, Hegel, Schopenhauer, and above all, Nietzsche—seemed to many to point in a similar direction (at least in so far as their determination to transcend the messages of the unaided intellect was concerned) and so, in the twentieth century, did those of Freud and Fromm, Heidegger and Sartre. These thinkers were not, of course, irrational, or, in any simple sense, antirational. But the thrust of their writings did suggest (to those who read them, and even more so, to those who heard simplified versions of them) that the human condition could no longer be understood in terms of a purely rational and intellectual analysis.

This erosion of faith in unadulterated rationality was buttressed in modern times from many sides by factors already discussed: the scientific advances of Einstein, Heisenberg, and others, the almost unfaceable outrages of Hitler's death camps, the unleashing of atomic power, and the affects on thinking processes of television and other electronic inventions.[51]

In the face of these onslaughts against traditional objective rationality, some people, particularly the young, groped towards new ways of communicating with each other. How can you be sure, they would sometimes wonder, that others experience the same things as yourself? How, indeed, can your own experiences be given any wider validity? It was no longer easy to take for granted that everybody was capable of the same processes of ratiocination or to be sure that experience could be communicated through rational exposition. Hence, partly as compensation for the erosion of faith in rationality, but partly too, as its sympton, cause, and effect, there was a growing emphasis in modern Britain and America on the importance of the experience of the senses.

PART III

7   Towards a culture of fusion

THE 'TRADITIONAL' AND THE 'NEW'

By the 1970s, when Lyndon Johnson, in retirement, grew his hair down over his collar, and the Ceylon Tea Centre in London invited you to 'Come To Our Pot Party', it looked as though some of the visual and verbal symbols of the 'new' values were taking permanent hold inside the bastions of the 'old'. Conversely, a young man or woman opening a boutique, a poster shop, or a macrobiotic restaurant might have looked like an embodiment of the 'new' culture, but the enterprise would hardly be a success unless its founder were at least partially devoted to such traditional virtues as hard work and self-reliance. From some perspectives it looked as though the adherents of traditional values were successfully incorporating the signs and slogans and practices of those of the new values; from others, it looked as though the process of incorporation was going the other way.

To a considerable extent, the 'traditional' and the 'new' social values formed two clusters of more or less consistent attitudes that were in conflict with each other. When we talked about American culture and the Puritan ethic, for example, we emphasized the importance of such virtues as self-abnegation, deferred gratification, and so on. These puritan virtues clearly conflicted with the 'new' ethic of self-indulgence. If the values of the Puritans (or those that later generations ascribed to them) concentrated upon the importance of work, the 'new' values gave greater prominence to the importance of play; puritan values emphasized that the time elapsing between desire and fulfilment should be long, the 'new' values, that it should be attenuated almost into nothingness. The 'new' value of participatoriness could clearly be something of a threat to the traditional British value of deference, while that of transitoriness would not be easy to maintain alongside, say, the virtue of loyalty to one's team or group.

Sometimes, the apparent clash between the old values

and the new even took on specific institutional forms. In America in the early 1970s, for instance, there was a dispute between people who believed in the policy implications of a traditional interpretation of the value of equality of opportunity (whereby blacks or women were thought to have the right to get to college or into political conventions on exactly the same principles as anyone else) and those who subscribed to the policy implications of one aspect of the 'new' value of participatoriness (whereby it was thought that such groups should benefit from 'affirmative action' to compensate them for having been largely excluded from society's deliberations for so long). In Britain, similarly, the traditional value of self-restraint was often invoked in various guises as a means of criticizing the CND marchers or the Stop The Seventy Tour campaign — both of which were, among other things, embodiments of some aspects of the newer values of participatoriness. When the clash of values made itself felt in this crude and overt sort of way, it often coincided with a convenient social or economic line-up: the old against the young, the rich against the poor, the producers against the consumers, the political right against the political left.

More commonly however, there was no such convenient social battle-line drawn between putative adherents to the old values and the new, for the very good reason that most people were drawn to elements of each. One might almost say, indeed, that it was part of the human condition to be drawn towards apparently inconsistent poles, and that it is a mark of individual maturity to be able to mediate between them. We are all familiar with the dilemma that faces us when we 'want' to do one thing but think that we 'ought' to do something else. Many of the greatest works of literature have dealt with the conflict between the demands of duty and love. And the inconsistency between the old and new values that we have been discussing does correspond, to some extent, to the sort of value conflict that any individual is likely to experience throughout life. What we have identified as the older values are loosely related to the demands of the 'intellect' or of the 'super-ego' or one's parent figures; the newer ones to those of the 'emotions' or the 'ego' or 'id' or one's picture of the demands of one's own childishness. It may be therefore that in distinguishing traditional values from those that appeared to be more dominant in recent times one is, in part at least, applying to social history the lessons of one's own psychic history and imputing to earlier generations an adherence to the sterner 'parent' values that we all accept to some degree, and to modern generations a primary allegiance to more permissive 'child' values.

Such an inclination would be understandable enough, but it is deceptively oversimplified. For one thing, some aspects of the 'new' values are not always inconsistent with some aspects of the 'old'. Participatoriness, for instance, is a re-emergence of a value that was supposedly prized in the very New England townships that acted as the crucible of the stern puritan values of old and is quite consistent with the proud localism that characterized those far-off days. Similarly, a society with 'the pursuit of happiness' in its founding document cannot really be said only recently to have discovered the value of self-indulgence. And Britain, an island nation that provided the world with far more than its fair share of sailors and explorers, was not unfamiliar with the virtues of transitoriness, or indeed, the advantages of a preoccupation with technique. Some aspects of the 'new' values represent genuinely new responses or new situations. But in some respects these values were merely new variations on time-honoured themes.

Furthermore, there are inconsistencies not only between some of the 'old' values and the 'new' but within each set as well. Mention was made, for example, of the opposite directions in which the American values of 'liberty' and 'equality' were capable of leading; in Britain, the impassioned adherence to freedom (particularly from foreign domination) could look strange alongside the belief that one should curb the expression of strong emotions or that one should give the benefit of the doubt to those who palpably wield author ity. And among the 'new' values there is some inconsistency between, for instance, the demands behind and the motives for the values of participatoriness, with its inclination towards personal familiarity with one's local physical and social environment, and that of transitoriness.

So the material in Parts I and II should not be summarized

in such a way as to imply that there is a clearly defined and consistent set of traditional values, one set in Britain and another in America, which came into conflict in modern times with a new international set of values. Our formulation is far more tentative: that by about the 1960s, a number of social values, all of them admittedly originating in the distant past but generally not widely or intensely espoused until relatively recent times, seemed to be competing, within society as a whole and within individual members of society, with more traditional social values generally held to have been the dominant ones in the past. Those traditional social values were markedly different from one culture to another. Although the puritan virtues and the idea of liberty were not unfamiliar to the British, and although American culture was not inimical to, say, certain forms of xenophobia or emotional self-restraint, it seemed wiser to treat the two traditional cultures separately. The emphasis was on contrast; traditional values were best elucidated in the context of separate — and different — national societies. In Part II, however, when discussing the 'new' values that seemed to be particularly characteristic of the post-war decades, it seemed more realistic to treat Britain and America together. This was not, of course, meant to imply that the two cultures had completely converged or that values dominant in the one society would necessarily or automatically become the ascendant values in the other, but merely that modern British and American, and no doubt other Western, technological, affluent cultures were characterized more by their similarities than by their dissimilarities. The emphasis was on comparison; the 'new' values could best be understood in an international context.

Thus the 'traditional' and the 'new' values were hardly a pair of coherent and consistent clusters. The two labels are analytically useful but do not represent accurate pictures of historical truth. As for the modern relationship between the two, there was a constantly shifting, kaleidoscopic interweaving of some aspects of the traditional values of both British and American societies with some aspects of the recently-ascendant values, like the patterns made by clouds on a squally but sunny day.

CONSENSUS, POLARIZATION, SYNTHESIS

From the perspective of the 1970s, it is clear that these cultural patterns were not entirely lacking in structure. The process of incorporation may have been in a number of directions, but it was not haphazard; some elements in the culture of American and British societies seem to have been in the ascendant at certain times while others were being at least partially submerged. In general, the predominant pattern in the post-war years seems to have been a broad progression from relative value consensus to value conflict and even polarization and then on towards a new and broader value consensus.

In the early years after the war, many in America and Britain continued to subscribe to a set of agreed values by and large consistent with those traditional to each society. Then, as the years passed and the technological and electronic revolutions and the post-war affluence seeped into most corners of society, various sub-cultures began to attach increasing importance to some of the 'new' values. In time, both the traditional values and the new appeared to be in a state of almost perpetual cultural confrontation, and by the late 1960s there was even talk of the coexistence of two or more utterly antagonistic cultures;[1] one heard of the 'Counterculture' and of an 'Alternative Society'. By the 1970s however, many of the cultural collisions appeared to have become less intense as there developed what looked to some like a mutual interpenetration of values that had hitherto sometimes seemed to be implacably opposed, and to others like a successful reassertion of the stern and traditional values of the past.

This somewhat abstract formulation is, of course, only an extremely rough approximation to a complex truth. It can, nevertheless, be traced through a number of historical processes. For example, it is worth examining some of the political confrontations of the post-war decades.

No era is without its political dramas, its heroes and its villains, its winners and its losers. There is hardly a year in the period since 1945 that did not contain some spectacular event or see the emergence of some controversial policy or personality. If one is looking for passion and confrontation on the national and international political arena, it is never hard to find. However, there was a difference in the quality of the popular response to the major public events as the years passed.

The early period contained some epoch-making political developments — Truman's cold war internationalism and the rise of McCarthyism in America, for example, and the austerity and the nationalization programme and the beginning of the end of Empire in Britain. These things certainly aroused the minds and passions of those who were informed and involved, but the popular response remained relatively muted — at least as viewed from the perspective of later decades. In part this may have been because many people, particularly in Britain, were still resting from the draining effort they had put into fighting the war and felt that postwar policy was of such a lower level of immediacy that it could hardly enlist their active involvement to anything like the same extent. Political divisiveness was probably also kept to a minimum in Britain by the constant hope, fed by countless rumours, that one day soon rationing and housing shortages would somehow be brought to an end and Britain would return to 'normal'. Under these circumstances, people felt an understandable reluctance to rock the communal boat. In America, there was sometimes the added element of fear; many who might have liked to express publicly their distaste for some of the more aggressive policies and pronouncements of the later 1940s and early 1950s felt that the virulent anti-communism of those days was so pervasive and indiscriminate that it was safer to keep quiet.

By the middle and later 1950s however, this pattern began to show signs of changing. It would not be true to say that entire adult populations became politicized; personal problems such as the family budget continued to take precedence with most people over the national and international dramas of the day. But there was a growing tendency for policies and politicians to evoke greater popular displays of sympathy or antipathy than had recently been the case. There is no denying the intrinsic dramas of Suez or Little Rock, or the real threat to American national esteem represented by the successful launching of the first Sputnik in 1957. Each of these events was replete with powerful implications about which reasonable people might radically disagree. But the vigour and intensity of the response, coming as it did after a period of relative political quiescence and acquiescence, must be explained, in part at least, in terms other than those suggested by the political issues themselves. It would be hard to argue, after all, that the stifling of freedom at Berkeley in 1964-5 was more fundamental than the threat to freedom embodied by Senator Joseph McCarthy a dozen years earlier; yet McCarthy aroused no demonstrations and counter-demonstrations comparable to those sparked off by Berkeley.

More than a series of political views was being expressed by the new political involvements and activisms of the later 1950s and 1960s. The members of the Campaign for Nuclear Disarmament in Britain were certainly against Britain's nuclear defence policy, and the members of the Student Non-Violent Coordinating Committee in America were implacably opposed to racial discrimination. But organizations such as these also exuded to their participants the warm sense of belonging to a select club of well-meaning and like-minded comrades. The shared experience became almost as important for many participants as the political beliefs that had brought them together in the first place.

A corollary of this sense of belonging was a sharp awareness of those to whom one was opposed. The people who argued *against* Britain's unilateral nuclear disarmament or *against* racial desegregation had to be not only opposed but even, it began to be argued with increasing vehemence, confronted and shown the error of their ways. Confrontations engineered by CND or SNCC in the early 1960s were generally mild contrasted with some of those of, say, the Yippies at Chicago in 1968 or the Stop the Seventy Tour campaign in Britain in 1970; opposition to the Vietnam war took more aggressive forms—even in Britain, a nation officially not involved— than did the political protests of a decade earlier. At times in America in the late 1960s, it even seemed to some observers as though the most dramatic confrontations—those associated with racial tensions and with the passions aroused by the Vietnam war—might tear society apart. The two factors were

seen by some as being related. The Vietnam war, claimed
some of its opponents, was among other things a war whose
horrors would never have been perpetrated against white
people; "gooks', so to speak, were yellow 'niggers'. Furthermore, it was often argued that domestic violence of the sort
that tore the heart out of Watts, Newark, Detroit and elsewhere was not exactly discouraged by the nightly TV
message that the way to deal with one's intransigent foes was
by the use of force; nor was the sensitive problem of race
relations helped by a society whose young manhood had
been brutalized by the experience of what many considered
an unjust war. The urban riots of the later 1960s badly shook
American self-confidence. 'Our nation', wrote Otto Kerner
in the introduction to the report of the US Riot Commission
in 1968, 'is moving toward two societies, one black, one white.'
He went on to suggest that 'to pursue our present course
will involve the continuing polarization of the American
community and, ultimately, the destruction of basic democratic values.'

Political expressiveness, participation, confrontation, and
even polarization were not confined to the 1960s, nor did
these things happen in exactly the same ways at the same
times in both the UK and the USA. Political conflict and the
polarization of opinions did not stop in either country at the
end of the decade. Far from it; the eruptions of student protest at Kent State in 1970 or Essex and Oxford in England in
1974, were as bitter as anything in the 1960s. History does
not fit conveniently into decades, and British and American
history do not progress in lock-step.

Nevertheless, confrontations in both Britain and the USA
were fewer in the 1970s and for the most part less violent than
those of the middle and later 1960s. Furthermore, much of
the steam that had fuelled the political confrontations of
the 1960s seemed, by the 1970s, to have become canalized in
directions of a more personal and less public or political
nature.[2] The people whose energies had been thrown into
the civil rights movement or the anti-war movement of the
1960s seem to have had younger brothers and sisters who,
by the 1970s, were more concerned with the right to say or
smoke or sleep with whatever or whomever they chose.

So, some time around the late 1950s and early 1960s, and then again about a decade later, substantial changes appear to have occurred in the configurations of British and American social values. Neither social institutions nor social attitudes, of course, change suddenly or dramatically, and probably the single most important thing about the values of the British and the Americans during the three decades or so after the war was the extent to which, for the most part, they did not change. Nevertheless, it is remarkable how frequently such changes as did occur can be traced back either to the period falling roughly between Suez, Little Rock, or Sputnik, and a few years later, the end of the Macmillan era and the assassination of President Kennedy, or to the years of the Heath government in Britain and the first Nixon administration in the United States.

Very broadly, one might say that while traditional social values seemed to be holding their position of dominance throughout this modern period, some aspects of the 'new' values obtained substantial adherence during the 1960s, and by the late 1960s were presenting a severe challenge to their more traditional rivals; many of the social upheavals and clashes in the later 1960s were, in essence, social or political manifestations of profoundly different sets of values. The apparent ebbing of the tide of confrontation and conflict in the 1970s was, similarly, an expression of the gradual emergence of a new value consensus.

This division of the cultural history of the post-war years into three segments is reinforced by a number of further considerations. In the first place, there were the various changes discussed in Chapter 5: the acceleration of the diffusion of technological (particularly electronic) innovation and the widespread belief that society-wide affluence had all but arrived. These quantitative changes, not always fully apparent in the years immediately following the war, were at their zenith during the 1960s. In particular, these years saw a substantial extension of the opportunities for cheap travel as well as the final near-saturation of British and American homes with television sets—a veritable revolution in the opportunities available to ordinary people for the widening of their direct and indirect experiences of other times, places, and people. By the late 1960s and the 1970s, as economic stagnation, spiralling inflation, and rising unemployment became increasingly familiar economic patterns, and as the ecological movement began to encourage people to question the advantages of some kinds of further technological or economic 'growth', there were signs that much that was characteristic of the sixties might be in the early stages of retreat.

A second factor concerns the demographic composition of society during these years. Between about 1955 and 1965 the number of adolescents rose spectacularly. In America in the 1960s, the number of people between the ages of fourteen and twenty-five rose by almost twelve million—an increase of a sensational 44 per cent over their numbers in the previous decade. The only economic conditions familiar to the baby-boom generation of the 1960s were those of technological and economic expansion. This coincidence of, on the one hand, so many youngsters with no memories of, or personal associations with, severe economic deprivations and shortages, and on the other hand, apparently booming national economies, led to the spawning of a whole range of consumer industries and advertising techniques designed especially for the huge new youthful market. This consumption boom enjoyed by the war-free, leisured, and relatively affluent youngsters reached far beyond the wealthy Carnaby Street set or the sons and daughters of Scarsdale or Orange County. An engineering apprentice from Blackburn[3] said, 'I'm going to have a bit of fun while I live. I mean, your parents didn't have it, did they, with wars and what-not, and you're in a society now where you've got your leisure. Only thing you've got to do now is use it.' A dramatic drop in birth-rates during the late 1960s and the 1970s ensured that the unprecedented prominence of so many affluent youngsters, and of the attitudes associated with them, would probably be unlikely to return.

Finally, this was the first period in history when the total obliteration of humanity was a real possibility. It would be foolish to suggest that the youngsters of the 1960s were enjoying themselves just because they knew that the world might blow itself up a year later. But this knowledge undoubtedly took its place as one factor among many that helped to attract people to the 'new' values. Jeff Nuttall's book *Bomb Culture* was a brilliant attempt to document this awareness among young people in Britain, one of whom, Caroline Coon (head of an organization called *Release* which gave advice to people on drugs charges), said in a BBC radio programme in 1970:

> The kids I see don't want to work because how can they be sure that some idiot at the top level isn't going to make some awful mistake? And of course, I mean if one is really sure that perhaps one is not going to live for another five years, what's the point in doing anything?

A few years later, fear of the bomb seemed to have ebbed somewhat as other concerns became more prominent, and some of the main features of 'bomb culture' subsided.

Thus the economic condition of the 1960s, the new opportunities for travel, the arrival of television on a big scale, the 'baby-boom' adolescents, the fear of the bomb—these and other factors had helped to provide the backcloth for the remarkable assertion of the 'new' values, values which embodied a response to both the positive and the negative aspects of those historical factors. In so far as those factors were perceived positively (the great affluence, for instance), the new values proclaimed the legitimacy of taking advantage of them; the negative aspects (the possibility of a nuclear holocaust) seemed to reinforce the message of the new values that it was up to you to involve yourself in whatever was going—while the going was good. However, by the later 1960s and the 1970s, the features that had helped to project the 'new' values into the ascendant began to fade. Under these circumstances there seems to have been not only a re-emergence to a position of relative dominance of the traditional values of British and American society but also a reduction of tensions between the proponents of conflicting sets of values. As the tide of the 1960s ebbed, there seems to have been a tacit or even unconscious realization on all sides that the confrontations and conflicts of that heady period were, in part at least, symptoms of a unique set of social circumstances that would probably never recur.

This cultural trend, from consensus to polarization and on to a new mutual acceptance, represents in the broadest outline the relationship between some of the more important trends in post-war America and Britain. It might be amusing and even instructive to illustrate this from a source that proved revealing in Part II, namely, advertising.

In the years immediately after the end of the second world war, particularly in Britain which was living under a cloud of austerity, advertisers would generally make a greater appeal than in later years to the 'traditional' social values. For instance, a glance through papers and magazines of the 1940s and early 1950s reveals frequent appeals to authority of various kinds. The Army was called in by Wisdom who, in their advertisement for 'the correct-shaped toothbrush', pictured little soldiers pointing out the virtues of their product. The slogan, a nice combination of military (and perhaps subconsciously, dental) authority and controlled efficiency, was 'Just the Drill, says the Army'. Other traditional virtues evoked by British advertisements in the 1940s and early 1950s included reliability ('Write through life with a Mentmore'); an almost touchingly absurd elitism ('Even the wealthiest cannot buy better than Bronco Toilet Paper'); family life ('If you would your family please, Make sure you're buying Benedict peas'), and a slightly playful insularity ('Britons Make It: It Makes Britons'). In Britain and the USA alike, there were more advertisements than in later years for quasi-medical products of various kinds and for ways of cleaning and tidying up your appearance, but very few for what became the staple fare of later years— luxurious holidays abroad, alcohol, or tobacco.

The 'new' values were not entirely absent from the advertisements of the early post-war period even in Britain. Lifebuoy Toilet Soap already made you 'feel fresh in every pore' while Persil would sometimes anticipate the full flowering of participatoriness and invoke those 'seven million housewives' who 'can't be wrong'.

In general, however, it was not until the 1960s that the 'new' values began to form the most conspicuous basis of many commercial appeals. Air France combined their 'certain style of service' with being the 'ultimate in technology' while Benson and Hedges featured the 'very special box' demanded by their product. Other cigarette advertising emphasized participatoriness: 'Notice the way people notice you' if you offer them a Marlboro, while you're 'never alone with a Strand'. Qantas showed a blonde sitting on a beach facing the sea, legs apart, and invited you to 'Fly away to your beautiful beach. . . Anywhere on five continents'. Schlitz beer ran an advertisement showing a man leaning out over the side of a yacht and holding a beer can. 'You only go around once in life', said the slogan, 'So grab for all the gusto you can.'

The advertisements of the age of affluence were, for the most part, thunderingly successful, for the 'new' values which many of them invoked had spread widely through British and American culture. However, this same period witnessed a heightened awareness on the part of consumers of some of the tricks of the advertising trade and a growing scepticism about the fundamental integrity of the advertisers. Vance Packard's *The Hidden Persuaders* (first published in the late 1950s) had alarmed many readers and their fears were hardly assuaged by David Ogilvy's *Confessions of an Advertising Man* (published in 1964). It was at this period that 'Madison Avenue' came to mean not so much a street as a gigantic and more or less omniscient and omnipotent industry of manipulation. Why should the advertisers have been so successful and yet be regarded with such distaste?

The principal answer is that they were learning the lessons of motivational research and couching their messages in the verbal and visual language of the 'new' values of the age of affluence at a time when many people were deeply concerned about the erosion of 'traditional' values. It might be hard to deny yourself the pleasures of the scantily-clad girl offering you a Martini; both, indeed, were, as the advertisement said, 'IRRESISTIBLE.' But wasn't it one's duty to try? And shouldn't the advertisers be admonished for being so cunningly seductive? The success of much advertising, in other words, arose out of the same consideration that made people uneasy about it: its appeal to values that many found both attractive and dangerous. The frequent ambivalence towards advertising—a subconsciously warm but overtly

dismissive response to a particular advertisement and a
bitter admiration for the cleverness of the profession—was
in part a re-enactment of the wider conflict that many were
experiencing between the attractions of 'traditional' and
'new' values.

By the 1970s, much of the tension of this ambivalence had
subsided. People knew enough about 'Madison Avenue' to
know that its machinations did not always succeed and, for
their part, advertisers were more inclined to temper their
appeal to the newer values with judicious references to more
traditional ones. In Britain, the Midland Bank appealed
to variously raised female consciousnesses with its message:

> I've decided to become a bank manager. And there's
> nothing to stop me. At Midland. we girls have equal
> opportunities with the men. . . . Of course, I may decide
> to become a housewife. But that's a good career too, and
> I can always come back afterwards.

The Leeds Building Society showed a picture of a genial hippie and the caption: 'The Leeds is one Society Pete Jenkins
decided he'd opt into.' There was no juxtaposition of values,
old and new, that was not grist to the mill of the imaginative
advertiser. In the Los Angeles area, the TV screens were
forever recommending that you buy a Dodge car from a hill-
billy figure named Cal Worthington. 'Cal Worthington
Dodge', Cal himself would remind you, as he sang folksy
ditties with a banjo or wrestled with a baby elephant; 'Go
See Cal. Open *every* night of the week till midnight!' The
recipe contained a touch of transitoriness, a heavy dose of
pseudo-personalization, and for the traditionally minded,
a reminder that Cal's automobile empire was the rightful
reward for an individual prepared to work long hours and
rely on his own resourcefulness.

One traditional value that appeared again and again alongside the new was 'liberty'. If you bought an Astronette Hair
Dryer, you would get not only 'Air Cushion Comfort' and
'Salon Dryer Efficiency' but also 'Unique Freedom'. An
American radio advertisement for Yamaha motorcycles—
a symbol of transitoriness if ever there was one — made use
of the same traditional virtue in its slogan 'Don't you

deserve a little freedom before you lock yourself up for the day?' Sometimes a traditional value like freedom was given an up-to-date sound by simply coupling it with an appeal to the value of novelty: above a picture of Scholl sandals was the legend: 'The New Scholl Liberation Movement'.

The combination of the old and the new could sometimes be even more streamlined, and the very concepts of oldness and newness could themselves form the basis of a commercial appeal. Ads for new cars, for instance, would often emphasize that the latest model contained all the advantages of its predecessors ('what we have here is a Vega that still looks like a Vega, still handles like a Vega' or the Pinto Wagon which is 'the basic wagon idea all over again') — with the addition of some marvellous new improvements.

In the 1970s, as in the 1940s, the voices of commerce spoke sometimes in traditional tones, sometimes in the language of the 'new' values, often in both. A few advertisements do not prove anything. But it does appear as though, in the decade or so after the war, there was probably a preponderant appeal to the older virtues; by the 1960s, the emphasis was increasingly on the new values; by the 1970s, there appears to have been a stronger inclination than before to effect a judicious combination of the two.

CULTURAL FUSION

Traditional values had not been absent from British and American culture in the 1960s; merely threatened by rival attractions. By the end of the decade, they began to show signs of renewed strength. This reassertiveness of traditional values took a number of forms, some of them dramatic. There was the return to political power in America (in 1968) and Britain (1970) of forces widely perceived at the time as representing 'law and order'; there was the success of pressure groups (such as Mrs Mary Whitehouse's National Viewers and Listeners Association) designed to protect the traditional moral fibre of society; and there were even a number of police seizures and subsequent prosecutions of certain films (Warhol's *Flesh*, *Deep Throat*), art exhibits (some of John Lennon's lithographs), and underground newspapers (issues of the *International Times* or *Oz*) that were thought to be among the more conspicuous symbols of the 'new' culture of the 1960s.

But the forces of tradition would generally use subtler means to undercut or to neutralize the values of those to whom they were opposed and would characteristically try to promote greater value consensus. In particular, they would often adopt what might be called pre-emptive imitation, or liquidation by flattery. This may constitute at least a partial explanation of, for instance, the occasional adoption of the sartorial symbols of the new culture — the long hair and the jeans — by figures whose sympathies were predominantly with the more traditional culture. Pre-emptive imitation can work both ways, however, and may also provide a partial explanation of the radical youth who would get, say, a law degree at a respectable university in order to be able to go on and change the sort of society that attaches importance to things like university degrees. The trouble with pre-emptive imitation is that it is sometimes impossible to know which culture is imitating which. Take the pot-smoking, student-screwing professor; was he an adherent of 'traditional' values adjusting to the requirements of what he perceived of the 'new' — or vice versa? And what of the eminently reasonable minister of religion who was quite prepared to acknowledge the possible non-existence of God?

Adjustments and compromises between alternative and often conflicting beliefs are, of course, bound to be made all the time by any reasonably functioning society or individual. Perhaps, therefore, all that was indicated by the prevalence of pre-emptive imitation, by Lyndon Johnson's long hair, by the Ceylon Tea Centre's 'Pot Party', or by the radical student chasing the law degree, was that British and American societies in recent years could tolerate and even encourage adjustments and compromises between alternative sets of values, and that both societies, therefore, were continuing to function in a reasonably healthy and even dynamic way.

However, this theme of fusion, of compromise, of accommodation between pairs of competing claims is one that has recurred in many guises throughout this investigation. We noticed, for example, the adjustments between the sometimes

conflicting demands of equality and of liberty, and of centrifugal (or 'Celtic') and centripetal (or 'Roman') forces in
American culture; we discussed the partial erosion in recent
decades of barriers between 'us' and 'them' in social, artistic,
educational, and even religious hierarchies; mention was
made of Kammen's 'biformities' and also of Erikson's
'dynamic polarities'. And underlying the entire argument
has been a consideration of the relationships between
'traditional' values and 'new' values, American culture
and British. Throughout the writing of this book, the image
of pairs of magnets — and occasionally of reverse magnets —
has arisen intermittently in my mind.

To some extent, the recurrence of this theme can be attributed to the nature of the book, a work that depends for
its very structure upon the comparison and contrast of pairs
of concepts. However, as one surveys the culture of modern
Britain and America, it is hard not to be struck with the
thought that, underlying the entire story, there is an irrepres-
sible motif of something not unlike fission, and above all,
fusion. It is partly a question of the — sometimes successful
and sometimes unsuccessful — pre-emptive imitation of
one culture by another, a 'now' culture by a 'then' culture,
or a 'here' culture by a 'there' culture, and the occasional
development of cultural patterns that seem entirely new.
But it is deeper than that. As one distances oneself from the
details of the argument and surveys the general sweep of
British and American cultural history, what one observes is
an increasing tendency for the firm line between traditionally accepted cognitive categories to be challenged and even
to dissolve. In other words, many of the social conflicts of
modern British and American history raged around not
only competing sets of social values but around categories
of perception that were not infrequently tending to disintegrate and to be replaced. The instability of categories of
perception is prior to the instability of values and may be
said to lie at the root of much of the turbulence of modern
history.

An example is the distinction between the 'real' and the
'imaginary'. People used to say that a bar of soap or a house

or a parliamentary or presidential candidate or a political demonstration was something 'real', while a novel, play, joke or cartoon was a product of the 'imagination'. But the thrust of much modern history tended to militate against so straightforward a view. Two forces, in particular, appear in retrospect to have helped to throw the relationship between the 'real' and the 'imaginary' into some confusion. The first was the development of psychoanalysis and the growing appreciation of the workings of the subconscious; many people began to feel that if you believed that you brought your own (often subconscious) predispositions to bear upon what you perceived, it might be correspondingly more difficult to believe that you could ever perceive something that was objectively real. The second factor was the camera. On the television screen, in particular, ostensibly impossible juxtapositions of time, place, object and sound could be effected. As a result, 'reality', confounded by the electronically created 'imaginary', would sometimes try to imitate it. Art had always imitated life and life had sometimes and in some ways repaid the compliment. But such a symbiosis between the real and the imaginary was new.

There was nothing new in the inclination to question the existence of 'objective reality' or to consider the line between reality and imagination to be in part a product of one's own perceptions; this topic is found throughout the philosophical literature and it formed the basis of Plato's famous Cave Allegory. But it was a problem that, instead of occupying the minds of a few abstract thinkers, came, in modern Britain and the USA, to occupy a central position among the concerns of society at large. It was one thing to be squabbling about the respective merits of self-abnegation or self-indulgence, a work ethic or a play ethic, equality or freedom; it was a problem of an altogether prior order, however, if one could no longer be sure that such concepts as work or play or freedom had their basis in anything more 'real' than one's own carefully cultivated imagination.

The problem is illustrated by the Japanese play *Rashomon*, in which the same scene (the encounter of a husband and wife with a bandit in a forest, the seduction of the wife, and the killing of the husband) is re-enacted several times.

Each scene shows the events in a forest as seen by one or other of the presumed participants and, of course, each scene shows all the characters in a completely different light. Anybody who has attended hearings in a court of law will be familiar with this 'Rashomon effect'.

So will anyone reasonably familiar with the modern cultural history of Britain or America. The confusions between different levels of reality appeared again and again. For example, John Fowles titillated readers of his best-selling novel *The French Lieutenant's Woman*, a book set firmly in the nineteenth century, by constant references to the present day; just as one is settling into the spirit of Victorian England, one reads of Mary whose great-great-granddaughter 'is twenty-two years old this month I write in' and whose face 'is known over the entire world, for she is one of the more celebrated younger English film actresses'. Fowles also jerks the reader out of the 'reality' of the novel by discussing the dilemmas of the novelist and writing a pair of alternative endings. John Osborne's play *The Entertainer* was a sustained bitter joke about its principal character's capacity for self-delusion. 'You don't think I'm real, do you?' asks Archie Rice; 'Well, I'm not.' The same sort of sentiment appeared in American fiction and drama. 'Truth or illusion,' says George to Martha in *Who's Afraid of Virginia Woolf?* towards the end of their notorious all-night battle of cruel make-believe, 'who can know which is which?'

The 'Rashomon effect' was particularly conspicuous in the culture of politics.[4] Popular books like Vance Packard's *The Hidden Persuaders* and Joe McGinniss' *The Selling of the President* suggested that different people could be conditioned into perceiving a given object or person in a variety of ways or even into perceiving a variety of objects or persons as being all pretty much the same. McGinniss probably expected that his book would shock people and make them consider that in Nixon they had been sold a fraudulent bill of goods, that he was not as most people had been induced to perceive him during the election campaign. But, in fact, there was no great sense of outrage. If anything, many of McGinniss' readers probably felt some relief that at least their new President was now more adept at presenting a favourable TV

image than he had been in earlier elections. Indeed, one of
the by-products of television was that (particularly in image-
conscious California) it helped to enable people like Ronald
Reagan, George Murphy and Shirley Temple, famous for
their illusion-creating capacities, to become legitimate
candidates for office in the real world of politics. If you could
slip from the world of the imagination to the world of reality
the reverse journey could also be undertaken. Audie Murphy,
for example, a real-life hero of the second world war, became
even more celebrated once he had entered his new post-war
profession as a film star and portrayed his own exploits on
the screen.

Advertisers made use of the increasingly blurred line
between what was thought to be real and what was thought
to be imaginary. Film advertisements, for instance, exploited
the technique of telling people that (to take an instance from
the early 1960s) 'Paul Newman *is* HUD'. Another increasingly
common advertising technique was to print, in a magazine or
newspaper, what to all intents and purposes looked like a
feature article but which was, for veracity's sake, headed in
very small print with the word 'Advertisement'.

Styles of humour, too, particularly on or about film or
television, reflected a similar dissolution of the barriers between the real and the imaginary. 'Is this real, Daddy,' asked
the little girl watching TV, 'or are we on tape?'[5] There were
jokes after the six day war of 1967 to the effect that, as the
Israelis had got the war out of the way so quickly, could Moshe
Dayan kindly run it through again for the benefit of reporters.
And there were frequent cartoons (in the British *TV Times*,
for instance) around the theme of the man in the living room
being shot by the arrows of the Indians on his TV screen.

Another manifestation of the interrelatedness of the real
and the imaginary was the so-called New Journalism of the
1960s and its characteristic attempt to graft reality onto works
of the imagination, and conversely to apply creative techniques to the presentation of real events.[6] Norman Mailer,
for instance, wrote imaginative accounts of 'true' events—
political conventions, boxing matches, the 1969 moon landing — that had recently occurred but which, without his illum-
inating approach, would have been less vividly imprinted

upon the minds of his readership. In *The Armies of the Night* (as in Tom Wolfe's *Electric Kool-Aid Acid Test*), the events described did take place but were in part stimulated by the fact that the principal participants knew that their activities were being recorded by film cameras. The real and the imaginary were deliberately cross-fertilized in such a way as to enrich — and add to — each. Thus, when Mailer gets himself arrested outside the Pentagon knowing that he is being filmed and will later write about the incident, or when Kesey's Pranksters tell themselves while high on LSD to 'let it come out in front' and 'not to fight it' — while knowing that they are filming themselves and their pranks, and that they are later to be reported by Tom Wolfe, the once water-tight worlds of the 'spontaneous' and the 'staged', the natural and the artificial, the real and the imaginary, become impossible to disentangle. Even the most self-revealing spontaneity is a test, an experiment to be recorded and filmed. Film itself could add further skins to the onion. In Antonioni's *Blow-Up*, the central theme was the confusion between what one thinks one has seen (and just to add a further level of confusion, photographed) and that which might in reality have been there. And, back in the political world again, there were two excellent fictional movies shot against the genuine background of the events in Chicago at the time of the Democratic National Convention in 1968 — *Prologue* and *Medium Cool* — in both of which, as in the pioneering films of John Cassavetes, there were important scenes shot unscripted.

This apparent weakening of the barriers between the comfortably separate categories of the real and the imaginary caused some confusion. 'We risk being the first people in history', wrote Daniel J. Boorstin,[7] 'to have been able to make their illusions so vivid, so persuasive, so "realistic" that they can live in them.' This risk was taken seriously by those who feared that a clever public relations firm might succeed in selling a car or a holiday, a president or a prime minister, that was an absolute dud.[8] The confusion between the imaginary and the real sometimes reached the point where some student rebels or political radicals seemed to believe that if only their activities could be reported on television their cause would be as good as won, while some of their more naïve critics would talk as though they believed that student activism or radical politics had been invented by television and had only to be ignored by the media to die a natural and irrevocable death. The belief that images *were* realities, that maybe in some sense Hud and Paul Newman *were* essentially one and the same, was one of the currents running through modern cultural history.

A further tendency was for people to undermine the distinctions between traditionally clear and separate social roles—the ways, for instance, in which 'adults' and 'children' or 'males' and 'females' were supposed to behave.

Prior to the nineteenth century, children tended to be treated (by their parents, by novelists, by their portrait painters, by their employers) as mini- or potential adults, little allowance being made for the fact that they were actually a different type of being. But for well over a hundred years, there has been a recognition and acceptance of the qualitative differences between the physical and psychological requirements of children and adults. In recent times, however, there were signs of a new convergence of the roles of adult and child, this time taking the form of an occasional preparedness by adults to adopt the manners of children.

The Americans had always had fewer inhibitions in this respect than the British. One thinks, for instance, of the songs and slogans associated with men's luncheon clubs in the USA, or of the use of diminutives and personalized abbreviations whether for common nouns ('movies', 'cookies'), great corporations (Con Ed), or brand names ('Wheaties'). There were the funny hats, the cheer-leaders, and the balloons at sporting occasions and political conventions. Radio and television advertisements would sometimes feature adults speaking with children's voices; the housewife who needed a water softener was advised to call the 'Culligan man'— and proceeded, with the voice of a pre-adolescent schoolgirl, to yell plaintively: 'CULLIGAN MAN!'. Jokey gadgets were widely advertised and bought; a chain-store was called the 'Piggly-Wiggly'; diplomats and academics at parties would vie with one another to see who had been to Disneyland most often, who knew the latest elephant jokes or 'swifties', who had seen this or that Marx Brothers film most frequently.

Americans, from the Ku Klux Klan to Jerry Rubin (who wrote about 'Amerika'), would play games with the language and its spelling. The most serious political causes would be buttressed with amusing slogans or bumper stickers or buttons (for example, those about Vietnam: 'Draft beer, not people', 'War is Profitable: Invest Your Son' or 'Pull Out LBJ—Like Your Father Should Have Done!'). Earnest young couples would learn about 'War Games' and read about 'Games People Play'. In John Updike's *Couples*, the characters play word games and sex games with each other's husbands and wives; they do the same in Albee's *Who's Afraid of Virginia Woolf?* and call the games 'Humiliate the Host' and 'Get the Guests'. American women would often refer to each other as 'girls' (as in the television show entitled *Girl Talk*); American men, similarly, would often think of each other as 'boys'. One of the secrets of the phenomenal success of Disneyland ('the Happiest Place On Earth') and Disney World was that these were places where adults could legitimately shed their responsibilities and give themselves over to the delights of a 'Magic Kingdom' apparently run by and for children.

All this may have something to do with the fact of American society (but not the USA as a political unit) being relatively 'young', though analogies between the development of individuals and that of great nations are suspect. It may also be related to the necessarily uninhibited *bonhomie* and the emotional innocence[9] that were legacies from frontier days, or perhaps to the regression to childhood values that was likely to characterize the uncomfortable elderly foreign immigrant who had merged his identity with that of a group of his compatriots rather than make the enormous effort to adjust to the demands of his newly-adopted country. It has also been suggested that some of the apparent infantilism of American behaviour resulted from the tendency among mothers to give more attention to the child than the father; if you grew up feeling that it was children who got the attention, then one way of trying to keep the attention was to continue to act in some ways like a child. Acting as a child could also be a way of trying to avoid the fierce competitiveness associated with adulthood. If all your heroes were people

who had 'made it' but you had doubts about your own capacity to 'make it', one way out would be to retain the characteristics and values of the relatively uncompetitive—or
pre-competitive—period of life, childhood. Childhood is
the period when one first experiences the great tug of war
between one's desire for a *persona* of one's own and a desire
to fuse onself with one's environment. Fusion involves love,
warmth, and dependence—qualities sometimes provided
by a mother, but rarely by adult society; so that anybody with
strong fusion desires was bound to find the shift to adulthood
hard to achieve. Furthermore, since the discontinuity between 'childhood' (when one is permitted to be dependent)
and 'adulthood' (when one is supposed to be independent)
was often very sharp, many people, even as physical adults,
would exhibit powerful dependency needs which often
expressed themselves in childish ways.

These factors help to explain why there was often a streak
of childishness in the behaviour of American adults. But the
circumstances of the modern world considerably strengthened this tendency and helped to transport it across the
Atlantic. First, the enormous post-war baby boom and the
re-adoption of permissive child-rearing produced a new
modus vivendi between parents and children in which the
demands of the latter received more consideration than
hitherto. Second, with the subsequent extension of education to larger and larger segments of the population, a
person's period of childhood, or legitimate dependence,
was also extended; for while education can prepare people
for the adult world, it can also immure them from it. Above
all, however, the material abundance of the post-war decades
enabled many adults to indulge in an unaccustomed spree
of relatively unrestrained and child-like acquisitiveness—
often in the presence, and therefore under the watchful and
unsubtle guidance, of their children. In the supermarket,
the eyes that the manufacturers were primarily trying to
attract tended to be not five feet but three feet from the floor
—hence the bright colour and striking design of so many
objects on the lower shelves. Children were also great
television-watchers. If you wanted to sell something, the
thing to do was either to appeal directly to children or to tell

adults that the product was one from which children would benefit.

Modern adult society was in many ways suffused by a toy culture, a nursery culture.[10] Take one of its proudest achievements and in many ways its most archetypal, air travel. The luxurious experience of the businessman in flight is instructive. He is strapped into a seat, given instructions on how to behave 'in the unlikely event' that anything should go wrong, offered an occasional drink or candy, and, in general, invited to place his trust, hope, and admiration in the visibly capable hands of a team of super-mother-and-lover surrogates. As his attention wanders during flight, he might turn to look at the absurdly fragile-looking plastic walls, often embellished with nursery designs, little pictures of the Empire State Building or the Eiffel Tower. Perhaps he is given piped music or a movie. The time comes when a meal is produced—the carefully chopped and shaped elements of which are each slotted into their carefully chiselled places. The meal is on a tray which, as when he was a small child or a hospital invalid, is either fitted carefully onto a little folding table or perhaps fixed on either side of him to the sides of his seat. Anything he wants? He just has to ring. The whole thing is a sort of game in which ultimate authority and responsibility are kept at a distance. As a passenger, one may be an adult but there is no alternative but to play the role of dependent and irresponsible child. One may be on a business trip and spend the journey studying papers important for one's work. . . but the trip itself is a form of play.

'Play' was once thought the prerogative of children and sportsmen, people without fundamentally serious things to do and without major responsibilities to any ultimately answerable authority. 'Work', on the other hand, held an exalted position in the pantheon of traditional social values, particularly in America. However, as perceptions of adulthood and childhood became blurred and somewhat interdependent, so did perceptions of work and play. At his place of work, a man would find himself required to acquire and implement the skills of relaxed social intercourse; much of his time at his store, factory, office, or places of call would be spent playing social games with other people, flattering them, persuading them, winning away their allies, giving them food or drink or cigarettes, introducing them to other people. Less and less time would be spent alone, simply and straightforwardly doing some sort of solitary work. And as the preponderant proportion of the work force in post-war Britain and America shifted away from the manufacturing industries and the manual and 'blue-collar' jobs towards the service industries and the clerical and professional and 'white collar' jobs, the injection of play elements into work situations correspondingly increased.

If one shifts one's attention to play, one sees a complementary injection of values associated with work. Sports, for instance, became more serious, organized and coordinated affairs than they had once been. They became professionalized.[11] Any nineteenth-century Rip Van Winkle would have been astonished to discover, on awakening in the later twentieth century, the extent to which every athlete, footballer, or tennis player—even if his team was merely the local junior school—would feel obliged to make a great show of the exhaustive and abstemious period of training that he had undergone. Similarly, while he would no doubt appreciate the earnest seriousness with which people who invented children's toys or wrote reading books for tiny tots would often approach their important work, he would probably be surprised at the (to him) almost whimsically playful end-product of so many of their labours.[12] Work and play, it seemed, had become inseparably intertwined.

Another of the partially merging social categories at which our nineteenth-century Rip Van Winkle would probably rub his old eyes with bemused incredulity concerned the traditional sex roles. During the years immediately after World War II, women who had had to take on men's jobs generally appeared anxious to relinquish them and to revert to being 'women'. They would take off their khaki uniforms or their factory overalls, put their hair in curlers and their bodies into the 'New Look', and give themselves over to what Betty Friedan was to call the 'feminine mystique', while their demobilized men kept their hair short and tried to develop strong biceps. But this resumption of traditionally distinct roles did not long go unchallenged.

In Britain as in America, most children had for generations been brought up primarily by their mothers and by their (generally) female school teachers. In the post-war world, with the development of high rates of male employment and the increasing amounts of time and distance that men would be prepared to devote to their journeys to and from work, many children—particularly those from middle-class suburban homes—would tend to be even less likely than in earlier times to come into frequent contact with their fathers. Such children would grow up with almost exclusively female models and this could impose severe strains on, for instance, the young boy who, with puberty, would suddenly be expected to adopt all the traditional trappings of male sexuality. The models of masculinity with which generations of boys had grown up in the past had often derived from myths in which women, if present at all, were either unassailable virgins or abandoned temptresses. But with the gradual emancipation of women in the post-war world and their growing demands for equality with men, these traditional models of womanhood and of the corresponding male roles were no longer operative. By the 1960s, many young men were coming to grow their hair longer than their fathers had generally done, and were prepared to wear brightly coloured and sensitively textured clothes and to speak with gentle voices. Kenneth Keniston[13] was quoted as saying that, for many of the young men of the recent period, 'the old notions of masculinity are not an attractive ideal any more, and . . . there is much more acceptance of what were traditionally considered—and this has to be put in quotes—"feminine" qualities of . . . empathy, sympathy, compassion, love, tenderness, and so on.'

Young women, on the other hand, were increasingly likely to adopt characteristics that traditionalists might have thought to be 'masculine'—to wear trousers, for instance, and their men friends' sweaters, or to apply for jobs in hitherto all male professions.[14] As more and more women took advantage of contraceptive pills or other forms of female contraception, they could begin to take sexual initiatives and to show sexual appetites that, in previous ages, would have been widely considered both indelicate and dangerous.

They were able to plan and to restrict as never before the amount of time put aside for child-rearing, with the result that more and more women found that their reproductive role went only a small way towards the achievement of any real fulfilment in life. Many women, particularly those with under-utilized educational and professional qualifications, began to feel an uneasy frustration if their lives were largely restricted to the performance of those roles traditionally thought to be 'feminine'.

Dr Fred Brown of Mount Sinai Hospital was reported (*Newsweek*, 6 September 1971) as having discovered that the reaction of young men and women to a gender identity Rorschach blot had more or less reversed in just a few years. In the 1950s, the aggressive and sharply-curved image had been generally identified — by males and females alike — as masculine; by the late 1960s, according to Dr Brown, young male and female patients tended to identify the blot as feminine.

This blurring of traditionally clear and separate sex roles was only partial, of course, and for many people was of sufficiently little serious consequence that it could cause more amusement than genuine confusion or disturbance. There were jokes about long-haired and gentle couples, arm-in-arm, and how you couldn't tell which was which. And the commercial interests weighed in with 'Unisex' clothes and sauna baths.[15] But there were serious — even semi-political — manifestations as well. There was, for instance, a 'Gay Liberation' movement that demanded the right of (primarily male) homosexuals to relate to each other with as much social freedom as did heterosexuals. And there was the much stronger (though in many ways fissiparous) 'Women's Lib' movement whose unifying theme was the insistence that women should be liberated from what they saw as their traditional role as, primarily, object rather than subject. In the women's movement there were, inevitably, the extremists whose chief aim sometimes seemed to be the total elimination of men from their lives. But millions of intelligent women, upset by the vacuous existence to which they felt society had condemned them, were beginning to make a determined effort to obtain the social and economic and

sexual equality with men to which they considered themselves entitled.

It is important not to exaggerate this partial dissolution of
traditional conceptual categories. Most people in Britain
and America usually had a pretty good idea of what they
meant by the difference between 'real' and 'imaginary',
'adult' and 'child', or 'male' and 'female'. Indeed, as various
elements in the culture seemed to blend with one another,
powerful contrary forces developed that were largely designed to give renewed prominence to, for instance, hitherto
partially submerged ethnic, religious, sexual, or geo-political
distinctions. It would certainly be going too far to suggest
that the culture of modern Britain and (above all) America
was, *tout court,* a 'fusion' culture.

Nevertheless, there does seem to have been a strain towards convergence, towards accommodation, towards the
partial synthesis of apparently distinct categories in modern
British and American culture. This is hardly surprising, for a
period of rapid material change is inevitably likely to create
circumstances within which new cultural accommodations
need to be sought. As it became easier for millions of people to
hear and see — and even to go and get first-hand experience
of — cultures other than their own, some of the dictates of
their own familiar culture were bound to be called into question and even undermined. If their own culture was not to
be completely overthrown, people had to develop values
that would permit them to retain elements of the culture
with which they were familiar while at the same time to be
receptive towards elements in those that were new to them.
This type of cultural accommodation was clearly facilitated
by some aspects of the 'new' values — the value of 'participatoriness', for example, with its tendency to reduce the importance of distinctions between 'us' and 'them'; or the value
of 'transitoriness' which helped to make it possible for
people to question traditional categories of time and place.
Similarly, if one valued 'technique' and was less concerned
with 'content', one could open oneself to a variety of inconsistent cultural messages and receive and digest them all while
minimizing the discomfort that would result if one were

more receptive to matters of substance. Finally, the value of 'self-indulgence' could in part be a way of reassuring oneself that one's heart or senses should be used in conjunction with one's mind; that one's ego and id counted for just as much as one's super-ego, and that the best ethic to adopt was one that was warm, undemanding, all-embracing.

The culture of modern Britain and America was a culture the driving tendencies of which seemed to be seeking (with varying degrees of success) for bridges rather than moats, inclusiveness rather than exclusiveness, synthesis rather than analysis, maybe even fusion rather than fission. It is possible that when the history of our times finally comes to be written, people will say that our thermo-nuclear physicists gave us not only our weapons of ultimate destruction, but also the best metaphor with which to describe our ultimate social strivings.

8 The Americanization of British Culture?

INTRODUCTION

All the test-match cricketers at Lord's now seem to chew Wrigley's Spearmint. T. S. Matthews, *TIME* Magazine, 1974.

As this essay has swung hither and thither, back and forth across time and the Atlantic, two equal and opposite temptations have frequently arisen.

On the one hand, how much easier the writing of this book would have been to an author who agreed with H.A.L. Fisher,[1] to whom history contained no plot or rhythm, no patterns or harmonies. For Fisher, there could be 'only one safe rule for the historian: that he should recognize in the development of human destinies the play of the contingent and the unforeseen.' With such a view of the past, this book would have represented an attempt to chronicle the collective experience of the British and American people and to leave to others what is loosely called interpretation. The 'facts', in such an exercise and according to such a philosophy, would have been left largely to speak for themselves.

The problem with this approach is that, unfortunately, facts do not speak for themselves, or rather, they can be capable of appearing to speak in all sorts of ways unless they are to some extent controlled and directed by the historian who presents them. A 'fact' can mean all or nothing depending upon the context within which it is embedded. And a total lack of context generally represents a greater violation of the truth than the context chosen by a careful and honest historian. Furthermore, the very process of choosing which facts to include and which to omit normally presupposes a guiding principle on the part of the historian. For these and other reasons, an approach based on the purely unstructured and indiscriminate presentation of 'facts' with no 'interpretation' was never seriously entertained in the preparation of this book.

257

The other frequent temptation was to overstructure and to over-interpret. How clever of Karl Marx, Walter Bagehot, Frederick Jackson Turner, David Riesman, or talented popularizers like Vance Packard, Charles Reich or Alvin Toffler to come up with key concepts or phrases that could unlock so much. How convenient it would be, one sometimes felt, to hit upon some simple formula which would explain *everything*. But here too there would have been dangers. Just as the unstructured presentation of facts can seriously distort historical truth, so the overstructuring of facts can lead to an equally misleading picture. There is no single 'truth' about the past, and each generation, it has been well said, has to write its own history. But that history must always steer between the Scylla of too little interpretation and structure and the Charybdis of too much.

This balancing act is particularly difficult in a book whose structural elements are as complex as those with which we have been juggling. They involve, in this book, both comparisons and contrasts along two separate axes, those of time and of place. As regards *time,* we looked at what were called 'traditional' values and also at 'new' values and suggested that the former were developing over the past few centuries while the latter tended to come most strongly into prominence in the 1960s. By the mid-1970s it looked as though something of an accommodation between the two was gradually developing.

There remains one final link in the chain of argument that has still to be forged, and that is the element of *place.* The cultures of America and of Britain have in some ways been sharply at variance and in other ways remarkably similar. The question that has now to be faced concerns the geographical directions of cultural change as between the two societies.

One of the clichés of the post-war years was that the British were becoming Americanized.[2] This theme is susceptible to many variations and has recurred, along with its mirror-image of an Anglicized or Europeanized America,[3] throughout the history of the relationship between the Old World and the New. The idea of the Americanization of Britain can evoke an enthusiastic smile or a disgusted scowl and can be applied as easily to the field of economics or science as to fashions in food, clothing, or speech. The recurrent theme was that whatever happened in America was likely to happen in Britain and elsewhere a short while later and whatever happened in Britain had probably happened in America first. American society, wrote Zbigniew Brzezinski,[4] 'is the one in which the great questions of our time will be first tested through practice'. And, as Kenneth Keniston[5] added, 'we suffer from being a vanguard society; our example constitutes a model and a caution to other societies, but we ourselves have no models.'

In any large society, there are likely to be factors that facilitate the export of aspects of its domestic culture and others that tend to inhibit this process. Similarly, there are likely to be some factors that tend to predispose a society to be receptive towards the cultural influences that reach it from elsewhere, and others that tend to make it resistant to external cultural influences. British and American societies no doubt each had their fair share of all of these factors. However, British culture was probably the more receptive of the two to external influences while American culture was the more inclined to try to export itself. This is no more than an impression, but it is one for which explanations are not hard to find.

THE BRITISH AS CULTURAL IMPORTERS

In Chapter 3, some traditional British values were discussed: self-restraint, unflappability, secretiveness, deference, the control of aggression, insularity. The general picture was of a comparatively tightly-knit and hierarchical culture, one in which people tended to know their rightful place and expected (and were expected) to stay in it. Not a completely monolithic culture and certainly not as closed a society as many another; but at least as compared with America, a culture that tended to gravitate towards a few clearly defined and almost universally acknowledged nodal points. Above all, one within which internal lines of communication— particularly to and from the nodal points—were quick and efficient, while influences from outside tended to be

controlled and even resisted. This cultural pattern was
manifested in and supported by a centralized and hierarchical social and political system, and largely financed by
a series of overseas possessions.

By the middle of the twentieth century, several of the
elements that had provided the underpinning for this
apparently solid and stable British culture were showing signs
of falling apart. In particular, there was an enormous drain
of financial resources resulting from the effort of the second
world war followed by the shift from an economically
subordinate Empire to a more loose-limbed and independent Commonwealth. In time, people began to formulate
questions about their own relationship to the wider society
and about Britain's relationship with the world, questions
that earlier generations had not usually felt the need to ask.
These questions were characteristically couched in political
terms, but behind them would often lie doubts concerning
fundamental social values. For instance, the pros and cons
of British insularity constituted one of the issues underlying the passionate debate over Britain's membership of the
Common Market. The traditional deference of the British
also seemed to be tottering in some quarters during these
years: a case in point was the defiance of the 1971 Industrial
Relations Act and of the Industrial Relations Court by the
Engineering Union, action that, though clearly illegal,
nevertheless received considerable public and political
support.

Despite examples of this sort, and notwithstanding the
unusual degree to which traditional political assumptions
might have been questioned, the major institutions of British
society remained substantially unaltered. Throughout
the post-war years, the official political, cultural, and social
leadership of Britain and the various mechanisms of social
control remained firmly in the hands of a fairly small predominantly London-based, educated elite. Despite all the
protest and the romantic idealism, there was, in 1975 as in
1945, no Scottish or Welsh parliament. Many people continued to prefer a national newspaper to a local or regional
one. The BBC continued to link every part of the country
with an interlocking network of communications; local and

regional radio and television (BBC and commercial alike) never achieved the popularity of nationally-beamed networks. Most 'top' jobs still went to men—and to men with 'good' accents and an acceptably traditional education.

Thus, in the post-war decades, traditional British values were being questioned on a wide scale but the institutions of cultural influence and diffusion remained almost as centralized as ever. Such a situation provided fertile ground for the planting of cultural seeds from outside. If the British were questioning their traditional values, they were more disposed than usual to entertain alternative ones; but if at the same time their institutions remained efficient and centralized, new values, like the old, were likely to be diffused rapidly and efficiently throughout the culture. Thus the very mechanisms that had been so effective in insulating British culture at times of political and economic strength and independence facilitated the absorption of external influences once the British had embarked upon a period of self-questioning.

In a society like America, with its strong tradition of cultural pluralism, the periodic questioning of accepted values was never normally likely to lead to any single new nationwide pattern. But in a more tightly-packed and centralized society such as that of Britain, the pressures for a more or less homogeneous set of social values were never far from the surface. Thus the British were not only prepared, by the 1950s and 1960s, to question and challenge some of the values with which their society had been so deeply imbued for so long; they also had a strong inclination, backed up by institutional arrangements, to spread throughout their society with great speed and efficiency such external cultural messages as may have penetrated their still not inconsiderable insularity.

This relative receptivity to the messages of other cultures was partly a result of a positive outlook; Indian restaurants and Italian shoes, Greek handbags and Spanish holidays were pleasant enough. But it often had a more negative connotation and was a form of sour *faute de mieux*. If you could no longer subscribe wholeheartedly to the traditional values of your own society, and if, in particular, its cultural insularity was no longer easy to justify, maybe you could do worse than accept some of the cultural messages of other societies. It was with something like this attitude that many white people in Britain, if they were not openly hostile to non-white immigrants, tried to make gestures of toleration, acquiescence, and even welcome to the Indians, Pakistanis, West Africans, and West Indians whom they found in their midst. The crude imitation of certain black styles of speech or clothing or the occasional adoption by whites of an 'Afro' haircut or a 'rhythmic' walk would not infrequently be undertaken in such a spirit, one that mixed some genuine approval for the symbols of the immigrant culture with a gnawing disenchantment with the symbols of traditional British culture. And it was no doubt in something of the same spirit—though of course the political connotations would often be different—that some sections within the wider British culture came to be particularly receptive to transatlantic messages.

In the earlier post-war years, above all, it was to America that many British people seem to have looked for cultural leads. This was natural enough. After the legendary camaraderie during the war and the Anglo-American heroization of Roosevelt, Marshall, and Eisenhower, and of Churchill and Montgomery, the idea of a 'special relationship' took a firm hold among opinion leaders on both sides of the ocean. In those years, the heady concept of a north Atlantic alliance of two great English-speaking nations achieved great popularity in both countries and it paved the way for what many leaders hoped would prove to be considerable cultural interpenetration.

The traffic went both ways. But from the first, the major cultural initiatives and influences came from the bigger, richer, less war-weary of the partners, the USA. American political, military, and economic power were, after all, far greater than their British counterparts by that time and the force of America's cultural influence was scarcely unrelated to these other factors; a cultural programme such as the Fulbright scholarships cannot be fully understood except as an outcome of a political atmosphere which also produced the Marshall Plan and NATO. In the post-war world, Anglo-American cooperation, whether cultural or political, economic or military, generally meant British acquiescence and participation in schemes originated in and financed by the USA. If the British had any illusion that they could, if they wanted to, go their own independent way, this was most dramatically shattered in 1956 when it was American pressure above all that caused the British and their French allies to withdraw from their adventure in Suez.

The impetus of the early post-war years was not kept up. Nevertheless, as the British continued to wonder about their society and its role in the modern world, their receptivity to cultural influence from abroad remained unabated. Some of them may not have liked American accents or Bermuda shorts or chewing gum or, more seriously, the way some white Americans treated their black compatriots. But even those people in Britain who were politically most critical of the United States often found it hard to resist the attractions of the increasingly ubiquitous American goods in the shops, or the countless expressions and gestures that, between them, amounted to a not inconsiderable 'Americanization' of Britain.

British receptivity to the products of American culture was not slavish or indiscriminate. Nor does it appear to have been as conscious or as wholehearted as was that of some other societies — particularly in parts of the developing world — where susceptibility to the blandishments of 'Coca-colonization' could at time seem almost total. Nevertheless, it remains broadly true that the British in the post-war decades were more open to cultural messages from abroad than they had generally been in the past, and that the cultural messages to which they appear to have been most receptive were those emanating from the United States.

THE AMERICANS AS CULTURAL EXPORTERS

There was nothing really new about the predisposition of American culture to export itself. Throughout American history, there recurred from time to time a zealous determination to inculcate into others the attitudes, values and styles of American life.

Indeed this crusading moralism can be said to have been part of the birthright of a nation originally conceived as a 'city on a hill' to which everybody else would look for an example. Sometimes, as in the 1840s, cultural imperialism was furthered by military conquest; in the early twentieth century the export of American culture was primarily a by-product of an expansionist economic policy. Every now and then, idealistic (if presumptuous) voices would be raised to the effect that American culture should be exported simply because it was — or ought to be — the model for everybody else's. President Woodrow Wilson, for instance, in his speech proposing a League of Nations in January 1917, advocated what he called 'American principles, American policies'. These, he said, 'are also the principles and policies of forward-looking men and women everywhere, of every modern nation, of every enlightened community. They are the principles of mankind and must prevail.' American involvement in the affairs of other nations, whether military, economic, political or cultural, would characteristically take on the tone of a moral duty to help the less favourably endowed foreigner to enjoy the advantages bestowed upon those lucky enough to be Americans.

With her enormous accretion of power in the post-war world, America's opportunities and wherewithal for acting upon her missionary inclinations were greater than ever before. The massive export of America's economic and military might is easy to document, and there was scarcely a part of the globe (outside the communist orbit) that did not feel the influence of this colossal expansion. But equally significant though less tangible was the extent to which American attitudes and values were gradually spread throughout the globe, a tendency easy to illustrate, impossible to quantify and incalculable in its effects.[6]

It has sometimes been suggested that if societies other than the USA began to display 'American' characteristics, this was not so much because of conscious American cultural imperialism as because they were all, including America, being subjected to similar social and economic influences.

According to this line of argument, the USA, like Britain or
Japan, was heavily industrialized; like them, it was experiencing a shift in emphasis from blue-collar to white-collar
occupations, from manufacturing industries to service industries, from a preoccupation with the values of production
to an espousal of values of consumption. This combination
of circumstances was no doubt further advanced in the USA
than elsewhere, but other societies were in hot pursuit. Japan,
Canada, Sweden and the rest would, in time, take on the
characteristics of the USA, and the process would be followed
thereafter by the countries of western Europe, Australia
and New Zealand, and eventually, one assumes, the whole
of the rest of the world. A number of American and other
thinkers devoted much time, money, and intellectual energy
to the problems of analyzing these changes, forecasting their
likely effects, and assessing the probable timetables of various
societies as they followed the path towards 'post-indus-
trialism'.[7]

There is much to be said for this approach; the economic
and social processes that Japan, say, or Sweden experienced
in common with the USA undoubtedly helped to encourage
them, too, to develop a culture that emphasized the virtues
of technique and replication, participatoriness, transitoriness, and sense-gratification. Nevertheless, the suggestion
that the USA was the cultural leader because it was the economic front-runner is suspect on a number of counts. For
one thing, the content of 'post-industrial' culture contained
many ingredients that were clearly and characteristically
American in origin. Furthermore, the attitudes and values
specifically associated with other economically advanced
societies were far less prominent outside their own national
boundaries than were those of America. Then again, American cultural influence was by no means confined to those
societies that were in the first rank in the rush towards 'post-
industrialism'; none of the post-industrial theorists, for
instance, considered Britain to be in the top league along
with the USA and Japan and Sweden, but this did not prevent
a growing — and largely unreciprocated — tendency by the
British to try on many of the cultural clothes of the Americans. Thus while America may have been the archetype of

the post-industrial society, one cannot attribute to this fact alone the spread of American culture to so many parts of the globe.

This is not, however, to argue that American cultural imperialism was always the product of conscious policy. American leaders did not sit down and say to themselves 'Here we are, we believe in the work ethic or in liberty and equality (or, as it may be, in participatoriness or transitoriness) — let's see what we can do to get other people to believe in these things.' Matters such as these are often, in the nature of things, almost as hidden from the cultural exporters as from the importers. But with her accretion of wealth and power, the American tradition of cultural expansionism was given new scope.

This is clear if one examines in detail one or two aspects of the American cultural influence upon Britain. Take, for instance, the question of language — a primary carrier of cultural values. The British and the Americans spoke more or less the same language; although some ten to twenty American words or constructions became accepted by British English for every one ('gremlin', 'gadget') that went the other way, many of them crept in almost unnoticed. By the later years of our period, even the most hardened anti-American in Britain might have been heard putting the stress on the first syllable of words like 'television' or 'research',[8] using the adjective 'commercial' as a noun, and referring to the 'incumbent' prime minister. As for such neologisms as 'motel', 'astronaut', or 'teach-in', these were by now firmly accepted parts of British English. As I write, I feel the imminent arrival of 'senior citizens', while the 'supermarkets' already have 'cans' alongside the 'tins' and the 'highways' reverberate to the noise of 'trucks' alongside the 'lorries'. Before long, British politicians will surely start to imitate their more dynamic American counterparts and 'run' for office instead of merely 'standing'.[9]

Many 'Americanisms' were ways of dealing linguistically with concepts that were themselves of largely American origin. A social phenomenon would occur in America, an American word would be coined to describe it; the fact and then the word would cross the Atlantic to Britain. As examples of this process, one might cite the words 'baby-sitter' and 'teenager' and the social and economic implications that these words and their usages carried. Or take the linguistic exigencies of the suburbanization of the British middle classes. By the 1960s, expressions were needed for the process — long since familiar in the USA — of travelling daily in and out of town to work and back and also for the people who had to do it. As the need for new words grew, the resistance to 'commute' and 'commuter' ebbed away.

The cultural influence of America was not restricted to matters of accent and vocabulary. The British learned to eat hamburgers (and what they began to call 'french fries') and cole slaw, to drink milk shakes, and to wear blue jeans. Above all, they continued to appreciate those two most authentically American cultural products, jazz and what Americans called the 'movies'.

The combined cultural message of things American, the handy neologisms, the hamburgers, the jeans, the jazz and the rest, often seemed to amount to something like this: you could be 'cool' (rather than 'uptight'); you could eat and dress and talk snappily while on the move; you could minimize distinctions between your own styles and those of others around you — and yet you could sit back and enjoy the fruits of your society, safe in the knowledge that the underpinning was technically secure. On the surface, all may have appeared casual, transient, informal, improvised, rough, fragile even; underneath, all was efficiency itself. Superficially, things might have appeared playful or even capricious; fundamentally, however, you could be confident that everything worked.

This was what one might call the 'Disneyland principle'. A ride at Disneyland would typically involve movement (sometimes in a direction or at a speed that was at first deceptive), a degree of informality or even casualness in which everybody had to join, a built-in hazard sufficiently alarming to get some of the women and children excited, and ultimately a reassuring reassertion of the infallibility of the technology in which you had initially placed your trust. This principle looks more and more familiar as one examines it closely. 'Child' values on the surface backed up by 'adult' values, 'play' supported by something known to 'work'. Indeed, the Disneyland principle involved a fusion of all the 'new' values: various types of transitoriness, participatoriness, and self-indulgence backed up by a fundamental reliance on technique.

British receptivity to the Disneyland principle was not always conscious nor was it unqualified. Nevertheless, as the British passed through a sustained period of self-questioning and self-analysis, it is easy to understand the appeal of this type of American-born message. If there is one thing that people probably want to hear when they are worried it is that things are all right, or 'OK', that the apparently unstable and improvised nature of things masks a fundamental reliability. It was a message not unlike this that people in Britain so often seemed to want to hear from the American words and phrases and foods and clothes and films and records that many of them were increasingly avid to consume. And it is hard to resist the conclusion that this was the message, too, that many Americans were equally avid to export.

Chronological table
Acknowledgements
Notes
Index of Authors and Sources
General Index

Chronological table

	USA	International	Britain
1945	Death of Roosevelt Truman President	Hiroshima End of world war II UN established	Labour win election under Attlee
1947	Marshall Plan inaugurated	Independence of India and Pakistan	
1948	Truman re-elected President	State of Israel Berlin blockade	National Health Service
1949		NATO Federal (West) and Democratic (East) Republics of Germany People's Republic of China	
1950	H-bomb programme begun	Korean War begins	Labour win election with tiny majority
1951			Festival of Britain Conservatives win election under Churchill
1952	Eisenhower elected President	Egyptian coup ousts Farouk	Death of King George VI
1953		Death of Stalin Truce in Korea	Everest climbed Coronation of Queen Elizabeth II
1954	H-bomb exploded at Bikini *Brown v. Board* (desegregation decision)	Dien Bien Phu	
1955	Salk polio vaccine Contraceptive pill		Eden replaces Churchill as Prime Minister and wins election victory Gaitskell replaces Attlee
1956	*My Fair Lady* Eisenhower re-elected President	Khrushchev denounces Stalin Hungarian uprising	*Look Back in Anger* Suez
1957	Little Rock	Ghana first independent African state First Sputnik	Macmillan replaces Eden
1958	Marines to Lebanon	Pope John XXIII elected De Gaulle becomes President of France	CND launched
1959		Castro overthrows Batista	Conservatives win election under Macmillan

271

	USA	International	Britain
1960	Kennedy elected President	Sharpeville Independence of Congo Paris Summit Conference U-2 incident	
1961	Bay of Pigs operation	Gagarin first man in space Berlin Wall	Application to join EEC South Africa leaves Commonwealth
1962	Cuba missile crisis	Vatican II begins	Commonwealth Immigrants Act *That Was The Week That Was*
1963	Civil Rights march on Washington Kennedy assassinated Johnson President	Death of Pope John Test Ban Treaty	De Gaulle vetoes EEC application Death of Gaitskell; Wilson leader of Labour Party Profumo scandal Great Train Robbery Home replaces Macmillan as Prime Minister Beatlemania National Theatre at Old Vic
1964	Civil Rights Act Johnson re-elected President	Death of Nehru Tonkin Gulf incident Khrushchev replaced by Brezhnev and Kosygin	Labour win election under Wilson
1965	Malcolm X assassinated Escalation of US presence in Vietnam Watts riots		Death of Churchill Race Relations Act 'Swinging London' Rhodesia's UDI Beatles receive MBE
1966	'Black Power'		Labour win election England win soccer World Cup
1967		Military coup in Greece Six day war Nigerian Civil War begins	Homosexuality and Abortion law reform
1968	Martin Luther King and Robert Kennedy assassinated Democratic convention in Chicago Nixon elected President	*Evènements* in Paris Russians invade Czechoslovakia	Kenya Asians Act Enoch Powell speech Civil Rights Movement in Northern Ireland

	USA	International	Britain
1969	Manson murders First moon landing Chappaquiddick		Investiture of Prince of Wales
1970		End of Nigerian Civil War Death of Nasser Allende President of Chile Revolt in Poland	Conservatives win election under Heath
1971		Indo-Pakistan War; Bangladesh	
1972	Nixon visits China Nixon overwhelmingly re-elected President	Israeli athletes killed at Munich Olympics	'Bloody Sunday' in Derry Tutankhamun exhibition (1.6 million visitors)
1973	Watergate hearings	End of Allende regime Middle East War	Britain joins EEC Wedding of Princess Anne
1974	Nixon resigns Ford President	End of Caetano regime in Portugal Colonels' regime in Greece ends	Miners' strike 3-day week Two elections: Labour Government under Wilson
1975		Saigon taken by Viet Cong	Thatcher replaces Heath as Tory leader
1976	US Bicentennial	Civil war in Lebanon	New National Theatre opened Wilson resigns Callaghan Prime Minister Thorpe affair

Notes

Introduction (pages 9-15)

1 'I would like to express my objection to . . . the continual use of the word "America" to refer to the United States,' wrote a Canadian correspondent to *New Society* (8 Nov. 1973). 'Like many persons living in American countries other than the USA, I find this use of the term obnoxious. "Americans" (i.e. citizens of the USA) are notorious for their ethnocentricity, their abuse of the English language, and their belief that the United States is the centre of the universe. It is unfortunate indeed to find their attitudes creeping into the thinking of other peoples. While the editors of *New Society* may think of Canadians, Mexicans and other inhabitants of the New World outside the borders of the United States as banana republicans, we poor colonials know that the first step towards liberation is to rid ourselves of the colonial mentality diffused by imperial culture. I hope that you people will see fit to do your small part by using the terms "America" and "Americans" correctly at all times.'

2 Titles of books by H. S. Commager and W. J. Cash respectively.

3 Daniel J. Boorstin, *The Genius of American Politics*, University of Chicago Press, 1964 edn, p. 30.

4 Richard Hofstadter, *The American Political Tradition*, Cape, 1967 edn, p. xi.

5 For a convenient statement of this viewpoint in a single volume, see Barton J. Bernstein (ed.), *Towards a New Past*, Random House, 1968. The essays cover all periods of American history, and Bernstein's introduction discusses the 'dissenting' perspective from which the essays are written.

6 See Robert E. Lane, *Political Ideology*, The Free Press of Glencoe, 1962; Kenneth Keniston, *The Uncommitted*, Dell, 1965; Robert J. Lifton, *Home from the War*, Simon & Schuster, 1973.

7 'That is why', wrote Charles Hampden-Turner (*Radical Man*, Schenkman, 1970, p. 11) 'we have such detailed knowledge of mental illness, alienation, anomie, isolation, delinquency, sensory deprivation and every kind of human and social disintegration [but] know next to nothing of integration, wholeness, personality development, and complex mental syntheses and functionings.' The approach to social research as social pathology has been reinforced by the common tendency to recruit, as the individual

275

subjects of research, members of relatively downtrodden and powerless strata of society, its elderly, its sick, and its dependent members. See, for example, Herbert C. Kelman, 'The Rights of the Subject in Social Research', *American Psychologist*, Nov. 1972.

8 See, notably, E. P. Thompson, *The Making of the English Working Class*, Pelican edn, 1968, and the writings of Eric Hobsbawm, Raymond Williams, and the History Workshop at Ruskin College, Oxford, under the direction of Raphael Samuel.

9 'In the lower working class,' wrote Robert Roberts in his memoir *The Classic Slum*, Manchester University Press, 1971, p. 28, '"manners" were imposed upon children with the firmest hand: adults recognized that if anything was to be got from "above" one should learn early to ask for it with a proper measure of humble politeness. There was besides, of course, the desire to imitate one's betters.' Even in words of popular songs—scarcely embodiments of deference for the most part—the values and perquisites of the elite were scarcely absent.

10 By a person's 'opinions' we mean his tentative (i.e. legitimately reversible) views regarding particular topics. Opinions are of a more or less transient nature and are most likely to be cognitive (dealing with a person's perceptions of apparently static facts). 'Attitudes' are a person's clusters of opinions of a more general nature and are normally more durable than opinions. They are states of mind, changeable over the longer term but not likely to be substantially altered by the introduction of a particular item of information. Attitudes encompass personal priorities, for they indicate something about the items or artefacts or institutions that a person considers more or less important, good, attractive and so on. 'Values', finally, are a person's continuous and long-term predispositions regarding moral preferences. They are by definition evaluative and are in general likely to be internalized social norms. (Social norms are part of the social culture and are reinforced by social rewards and punishments, whereas values are part of the individual personality.) A person's values are normally more or less systematic and comprehensive; they are general frames of reference with which an individual feels that he can tie together the evaluative features of his attitudes. And they concern topics that the individual considers both broad and significant.

These definitions are obviously interrelated. Perhaps the clearest way of understanding the difference between opinions, attitudes and values is to consider them as lying on a continuum from the most transitory to the most permanent, the most specific to the most general, and from the most cognitive to the most evaluative. It probably extends also from the most conscious (for who is not conscious of his own opinions?) to the least conscious.

11 'No other people has been so curious about itself,' wrote Clyde Kluckhohn, 'nor so willing to subject itself to scientific analysis, nor so avid to read even the most sneering and superficial critici ms of outsiders.' (Article in Bruce Bliven (ed.), *Twentieth Century Unlimited*, Lippincott, 1950.) Nobody could have written that about the British — a fact that in itself suggests an important difference between the two cultures.

12 We become, in Daniel Bell's vivid phrase, 'squares by day and swingers by night'.

13 Advertisements do not, of course, give a picture of life as it really is; but they do embody some of the aspirations and fears of those to whom they are directed and in this way are an invaluable pointer towards the values that people espouse in their role as consumers. Marshall McLuhan wrote that 'historians and archaeologists will one day discover that the ads of our time are the richest and most faithful daily reflections that any society ever made of its entire range of activities.' (*Understanding Media*, Sphere Books, 1967, Chap. 23, p. 247.) Since American society was technologically and materially so advanced and culturally so influential, it seemed appropriate in Part II to rely extensively upon advertisements (alongside other types of data) from the USA. For further consideration of American cultural influence see Chap. 8.

Chapter 1   *The eye of the beholder* (page 23)

1   Richard Rose, *Politics in Britain Today*, Faber, 1974, p. 123.

2   The attempt to deal definitively with the problems of immigration eventually forced the British Government to consider for the first time defining what was meant by British citizenship (speech by Alex Lyon, Minister of State at the Home Office, to the Immigrants Advisory Service in Birmingham, 5 Apr. 1975).

3   By 1968, Otto Kerner was able to write, in the introduction to his *Report of the National Advisory Commission on Civil Disorders*, Bantam, 1968: 'Our nation is moving towards two societies, one black, one white — separate and unequal. . .[T]o pursue our present course will involve the continuing polarization of the American community and, ultimately, the destruction of basic democratic values.'

4   Lewis Yablonsky, *The Hippie Trip* Western Publishing Co., 1968.

5   Daniel Bell, *The End of Ideology*, The Free Press of Glencoe, 1962, p. 37.

6 See, for instance, E. E. Maccoby, R. Mathews and A. Morton, 'Youth and Political Change' in *Public Opinion Quarterly*, Spring 1954; R. Flacks, 'The Liberated Generation' in *Journal of Social Issues*, XXIII, 1967, pp. 52-75; Kenneth Keniston, *Young Radicals*, Harcourt, Brace, 1968.

7 G. Almond and S. Verba, *The Civic Culture*, Princeton University Press, 1963, pp. 346-63.

8 Quoted in Diane Divoky (ed.). *How Old Will You Be In 1984?*, Avon, 1965. The point was eloquently made, too, in a popular song by Tom Paxton:

> What did you learn in school today,
> Dear little boy of mine?
> What did you learn in school today,
> Dear little boy of mine?
> I learned that Washington never told a lie,
> I learned that soldiers seldom die,
> I learned that everybody's free,
> That's what the teacher said to me,
> And that's what I learned in school today,
> That's what I learned in school.

9 Kate Millett, *Sexual Politics*, Sphere Books, 1971, p. 43.

10 See, for instance, Robert D. Hess and Judith V. Torney, *The Development of Political Attitudes in Children*, Anchor, 1968. Patriotism of a traditional kind was not easy to sustain among adults in the USA and the UK as the post-war years wore on. By the later 1960s, American patriotism sometimes tended to follow two somewhat disparate directions. The old-fashioned super-patriots would raise 'Old Glory' with more grit and determination than ever before and proclaim that every citizen of America should 'Love It or Leave It', while many student rebels and anti-war protesters would denounce the words and deeds of their political leaders and rationalize their protest as arising out of a more authentic patriotism. In Britain, once the great days of the war, Churchill, and the Empire had clearly receded into the past, patriotism often became somewhat whimsical. The Union Jack would turn up on bras and shopping bags, while the 'I'm backing Britain' campaign of the mid-1960s became a 'jokey' slogan among the swinging youngsters.

Chapter 2 *America* (page 37)

1 Quoted in an article by E. Mansell Pattison in the *Los Angeles Times*, 9 Jan. 1973.

2   See, for instance, the article by Robinson and Converse in Angus Campbell and Philip E. Converse (eds.), *The Human Meaning of Social Change*, Russell Sage Foundation, 1972.
3   Geoffrey Gorer, *The Americans*, Cresset Press, 1948, p. 121.
4   For a superb treatment of this theme see J. K. Galbraith, *The Affluent Society*, Hamish Hamilton, 1958, esp. Chap. 9, 'The Paramount Position of Production'.
5   In every age people are nostalgic about some aspects of the age that preceded it. 'Most old folks', wrote Michael Wood (in an article entitled 'Nostalgia or Never: You Can't Go Home Again' in *New Society*, 7 Nov. 1974) 'can remember a time when beer was cheaper, . . . and people had more respect, and the corporation had not ploughed up those fields at the end of the street for council housing. Most of us remember odd patches of our lives with special affection . . . [that] provoke a sort of tenderness. . .' But in modern Britain and America, nostalgia seemed at times to have taken the place of patriotism as the one great socially acceptable emotion. 'I believe in yesterday' sang the Beatles, and scored a stunning success. In the late 1960s, all the young women seemed to be wearing the midi-length dresses, black stockings and even the berets of the twenties (the inspiration being perhaps *Bonnie and Clyde*) while the real enthusiasts for the sartorial past resuscitated the long skirts and high shoulders – and even the 'Grannie glasses' – of 1900. There was a vogue for high-backed wicker chairs and Beardsley, while in the States hundreds of thousands of people bought a reprint of the 1897 Sears, Roebuck catalogue. Cinemas found that they could do a brisk trade with the Marx Brothers, Buster Keaton and Bogart, while theatres on both sides of the Atlantic were sold out in the early seventies with revivals of *No, No, Nanette*. For a lengthy description and analysis of the nostalgia boom, see *Newsweek*, 28 Dec. 1970.
6   See Philip French, *Westerns*, Secker & Warburg and BFI, 1973, esp. p. 48.
7   Martha Wolfenstein and Nathan Leites, *Movies: A Psychological Study*, The Free Press of Glencoe, 1950, final chapter.
8   For an excellent analysis of the Western as a mythological embodiment of the values of the early Puritans, see Peter Homans, 'Puritanism Revisited: An Analysis of the Contemporary Screen-Image Western' in *Studies in Public Communication*, no. 3, University of Chicago, 1961. Homans emphasizes in particular the concepts of self-control and the confrontation with evil that pervade both New England Puritanism and the archetypal Western movie.
   For examples of the durability of the frontier legacy, consider (in addition to the continuing popularity of Western movies) the

American adoption, almost as a national dish, of the barbecue dinner and the (often slightly underdone) stea⊢, not to mention the griddle cakes and maple syrup on which Americans often like to breakfast. Consider, too, the universal adoption of jeans (even on 'Barbie' dolls, see Chap. 7, note 14).

9 Quoted in William Carlson Smith, *Americans in the Making*, Appleton-Century, 1939; repr. by Arno Press and the *New York Times*, 1970, p. 33.

10 Quoted by Michael Drake, 'We Are Yankeys Now' in *New York History*, vol. XLV, no. 3, July 1964.

11 William Carlson Smith, *Americans in the Making*, p. 27.

12 ibid., p. 324.

13 Quoted in Daniel J. Boorstin, *The Americans: The Colonial Experience*, Random House, 1958, p. 33. As early as 1717, John Wise in his essay 'A Vindication of the Government of New England Churches' wrote of man's 'Personal Liberty and Equality' which were 'to be cherished, and preserved to the highest degree, as will consist with all just distinctions amongst Men of Honour, and shall be agreeable with the Publick Good.' Wise considered it a law of nature 'that every Man Esteem and treat another as one who is naturally his Equal...' The essays of John Wise were collected and republished in 1772 and played their part in influencing those who were beginning to demand the independence of colonial America.

14 Alexis de Tocqueville, *Democracy in America*, Richard D. Heffner (ed.), Mentor, 1961, p. 55.

15 ibid., p. 117.

16 William Carlson Smith, *Americans in the Making*, p. 172.

17 See, for instance, Isaiah Berlin, *Two Concepts of Liberty*, Oxford, 1958.

18 American parents would characteristically encourage this attitude. 'The ambition to succeed . . . is the ambition of every parent for his child. It is emphatically an American ambition . . . the mainspring of activity.' I.G. Wyllie, *The Self-Made Man in America*, Signet, 1964, p. 63. One of Studs Terkel's interviewees, a steelworker, told him: 'I want my kid to look at me and say "Dad, you're a nice guy, but you're a fuckin' dummy." Hell, yes, I want my kid to tell me that he's not gonna be like me.' Studs Terkel, *Working*, Pantheon, 1974, p. 37.

19 This view that the values of equality and achievement are mutually reinforcing is not accepted by all observers of American society. The case *for* this symbiosis is argued by David C. McClelland, *The Achieving Society*, Van Nostrand, 1961. McClelland argues that, among other factors, 'other-directedness' (Riesman's term for

the peer-group approval that provides a major push towards equality among twentieth century Americans) can be a powerful incentive towards greater achievement. On the other hand, S. M. Lipset (*The First New Nation*, Anchor, 1967, Chap. 3) argues that equality — particularly when stimulated by other-directedness — is antipathetic towards achievement.
20 London *Evening Standard*, 15 Aug. 1969. For a British observation of the extent to which achievement in the USA is measured by wealth, see Geoffrey Gorer, *The Americans*, Cresset Press, 1948, Chap. 7, 'Success and the Dollar'.
21 Jack Newfield, *Robert Kennedy: A Memoir*, Cape, 1970, p. 304. Interestingly enough, black Americans were, by the end of the 1960s, substantially more sanguine about their country and about their own personal situation than were white Americans — either because blacks still espoused a traditional value system that many disillusioned whites were sloughing off or, perhaps, because they felt that their lot was so miserable that it could hardly fail to have been improving. See, for instance, polls published in the London *Daily Telegraph*, 4 Dec. 1969, and in the *International Herald Tribune*, 28 June 1971. See also Albert H. Cantril and Charles W. Roll Jr, *Hopes and Fears of the American People*, Universe Books, 1971, p. 27; and William Watts and Lloyd A. Free, *State of the Nation*, Universe Books, 1973, p. 25.
22 W. Lloyd Warner, *American Life, Dream and Reality*, University of Chicago Press, 1962, p. 127.
23 Erik Erikson, *Childhood and Society*, Penguin edn, 1965, p. 278.
24 Zbigniew Brzezinski, 'The Technetronic Age' (article condensed from *Encounter* in *Dialogue*, USIA, vol. 2, no. 4, 1969). Some of the ideas in this piece appeared in expanded form in *Between Two Ages: America's Role in the Technetronic Era*, Viking, 1971.
25 Michael Kammen, *People of Paradox*, Knopf, 1972.
26 Geoffrey Gorer, *The Americans*, p. 34.
27 See, for instance, Roderic Gorney, *The Human Agenda*, Bantam, 1973, pp. 505 *et seq*.
28 Erik Erikson, op. cit., p. 277. Similarly, W. Lloyd Warner after listing America's 'two basic, but antithetical, principles', goes on to say: 'I wish to assert that, paradoxical as it may seem, both of these antithetical principles . . . are necessary to the proper functioning of contemporary American democracy' (*American Life, Dream and Reality*, pp. 127-8).
29 Quoted in R. E. Park and E. W. Burgess, *Introduction to the Science of Sociology*, Chicago, 1924, p. 734.
30 W. Lloyd Warner, op. cit., pp. 61-2.

Chapter 3   *Britain* (pages 80-85)

1   By a myth I mean a belief or system of beliefs which, while perhaps untrue in a literal sense, may nevertheless contain an element of meaning which is true in a symbolic sense. A myth generally contains an element of moral persuasion, and often embodies an appeal to nature or the idea of the natural.

2   It was characteristic of the British to regard as heroes the men of the Light Brigade who made a suicidal charge in the Crimean incident that might in other cultures have been forgotten or perhaps considered as indicating in those particular cavalrymen a sheeplike acquiescence in orders that were patently foolish or wicked. However, within British culture the Charge subsequently took on the mythical status of an example of British sang froid at its most noble. A famous example from the early twentieth century of the inclination of the British to deal calmly with crisis and even the imminence of catastrophic defeat was the way in which Captain Oates, a member of Scott's last Antarctic expedition, faced death. Scott, soon to die himself, wrote of Oates in his diary:

> He took pride in thinking that his regiment would be pleased with the bold way in which he met his death. We can testify to his bravery. He has borne intense suffering for weeks without complaint, and to the very last was able and willing to discuss outside subjects. He did not — would not — give up hope to the very end. He was a brave soul. This was the end. He slept through the night before last, hoping not to wake; but he woke in the morning — yesterday. It was blowing a blizzard. He said, 'I am just going outside and may be some time.' He went out into that blizzard, and we have not seen him since. . . . We knew that poor Oates was walking to his death, but though we tried to dissuade him, we knew it was the act of a brave man and an English gentleman.

3   The appeal to the spirit of Dunkirk showed great tenacity and surfaced, for instance, during the difficult winter of 1973-4 when the Government anxiously tried to persuade people to put up with the economic discomfort into which Britain seemed to be plunging. The cliche was an unfortunate one, not only because Dunkirk was not a victory but a withdrawal, but also because the myth of a country united as never before was not even historically accurate. (See William Rankin, 'What Dunkirk Spirit?' in *New Society*, 15 Nov. 1973.) The pricking of an historical myth, however, has rarely prevented people from appealing to it.

4   Angus Calder, *The People's War: Britain 1939-45*, Cape, 1969, p. 188.

5   Charles de Gaulle, *The Call to Honour 1940-42*, Collins, 1955, pp. 62-3.

6 Stanley Baldwin, *On England (And Other Addresses)*, Holder & Stoughton, 1938, pp. 12-13. Quoted in Rupert Wilkinson, *The Prefects*, Oxford University Press, 1964, p. 86.

7 Bertrand Russell, with his usual wit and elegance, expressed this common English perception in a television interview with Woodrow Wyatt recorded in 1959:

> BR: I don't think they (the British) have the same inflexible dogmas that are very common in other countries. . . . When the French Revolution came French aristocrats were asked, 'Would you rather surrender your privileges or have your heads cut off?' and they said, 'Naturally, have our heads cut off', and they did. Whereas in England in 1832, the Reform Bill before Parliament involved the surrender of the privileges of the aristocracy. My grandfather himself, very much an aristocrat, brought in the Bill and got it through. . . And I think I may attribute to him the fact that my head is still on my shoulders. . . The continental approach is much more rigid. You are for this or for that and not for getting a suitable adjustment of the two.
> WW: Do you feel yourself to be British?
> BR: Indeed yes, and quite in the tradition. . . I think we like tradition unless it does some very obvious harm. Now take, for instance, the question of the naming of streets. In every continental country that I know of they change the streets every now and again because their politics have changed, and the great men they used to admire they no longer admire. If we were like the continentals we should knock down the Duke of York's column, because we don't admire the Duke of York.

(This quotation is from *Bertrand Russell Speaks His Mind*, Barker, 1960.)

8 Baldwin once told R. A. Butler that intellectualism was a sin worse than death. *The Listener*, 14 Mar. 1974.

9 Occasionally, the pressures and provocations reached breaking point and self-restraint was no longer possible. Hence, for instance, some of the rick-burning and machine-breaking in early nineteenth-century England.

10 For a discussion of the similarities and dissimilarities of British and American social values with special reference to deference and elitism, see S. M. Lipset, *The First New Nation*, Anchor, 1967, pp. 244-57.

11 Even at the height of the 'Captain Swing' disturbances of 1830, according to two of the most radical of modern British historians, 'the labourers and their sympathisers did not normally want a disruption of the old society, but a restoration of their rights within it. . .' Eric Hobsbawm and George Rudé, *Captain Swing*, Lawrence & Wishart, 1969, p. 61.

12 Quoted in Raphael Samuel, 'The Deference Voter' in *New Left Review*, Jan. 1960, p. 11.

13 Quoted in Eric Goldman, *The Crucial Decade — and After*, Vintage, 1960, p. 89.

14 Tocqueville, whose observations about America were so perceptive, also visited England and he found the English club a marvellous illustration of two opposite tendencies that he thought he could identify among the British — what he called the 'spirit of association' and the 'spirit of exclusion'. 'What better example of association', he wrote, 'than the union of individuals who form the club? What more exclusive than the corporate personality represented by the club?' From Tocqueville's *Journey to England* in J. P. Mayer (ed.), *Journeys to England and Ireland*, Faber, 1958, pp. 87-8.

15 The British postage stamp was virtually unique in that it did not say from which country it came!

16 'The secrets of the governing class of Britain', wrote Edward Shils, 'are kept within the governing class. . . . The British ruling class is unequalled in secretiveness and taciturnity. . . .What is spoken in privacy is expected to be retained in privacy and withheld from the populace. When journalists are confided in, it is with the expectation that the confidence will be respected.' Edward A. Shils, *The Torment of of Secrecy*, Heinemann, 1956, pp. 49-50.

17 Geoffrey Gorer, *Exploring English Character*, Cresset Press, 1955. The book suffers from a number of limitations — most of its data and much of its hypothesizing are based on a sample derived from a popular Sunday newspaper of the time, *The People* (though as a partial corrective Gorer also conducted a more scientific field poll) and the analysis is confined to the English and does not deal with the British as a whole. In addition, Gorer's questions were often little more than reflections of his own preconceptions about the English at a particular point in time, namely the early 1950s. Nevertheless, Gorer himself acknowledges the limitations of this study and it remains a useful source of information about English attitudes to such issues as child-rearing, love, sex, marriage, law and order, religion, and neighbourliness.

18 According to a public opinion poll reported in the *Sunday Times* in 1969 — shortly after policemen had been seen repeatedly fighting with demonstrators, and soon after *The Times* had published a big story about police corruption — the British people still thought, by figures consistently over 90 per cent, that the police were 'helpful', 'friendly', 'polite', 'honest', 'fair', and 'efficient'. Even when the figures were classified by age, class, and so on, they only dropped below 90 per cent once: of people between sixteen

and twenty-four, only 89 per cent thought that the police were usually polite.

19   George Orwell, 'The English People', *Collected Essays, vol. III, 1943-45,* Penguin edn, 1970, p. 17. Sir Arthur Bryant considered that one of the chief reasons for the Anglo-French wars of 1793-1815 was 'the British refusal to admit any Order not based on law'. (*The Years of Endurance,* Fontana edn, 1961, p. 9.)

20   Here are three newspaper reports all quoted in the *New Statesman's* 'This England' column:

> Plymouth City Council yesterday took away its £100 grants from two Church homes for unmarried mothers and teenage girls and gave them instead to Plymouth Dogs and Cats Home.

> One of the original kittens had been killed by the Mau Mau and his preserved body was flown to England, said Miss Cotton. She went on: 'He was the son of a cat whose picture appeared on National Savings Posters. We felt it was only right for him to be buried in his own country.'

> There ought to be a regular births and deaths column for horses. . . A regular column where people can keep up with the news of horses they once knew or rode is definitely needed.

> In my local park is a bench inscribed: IN MEMORY OF ENID MARGARET SIMPSON AND HER DOG YAWN. Alongside the forbidding battlements of Edinburgh Castle, I noticed a few years ago a sign announcing the site of a 'Cemetery for Soldiers [sic] Dogs'. (A book on British attitudes to animals is in preparation by Keith V. Thomas.)

21   Geoffery Gorer, *Exploring English Character,* p. 183.

22   Much of the British desire to control the aggressions of others was internalized; no people were more proud than the British of their capacity to endure with stoic silence the painful shafts that life could inflict. Indeed, there could be something almost masochistic about the British. In 1970, only about 15 per cent of British homes had central heating when the figure in France was 36 per cent. Or think of the extraordinary resistance of the British (and the instant receptivity of the Americans) to the adoption of soft toilet paper in the 1960s. According to the *New Statesman's* 'This England' column, there was once a report in the *Observer* saying that the Dartmoor prison debating society had passed a resolution asking for the reintroduction of corporal punishment and hanging!

23   Jeremy Seabrook, *City Close-Up,* Allen Lane, The Penguin Press, 1971, p. 115.

24   The English working class, it has often and rightly been pointed out, has historically tended to be more easily able to express its

aggressions than the more inhibited middle class. But see, for example, Robert Roberts, in his authoritative memoir *The Classic Slum*, Manchester University Press, 1971; despite gruesome stories of domestic brawlings and beatings, Roberts is still able to write (p. 134): 'Apathy, docility, deference: our village as a whole displayed just those qualities which, sixty years before, Karl Marx had noted, stamped the poor industrial workers—qualities which convinced him that the English proletarian would never revolt of his own accord.'

25 Rupert Wilkinson, *The Prefects*, pp. 89-90.

26 *The Memoirs of Field-Marshal Montgomery*, Fontana edn, 1960, pp. 101, 166.

27 Margaret Mead, *The American Character*, Penguin edn, 1944, p. viii. For an amusing description of British conversation by an observant and affectionate foreigner, see Hanoch Bartov, *An Israeli at the Court of St James*, Vallentine Mitchell, 1971, p. 17.

28 Emerson, in his *English Traits*, tells of an English lady on the Rhine who, hearing a German speak of her party as foreigners, exclaimed 'No, we are not foreigners; we are English; it is you that are foreigners.'

29 Arthur Bryant, *The Years of Endurance*, p. 225.

30 The American slang word for an Englishman, a 'limey', was derived from the fact that the ship-bound British would proverbially eat limes in order to try to avoid scurvy.

31 cf. the quotation from Stanley Baldwin cited on p. 87.

32 See Rupert Wilkinson, *The Prefects*. The kinship between life at sea and life at one of the more traditional 'public' schools is closer than one might think. I once produced a programme for BBC radio about Harrow School songs and was struck by how many of them invoked supposedly nautical virtues. At Eton, *the* song—possibly the most famous of all British school songs—is a boating song, and, of course, the established headgear at Eton, Harrow and elsewhere was a 'boater'!

33 *Cricket Quiz: Over 500 Questions and Answers About the 'King of Games'* compiled by Robert Tearle, Danceland Publications Ltd, 1945, p. 2. The vocabulary of cricket was often used in Britain to epitomize the highest and most characteristic of British virtues. An honourable person would be said to 'play with a straight bat' while the actions of somebody less admirable would be looked upon with some scorn as 'not cricket'. You could be 'caught out' or stumped' if not 'on your guard' and even (like Rommel by Montgomery) 'hit for six'.

34 Virginia Cowles, *No Cause for Alarm: A Study of Trends in England Today*, Hamish Hamilton, 1949, p. 24.

35 Neville Cardus, Prelude to *Cricket*, Longmans, 1930.
36 ibid.
37 Neville Cardus, *Days In the Sun*, Hart-Davis, 1948 edn, pp. 135-6.

Chapter 4 *Anglo-American mirror images* (page 106)

1 On the subject of Saint Monday, E. P. Thompson has written:

There are few trades which are not described as honouring Saint Monday: shoemakers, tailors, colliers, printing workers, potters, weavers, hosiery workers, cutlers, all Cockneys ... Saint Monday, indeed, appears to have been honoured almost universally wherever small-scale, domestic and outwork industries existed; was generally found in the pits; and sometimes continued in manufacturing and heavy industry. It was perpetuated, in England, into the nineteenth—and, indeed, into the twentieth —centuries for complex economic and social reasons.

(From 'Time, Work-Discipline and Industrial Capitalism' in *Past and Present*, no. 38, 1967, pp. 75-6.)
2 See Michael Young and Peter Willmott, *The Symmetrical Family*, Routledge & Kegan Paul, 1973, p. 126, where Young and Willmott quote studies by M. A. Bienefeld and by E. H. Phelps Brown and M. H. Browne.
3 Laslett even suggests that, alongside the occasional co-opting of people from lower status groups *up* to the ranks of the social elite, *downwards* mobility in pre-industrial Britain was probably rather more common. Peter Laslett, *The World We Have Lost*, Methuen, 1965, pp. 186-7.
4 This contrast is far from total. America's Brahmins (the hereditary ones and the industrial parvenus alike) were sometimes an even more visible 'leisure class' given to 'conspicuous consumption' than their discreet counterparts from pre-industrial Britain. And the British, by and large, never tried to distance themselves from the ordinary daily toils of life, or even of earning a living, as did some of the *ancien régime* elites of continental Europe. Indeed, the English gentleman, wrote Simon Raven (*The English Gentleman*, Blond, 1961, p. 53) 'has always been more flexible in his choice of occupation than his continental counterpart.' However, Raven concedes, the upper crust Englishman has traditionally been reluctant, except in an emergency or for a hobby, to work with his hands.
5 'Poets', in the words of one of the Harrow School songs (*Byron*),

'shouldn't have work to do!' Things were not always as easy as they might sound for all members of the English upper classes. While the elder son of an old aristocratic family would expect to inherit his father's land and status, his younger brothers might be at a loose and even impecunious end. You might, as it were, have been the son of an earl or a duke, but if you were not careful you might end up as merely the father of a clergyman or a yeoman farmer. Hence the tradition of the younger son embarking on a career—not too strenuous or menial a one to be sure—in the upper reaches of the church, the army, or politics. These were 'work' situations that none the less permitted or even demanded a great deal of the leisured sociability characteristic of the life of the landed aristocrat. In these professions, one's work was implicit rather than visible.

6 The first professional cricketer to captain an England team was Len Hutton in 1952. The appointment caused a lot of raised eyebrows at the time and although Hutton was generally conceded to have done a good job, he was succeeded by that epitome of the amateur the Rev. (later Bishop) David Sheppard.

7 Virginia Cowles, *No Cause for Alarm: A Study of Trends in England Today*, Hamish Hamilton, 1949, p. 24.

8 Attributed to the American baseball manager Leo Durocher. American sporting history is full of legendary *bons mots* of this ilk. 'Winning', said Vince Lombardi the football coach, 'isn't the most important thing—it's the *only* thing!' For a depressingly powerful account of the lengths to which American footballers can be prepared to go in order to win, see Anton Myrer, 'The Giant In the Tube', *Harper's*, Nov. 1972. A good introduction to the mores of American sport for British readers is provided by Paul Gardner, *Nice Guys Finish Last: Sport and American Life*, Allen Lane, 1974. One of the best statements of the ways in which American values can be encapsulated in sport is Michael R. Real, 'Super Bowl: Mythical Spectacle', *Journal of Communication*, vol. 25:1, Winter 1975. North American professional football, he concludes, (all in italics) 'is an aggressive, strictly regulated team game fought between males who use both violence and technology to gain control of property for the economic gain of individuals, within a nationalistic entertainment context.' He goes on (unitalicized) to say of the Super Bowl, the Cup Final of US-football, that it 'propagates these values by elevating one game to the level of a spectacle of American ideology collectively celebrated'.

9 Rupert Wilkinson, *The Prefects*, p. 15.

10 Simon Raven, *The English Gentleman*, p. 53.

11 Nelson Algren was also struck by this contrast:

I climbed into [a taxi] and off we went on a four-shilling ride to Half Moon Street, where I gave the driver a two-shilling tip. He said it was all right but thought I was going it rather strong. Only an English cabbie would resent being overtipped.

(Nelson Algren, *Who Lost An American?*, Deutsch, 1963, p. 77.) Algren goes on to complain, however, that the cabbie did not leave one of the shillings on the kerb when he drove off. 'Or both!'

By contrast an American cab-driver told Studs Terkel (*Working*, Pantheon, 1974, p. 199): 'A lot of drivers, they'll agree to almost anything the passenger will say, no matter how absurd. They're angling for that tip.'

12 The origins of this two-way bond—loyalty upwards and service downwards—may go back as far as Anglo-Saxon times. Dorothy Whitelock wrote of the intense loyalty of the man to his lord in Anglo-Saxon England. In return, she said, the man would get protection.

No one would be eager to molest a man who had a powerful lord ready to demand compensation or to take vengeance. The lord took responsibility for the man's acts; he had to produce him to answer a charge in court, or pay the damages himself, and it would be to his interest to defend his man from a wrongful accusation. He was held responsible even for deeds committed before the man entered his service, and would therefore be unwise too readily to accept an unknown man. . . The lord's responsibility for his followers is the aspect of this relationship which stands out most prominently in the laws. (*The Beginnings of English Society*, Penguin edn, 1968, pp. 36-7).

13 J. D. R. McConnell, *Eton—How it Works*, Faber, 1967, p. 60.

14 It is notoriously difficult to assess either the amount of mobility in a society or people's attitudes towards it. In a society that values above all wealth, the socially mobile are those who have (and take) opportunities of gaining (or losing) appreciable amounts of wealth, and social mobility can be discussed in terms of the extent of those opportunities. But in a society in which different and often contradictory values are espoused and where the predominant values of one section of the community are not those of another, this type of assessment becomes difficult, for it is less clear who is rising and who falling—and by what criteria.

In addition to the problem of which values to concentrate on, there is the question of which people to observe. Should one pick on, say, the biographies of 'successful' people of a generation ago and the present and see which groups had furthest to climb then and now? The problems with generational studies are that they concentrate exclusively upon the successful elite and tend to equate

different types of success and to assume that the criteria of success
are constant over time. Another approach is to examine a group of
people at the start rather than the end of their careers, and to
observe their achievements over a period of time. This method
can also equate the values of one era with those of another by failing
to take account of the fact that the child who achieves what his
parents wanted him to achieve might be considered a failure by the
society in which he is an adult. A third approach, and possibly the
most fruitful, is to concentrate upon some popularly admired
enclave in society—the upper echelons of the legal or medical professions, perhaps—and to see what sort of people have access to it
over a period of time. The classic study on Britain, one containing
articles on many aspects of this topic, is still D. V. Glass (ed.), *Social
Mobility in Britain*, Routledge, 1954.

15 E. C. Banfield, *The Unheavenly City*, Little, Brown, 1968,
p. 64.

16 The Robbins Report of 1963 showed that a manual worker's
child had only one-eighth as much chance of a degree-level education as the child of a non-manual worker. In 1968, children of
manual and agricultural workers formed 28 per cent of university
students—but their fathers formed 64 per cent of the 45-59 age
group in Britain (*The Universities Central Council on Admissions*,
Statistical Supplement to the Sixth Report, 1967-8). However, see
Herbert Hyman, 'England and America: Climates of Tolerance
and Intolerance', in Daniel Bell (ed.), *The Radical Right*, Anchor,
1964. Hyman writes: 'Contrary to usual belief, social mobility in
Britain, both upward and downward, has been substantial and not
very different in magnitude from mobility in the United States.'
This provocative sentence is backed up by a lengthy and source-
filled footnote (that goes some way, however, towards weakening
the impact it is ostensibly designed to buttress). Whatever the truth
of this complex matter, it probably remains the case that the British,
by and large, were characteristically less sanguine than the Americans about the opportunities for social mobility provided by their
society. It is interesting to note, in conclusion, that, in the context
of other comparable European countries such as France, West
Germany and the Netherlands, opportunities for social mobility in Britain appear to have ranked relatively high. See Frank
Parkin, *Class Inequality and Political Order*, MacGibbon & Kee, 1971,
pp. 107-14.

17 Unpublished communication to author. The supposed cultural
embourgeoisement of the British working class has been passionately
debated. For a statement of some of the bones of the argument, see
John H. Goldthorpe, David Lockwood, Frank Bechhofer and

Jennifer Platt, *The Affluent Worker in the Class Structure*, Cambridge University Press, 1969, pp. 21-9.
18 Peter Willmott, *Adolescent Boys of East London*, Pelican edn, 1969, pp. 170, 172. For a statement of the working class perspective on the apparently largely immutable British class structure, see John H. Goldthorpe *et al*, *The Affluent Worker in the Class Structure*, pp. 118-19.
19 This contrast was particularly striking when Britain had a Conservative government and could be a shock to an unsuspecting American observer. Tom Lambert, the *Los Angeles Times'* man in London, was clearly aware of this when reporting on the annual conference of the Trades Union Congress in September 1972:

> If an American trade unionist views profits as a source for wage increases, most of his British counterparts see them as despicable. If an American might increase his productivity to generate profit as beneficial ultimately for him, some of his British counterparts might ease up on the job.
> In essence, the TUC seemed . . . a class political session featuring denunciations and warnings to government and industry.

This contrast between the class perceptions of British and American workers is further revealed in the cultural aspirations of workers in the two societies. We have already noted reservations among members of the British working class towards cultural *embourgeoisement*; one of Peter Willmott's East Enders despised

> these so-called 'middle-class' people, who think they are higher than you because they live in higher-class places. People with bowler hats and umbrellas. They think they own the world. They look around with their noses in the air and talk to you as if you were nobody.

Peter Willmott, *Adolescent Boys*, p. 139. Contrast this with, for instance, this black woman from Harlem, one of David Riesman's *Faces in the Crowd*, Yale University Press, 1952, abr. ed. 1965, p. 126:

> I do part-time work because it doesn't keep me away from my children. I'm a housekeeper. And when I say a housekeeper I mean housekeeper. I don't mean a maid. I don't act as a maid for anyone. When people come to the door asking if the Madam is here, I give them a sharp answer and . . . tell them that I am Mrs Henderson. [Pause] I was married too.

20 David Riesman, *Faces in the Crowd*, pp. 624-5.
21 David Riesman, ibid., p. 95.
22 See Chap. 2, n. 18.

23 Michael Young and Peter Willmott, *Family and Kinship in East London*, Pelican edn, 1962, p. 173.
24 William H. Whyte, *The Organization Man*, Pelican edn, 1960, pp. 287-8, wrote:

> In an environment that seems to be homogeneous, one might think there were few distinctions one had to worry about. To the practised eye, however, there is much more diversity in the scene than the bystander sees, for the more accustomed one becomes to the homogeneity, the more sensitized is he to the small differences

—such as who has what modification of the basic ranch-house design, or the acquisition in this home of an automatic dryer or in that home of an unusually elaborate television set.

25 The foreign image of England as the home of liberty was one that reached as far as the ears of Mozart and the librettist of *Il Seraglio* who gave Blonde the splendid line, when resisting enslavement to the odious Osmin: 'Girls are not wares to be given away at will. I am an Englishwoman, born to freedom, and defy anyone who attempts to constrain me!' ('Mädchen sind keine Waare zum Verschenken. Ich bin eine Engländerin, zur Freiheit geboren; and trotz jedem, der mich zu etwas zwingen will.')

26 John Milton, *Tenure of Kings and Magistrates*. Edmund Burke, *Reflections on the Revolution in France and Speech at his Arrival at Bristol.* G. B. Shaw, *Maxims for Revolutionaries.*

27 'Liberty in the lowest rank of every nation,' said Dr Johnson, 'is little more than the choice of working or starving.' (*Works*, vi, p. 151).

28 According to Adam Smith, the duties of government ('the sovereign') as conceived in the late eighteenth century were threefold:

> first, the duty of protecting the society from the violence and invasion of other independent societies; secondly, the duty of protecting, as far as possible, every member of the society from the injustice or oppression of every other member of it, or the duty of establishing an exact administration of justice; and thirdly, the duty of erecting and maintaining certain public works and . . . institutions.

These three governmental functions derive from what Smith called the 'system of natural liberty'. Adam Smith, *The Wealth of Nations*, New York, 1937 edn, p. 651.

29 E. P. Thompson, *The Making of the English Working Class*, Pelican edn, 1968, p. 86.

30 E. L. Woodward, *The Age of Reform*, Oxford University Press, 1954, p. 212.

31 G. D. H. Cole, *The Intelligent Man's Guide to the Post-War World*, Gollancz, 1947.

32 The cowboy is perhaps the archetypal American myth figure, the lonely and rootless repository of so many of his society's virtues. Peter Homans, in his analysis of the western movie, emphasized that 'goodness' (of which the cowboy is the embodiment) 'lies in the power and willingness to resist temptation. It is the ability to remain in the presence of temptation and yet remain in control of one's desire.' Homans writes about the temptations of drinking, gambling, money, and sex—and shows how the Western hero can enjoy these temptations, but in moderation. Ordinary people indulge; heroes are 'good' and restrain or control their impulses. Peter Homans, 'Puritanism Revisited: An Analysis of the Contemporary Screen-Image Western' in *Studies in Public Communication*, no. 3, University of Chicago Press, 1961.

33 Some American football grounds even began to consider the installation of instant replay screens so that spectators could see controversial 'plays' immediately after they had occurred. The fans would no doubt feel that this device enabled them to keep a closer eye on the dubious decisions of the game officials, while the opportunities such a mechanism could provide for each coach to challenge calls against his team could prolong a game by as much as an hour or more. See Melvin Durslag, 'The Paying Fans Finally Get a Break' in *TV Times*, 11 Nov. 1972.

34 Officials of the New York subway can quote alarming figures to indicate the number of light bulbs that would vanish from their trains if the screw were not the reverse of that used in domestic fixtures. In London newspaper sellers can still leave a hat by their Kiosk for money to be deposited.

35 G. Almond and S. Verba, *The Civic Culture*, Little, Brown, abr. edn, 1965, pp. 169, 185. Even the political apathy and indifference that, as everywhere, was widespread in Britain and the United States, was not quite the same in the two societies. There was a greater tendency for the American to feel frustrated because, while he thought he understood the way politics worked, he was, nevertheless, unable to have a direct effect upon the way things happened. 'If you do speak up' says one of Robert Lane's Eastport interviewees in *Political Ideology* (The Free Press of Glencoe, 1962, p. 164), 'there's nothing done about it—they just go ahead', while another (p. 169) simply assumes that 'these guys are not someplace to make a buck'. This type of cynicism was common enough in Britain as well; Richard Hoggart (*The Uses of Literacy*, Pelican edn, 1958, p. 73) quotes working-class people talking about 'them', mysterious people who 'get yer in the end', 'aren't really to be trusted', 'are all

twisters really', 'will do y'down if they can' and 'treat y'like muck'.
But there was also the more characteristically British assumption
that political impotence was something ordained from above in
the interests of social stability and something, therefore, to which
the reasonable citizen would have to reconcile himself. 'I like to
be set an example and have someone I can look up to', says a British
worker quoted by R. T. McKenzie and Allan Silver in 'Conservatism, Industrialism and the Working-Class Tory in England' in
Transactions of the Fifth World Congress of Sociology, 1962.

36. See, for instance, Kenneth Keniston, *The Uncommitted*, Dell,
1965, Chap. 10, for the masculinity associations of, for instance,
'carrying a big stick', 'making overtures to potential aggressors',
and being 'afraid of being caught with our pants down'.

Annie Oakley, it will be recalled, complained, no doubt unaware
of the Freudian implications of her lament, that 'you can't get a
man with a gun.'

37 In Hugh Davis Graham and Ted Robert Gurr, *Violence
in America:* A Report Submitted to the National Commission
on the Causes and Prevention of Violence, Bantam, 1969, pp.
84-5.

38 James F. Kirkham, Sheldon G. Levy and William J. Crotty,
Assassination and Political Violence: A Report to the National Com-
mission on the Causes and Prevention of Violence, *New York Times/*
Praeger, 1970, p. 291.

39 James F. Kirkham *et al.*, *Assassination and Political Violence*, pp.
291-2.

40 Ibid.

41 However, *Moby Dick*, arguably the greatest work of fiction
produced by an American, is, in part, an allegory about the rapac-
iousness of the American people towards their natural environment.
And Melville's prime image for the American people is the body
of men aboard the ship, the *Pequod*.

42 See, for instance, S. M. Lipset and E. Raab, *The Politics of Un-
reason: Right-Wing Extremism in America, 1790-1970*, Heinemann
Educational, 1971, pp. 447-8.

43 In 1926, a time when the air was still thick with the cruel and
bloated rhetoric of extreme patriotism that followed the enormous
waves of immigration of the first years of the century, the world
war and the Palmer raids that followed it, the Rev. O.L. Martin, a
visiting Evangelist, said in Arizona:

> If I had my way there would be no language taught in the United
> States except English, and any foreigner coming here would be
> immediately sent back if he could not speak our language. I am
> 100 per cent American.

Then there was the editorial in New York's *American Standard* about opera:

> Were it not for Roman Catholic Italians, Russian and Polish Jews, and other Latin and Oriental aliens, who have swarmed into our country like a plague of locusts, grand opera could not live five minutes in the American atmosphere. From center to circumference, it is foreign to the decent Christian spirit of the United States.
>
> The Metropolitan Opera House is the most thoroughly foreign institution in this country. Standing at the back of the house and surveying an operatic audience, one can scarcely find an Anglo-Saxon face . . . Genuine Americans have no real feeling for it, and can neither produce operas nor act in them. To imagine George Washington, Benjamin Franklin, Thomas Jefferson, or any other such representative American paying to witness the horrors and sensualities of grand opera, is to imagine the impossible.

And finally here is a resolution unanimously passed at a meeting of the allied commanderies of the Patriotic Order, Sons of America of Berks, Pennsylvania, and reported in the Reading *Eagle:*

> Resolved, That we oppose the movement to place a statue of Christopher Columbus in Penn's Common, declaring that we only favor the placing of these marks of respect in honor of those who are native heroes and sons of the soil of America.

I wonder where in America they thought William Penn had been born. . . . These quotations are all from H. L. Mencken (ed.), *Americana 1926*, Knopf, 1926. The best short book on American nativism is John Higham, *Strangers in the Land: Patterns of American Nativism 1860-1925*, Rutgers, 1955.

44 A term used by William Kornhauser, *The Politics of Mass Society*, Routledge, 1960.

45 John F. Kennedy, *A Nation of Immigrants*, Hamish Hamilton, 1964, p. 3.

46 Tocqueville's *Journey to England*, from J. P. Mayer (ed.), *Journeys to England and Ireland*, Faber, 1958, p. 81.

Chapter 5   *An era of change?* (page 151)

1 'Our society is changing rapidly, deeply, and dramatically,' wrote Robert L. Kahn, ('The Meaning of Work' in Angus Campbell and Phlip E. Converse (eds), *The Human Meaning of Social Change*, Russell Sage Foundation, 1972, p. 201). He went on:

Some of those changes are generally seen as desirable: increased
longevity, physical convenience, increased education, gains in
productive efficiency. Some are of uncertain or at least debated
value: more television sets, expanded cosmetic lines, more
advertising through all media. And some changes are unarguably
bad: increases in violent crime, pollution of the air and water,
and crowding in areas already densely populated.

The belief that ours is an era of major change filtered down from
the social commentators to the language of day-to-day discourse,
and, to people less discriminating than Robert L. Kahn, the fact
of change seemed to be almost universally thought of as a constant,
probably as 'good', and in any case as irreversible.

2 Theodore H. White, *The Making of the President 1968*, Cape,
1969, pp. 416-17.

3 Donald A. Schon, *Beyond the Stable State: Public and Private
Learning in a Changing Society*, Pelican edn, 1973, p. 16.

4 There has been much controversy in American intellectual
circles concerning the scope and extent of change in American
values. See, for example, Leo Lowenthal, 'Biographies in Popular
Magazines' reprinted in William Petersen (ed.), *American Social
Patterns*, Doubleday Anchor, 1956, in which Lowenthal argued
that the heroes portrayed in popular magazines shifted, during
the first decades of this century, from being 'serious' and 'production' heroes to being primarily what he calls 'heroes of consumption'. David Riesman *et al.*, *The Lonely Crowd*, Yale University
Press, 1950, argued that there had been a shift from 'inner-
direction' to 'other-direction'. S. M. Lipset challenged views
such as these in *The First New Nation*, Basic Books, 1963, chap. 3;
so did Talcott Parsons who argued that 'there has been a notable
consistency in the basic orientations during almost the whole
of our national existence' (article in Eli Ginsberg (ed.), *Values
and Ideals of American Youth*, Columbia University Press, 1961).

5 Theodore H. White, op. cit., pp. 417-19.

6 Donald A. Schon, op. cit., p. 22.

7 At the beginning of February 1974, the verb 'to streak' meant
to impose stripes on something, possibly by moving fast over it.
Less than a fortnight later, there was hardly a soul in the whole
of Britain and the USA who did not know that it also meant to
run naked in a public place.

8 Roderic Gorney, *The Human Agenda*, Simon & Schuster, 1972,
pp. 556, 7. Bantam edn, 1973, pp. 638, ix.

9 Nik Cohn, *Pop from the Beginning*, Weidenfeld, 1969, p. 146.

10 Hilary Rose and Stevan Rose, *Science and Society*, Pelican edn,
1970, pp. xiv-xv.

11   In one of the most famous passages in one of the top-sellers of the early 1970s, this diminishing sense of the continuity and duration of time was taken to its logical conclusion:

Without warning, Chiang vanished and appeared at the water's edge fifty feet away, all in the flicker of an instant. Then he vanished again and stood, in the same milisecond, at Jonathan's shoulder. 'It's kind of fun', he said.

(Richard Bach, *Jonathan Livingston Seagull*, Macmillan, 1970, p. 55.)

12   Midge Decter pointed out (*Harper's*, May 1968) that 'ages' used to refer to periods as long as centuries whereas nowadays an 'age' usually means a decade or so.

13   Richard Hoggart, *The Uses of Literacy*, Pelican edn, 1963, pp. 191-2.

14   'Tomorrow's Paper — TODAY' proclaimed the advertisement for the British *Daily Express*.

15   See below, Chap. 7, pp. 236-7. Many observers were struck by the inclination of post-war Americans to become increasingly present-oriented. Why plan for the future (or learn from the past), people seemed to ask — an attitude that led some to condemn a ten-year old film as 'dated' and others to insist that college courses be 'relevant'. Margaret Zube (*Social Forces*, Mar. 1972) did a content analysis of selected issues of *Ladies' Home Journal*, 1948-69, which revealed that the values incorporated in the material in later issues were appreciably more present-oriented and less future-oriented than those in the late 1940s and early 1950s.

16   David Riesman, *Faces in the Crowd*, Yale University Press, 1952, abr. edn, 1965, p. 625.

17   'How dare Richard Neville claim to speak for *my* generation? My God, he's twenty-eight.' — Girl of nineteen, quoted by John Crosby, *Observer* 23 Sept. 1973.

18   And, of course, the technology-providers were themselves instrumental in keeping these expectations raised. You might think, for example, that nothing could (or need) be quicker than a direct-dialling telephone system that could link you with people thousands of miles away. But the telephone companies spent a lot of time and money in the USA in the early- and mid-1970s trying to persuade people to spend that much more and acquire 'touch-tone' phones. In the Museum of Science and Industry in Chicago, one of the most attractive exhibits enabled the young visitor to play with any number of futuristic phones — and to see on a timing device just how fast he could call by touch-tone.

19   The average official work-week in all non-agricultural establishments in the USA hovered around thirty-seven hours in the early 1970s and was just under forty back in 1950 (*Statistical Abstract*)

while the number of hours actually worked each week by the British manual worker only dropped from 45.2 in 1947 to 44.5 in 1968 (A. H. Halsey (ed.), *Trends in British Society Since 1900,* Macmillan, 1972, p. 120).

20 The proportion in 'professional and managerial' jobs in Britain, for instance, went up from 16 per cent to 20 per cent between 1951 and 1966, while those in semi-skilled and unskilled dropped from 33 per cent to 29 per cent. Michael Young and Peter Willmott, *The Symmetrical Family,* Routledge, 1973, p. 25.

21 International T. V. Almanac, 1970 edn, p. 26A; Roper Organization, Inc., *An Extended View of Public Attitudes Toward Television and other Mass Media, 1959-1971,* New York, Television Information Office, 1971, p. 5.

22 *Social Trends,* HMSO, 1973, p. 169.

23 *Historical Statistics of the United States of America,* US Bureau of the Census, series 932.

24 'The celebrity', wrote Daniel J. Boorstin (*The Image,* Pelican edn, 1963, p. 67), 'is a perso who is known for his well-knownness.'

25 Percentage of dwellings in the USA with electric service:

	1907	*1920*	*1930*	*1940*	*1950*
All dwellings	8.0	34.7	68.2	78.7	94.0
Farm dwellings		1.6	10.4	32.6	77.7

Source: *Historical Statistics of the United States of America.*

26 In 1900, the median American lived in the countryside. By the 1920s, more Americans lived in urban than in rural areas, though the definition of an 'urban' area given by the US Bureau of the Census was quaint: any community with a population of a mere 2,500 or more! By 1950, two-thirds of all Americans lived in urban (including the new and burgeoning suburban) areas and by 1970 the figure was 73.5 per cent. In Britain the most intensive period of urbanization had been in the earlier part of the nineteenth century. The combined population of London and other towns (102 of them) of more than 20,000 inhabitants had grown from nearly 3½ million in 1821 to over 9½ million by 1871. However, the proportion of the population living in urban areas stabilized in mid-Victorian times at between 75 and 80 per cent and has remained there. For an attractive evocation of the modern city and the ambivalence towards it, see Jonathan Raban, *Soft City,* Fontana edn, 1975.

27 Philip Kotler, *Marketing Management: Analysis, Planning, and Control,* Prentice-Hall, 2nd edn, 1972, p. 95.

28 *Statistical Abstract of the United States,* 1973; A. H. Halsey (ed.), *Trends in British Society Since 1900,* p. 90.

29 This expectation continued, largely unabated, well into the ecologically- and environmentally-conscious 1970s, particularly in the USA. Despite every article, speech and statistic warning that valuable resources were being used up and should be conserved, people continued to leave lights on in their homes when they went out or in rooms that were not being used, and were far more prodigal with their heating units than the exigencies of comfort really required. During the oil-crisis-ridden 1970s, I was frequently struck by the sight of American truck-drivers, bus-drivers, and above all policemen, driving up to, say, an ice-cream counter and simply leaving their vehicle running, unused.

30 The shift of emphasis from 'giving' and 'doing' to the more passive stance of 'receiving' and 'being' is documented in, for instance, the article already cited by Margaret Zube (*Social Forces*, March 1972), a content analysis of selected issues of *Ladies' Home Journal*, 1948-1969. A further indication of this suggested shift of values might be found in language. Air New Zealand advertised its cheap flights on American radio and added, as an additional attraction, that you can 'take in Australia as well'. We don't only 'take in' countries and films and concerts; there are other examples of receptivity or passivity in the modern vernacular — particularly in vulgar speech. We talk, for instance, of getting 'stoned' or 'ripped off' or 'laid'. Daniel Yankelovich, writing of American students in the later years of our period, talks of their tendency to embrace 'the existentialist emphasis on being rather than doing or planning'. (*The Changing Values on Campus*, Washington Square Press, 1972, p. 170.)

31 One graphic way of illustrating this tendency is to take a look at a pair of family magazines, British or American, one from the late 1940s, the other from the late 1960s. The former will be full of hygiene and beauty ads of various kinds, devices for the home, and clothes; in the latter, by far the biggest advertising categories (other, perhaps, than holidays) tend to be the drinks and smokes.

32 Towards the end of Mordecai Richler's *St Urbain's Horseman*, Panther, 1972, p 377, Duddy Kravetz says:

> The first time Marlene blew me I was actually ashamed for her . . . The first time she sucked me off I thought, oh boy, lucky Duddy, you're really marrying a hot one. This is something really special. Now you open a novel or go to the movie and they're all going down on each other from the opening chapter or scene. The whole world going gobble, gobble, eat, eat.

For more on this subject, see Paul Ableman, *The Mouth and Oral Sex* Sphere Books, 1972.

33 John Updike, *Bech: A Book*, Fawcett, 1970, p. 116.

34 Clellan Ford and Frank Beach, *Patterns of Sexual Behavior*, Harper, New York, 1951, pp. 85-90.

35 The supermarket is an easy metaphor for many aspects of the culture of suburban America (and of metropolitan America, too; see the section 'The Metropolis as a Department Store' in Paul and Percival Goodman, *Communitas*, Vintage, 1947 and 1960, pp. 125-8). But in Britain, too, the 'supermarket culture' took considerable hold. The number of supermarkets in Britain shot up from 175 in 1958 to 2,803 in 1967. The percentage of food sales taking place in supermarkets in Britain was between three and four at the beginning of the 1960s and about twenty by the end of the decade—by which time the percentage of food sales taking place in supermarkets in the USA was in the region of eighty. (See *Strategic Plan for the South East*, HMSO, 1971, vol. 2 para. 1.46.)

36 Kenneth Keniston, *The Uncommitted*, Dell, 1965, p. 234.

37 Automobile manufacturers often resorted to supposedly attractive names as a means of trying to get through to various types of buyer. For the aggressive loner there was the Avenger, the Maverick, the Scimitar, the Mercury, the Jaguar, the Triumph; gentler types might have preferred the Rover or Rambler or, if they had aristocratic predilections, the Princess. Those who liked exotic names with a Latin flavour could buy a Capri, a Ford Corona, an Austin Marina, a Ferrari, an Alfa-Romeo, a Gran Torino or an Eldorado.

38 See, for instance, S. H. Britt, *Consumer Behavior and the Behavioral Sciences: Theories and Applications*, Wiley, 1966, p. 186; for an analysis of the different self-perceptions of Volkswagen and Pontiac owners see E. L. Grubb and G. Hupp, 'Perception of Self, Generalized Stereotypes, and Brand Selection', *Journal of Marketing Research*, vol. 5, Feb. 1968, pp. 58-63.

39 Manufacturers were, of course, acutely aware that much commodity shopping was in essence self-image shopping. A major shoe manufacturer said that people bought his product 'because of the way the shoes make them feel—masculine, feminine, rugged, different, sophisticated, young, glamorous, "in". . . . Our business now is selling excitement rather than shoes.' Sometimes shopping could appear, at least to manufacturers, to take on something of the character of a religious quest. Charles Revson, President of Revlon, was quoted as saying 'In the factory we make cosmetics, and in the drugstore we sell hope.' Philip Kotler, *Marketing Management*, pp. 423, 623.

40 Tom Wolfe described the ease with which young working-class Londoners could drop out of 'the system' and into 'The Life' at lunch-time and adopt exciting new roles such as 'Knights of the

Codpiece Pants' and 'Molls of the Mini Mons'. ('The Noonday Underground' in *The Pump House Gang*, Bantam, 1969.)
41 For indications that class distinctions tended to be lessened by rising incomes, see, for instance, Frederick C. Klein's article in the *Wall Street Journal*, 5 Apr. 1965; 'Customer Shopping Center Habits Change Retailing' in *Editor and Publisher*, 96, 26 Oct. 1963; and S. U. Rich and S. C. Jain, 'Social Class and Life Cycle as Predictors of Shopping Behavior' in *Journal of Marketing Research*, vol. 5, Feb. 1968, pp. 41-9.

Chapter 6 *The 'new' values* (page 185)

1 The long-term fate of traditional British and American values is not something that can be realistically assessed for many decades to come. However, it is entirely possible that the tumultuous developments of the 1960s permanently altered and even helped to erode aspects of the traditional culture of both societies. By the mid-70s, for instance, there was little evidence of younger people in Britain returning to the deference patterns of their predecessors or, indeed, of their elders seriously expecting them to do so. On the contrary, it was beginning to look as though some of the traditional deference of the British or the work ethic historically so important to the Americans might have been permanently knocked off their respective pedestals.
2 For an attractive and sensitive treatment of the subtle relationship between technique and substance, see Robert M. Pirsig, *Zen and the Art of Motorcycle Maintenance*, Bantam, 1975. For the subordination of substance or quality to the criteria of packaging, consider the gradual substitution of frozen vegetables for fresh ones. There were, of course, economic reasons for this. But, in addition, market research clearly indicated that customers preferred the artificially coloured and flavour-boosted products to the natural ones.
3 Tocqueville, *Democracy in America*, Mentor, 1961 edn, p. 164. A century later, Salvador de Madariaga wrote in an essay entitled *Americans Are Boys* that to Americans 'principles and theories . . . are dangerous things. God knows where they might lead.' And a few pages later: 'They love "research" and recoil instinctively from speculative thought because research is the most material form of intellectual exercise.' Quoted in H. S. Commager (ed.), *America In Perspective*, Mentor, 1964, pp. 256, 269.
4 Roderic Gorney, *The Human Agenda*, Bantam, 1973, pp. 524-5, Simon and Schuster edn, pp. 460-1. It is to Gorney that I am

indebted for the term 'technique infatuation' (see *The Human Agenda*, Chap. 21).

5 For a powerful and disturbing treatment of the theme of killing as a technique see Philip E. Slater, *The Pursuit of Loneliness*, Beacon Press, 1970, Chap. 2.

6 A casual glance around the shelves of a local bookshop in the USA in June 1973 revealed, *inter alia: The Sex Book: A Modern Pictorial Encyclopedia, The Incompatability of Men and Women and How to Overcome It, Variations in Sexual Behavior, Sex Without Fear, Sex Without Guilt, The Marriage Art, How to Make Love, The Mistress Book, The Troubled Bed: How to Overcome Sexual Failure in Marriage, 101 More Intimate Sexual Problems Answered, Everything You Always Wanted to Know About Sex But Were Afraid to Ask, The Medical Guide to Sex and Marriage, Any Woman Can!, The Art of Erotic Massage, Sexual Marathon, Encyclopedia of Modern Sex and Love Techniques, The Love Game, Understanding Human Sexual Inadequacy, New Approaches to Sex in Marriage* and *The Joy of Sex: A Gourmet Guide to Love-Making*. When Roussy de Sales wrote his famous essay *Love in America* back in the 1930s (reproduced in H. S. Commager (ed.), *America in Perspective*, pp. 280-90), he too was struck by a tendency to emphasize sex technique rather than the quality of love. But the books that caught his attention had such relatively subdued titles as *Love and Happiness, So You're Going to Get Married*, and *Getting Along Together*.

This concern with means rather than ends reached some absurd lengths. Writing about the manufacture of the house-hold cleanser Vim, Polly Toynbee said that it required seven men to make it and a hundred to package it. 'The packaging', she quoted an administrative manager as saying, 'is, after all, more important in an industry as competitive as ours.' (Polly Toynbee, *A Working Life*, Hodder & Stoughton, 1971, p. 101.) And even in the rarefied air of academe, Austin Ranney claimed that 'at least since 1945 most American political scientists have focused their professional attention mainly on the *processes* by which public policies are made and have shown relatively little concern with their contents.' (Austin Ranney [ed.], *Political Science and Public Policy*, 1968, Introduction.) In philosophy, similarly, there was a noticeable switch towards the analysis of language and meaning and a corresponding tendency to avoid, for instance, the fundamental questions of ethics.

7 Marshall McLuhan, the entire corpus of whose writing was devoted to the proposition that 'the medium is the message', that the 'content' of a message had less impact than the form or technique or medium by which it was transmitted, had some withering

(but not always entirely fair or logical) things to say about this attitude. He quoted the founder of RCA, David Sarnoff, as saying 'The products of modern science are not in themselves good or bad; it is the way they are used that determines their value.' That, says McLuhan,

> is the voice of the current somnambulism. Suppose we were to say, 'Apple pie is in itself neither good nor bad; it is the way it is used that determines its value.' Or, 'The smallpox virus is in itself neither good nor bad; it is the way it is used that determines its value.' Again, 'Firearms are in themselves neither good nor bad; it is the way they are used that determines their value.' That is, if the slugs reach the right people firearms are good. If the TV tube fires the right ammunition at the right people it is good.

(Marshall McLuhan, *Understanding Media*, Sphere edn, 1967, p. 19.)
8   The story of the Xerox Corporation was astonishing. In a cover story (8 Nov. 1965), *Newsweek* reported a rise of annual sales from $33 million in the late 1950s to $385 million by the mid-sixties. Nor was this boom confined to the USA. The annual turnover of the British-based Rank Xerox grew from £2.5 million in 1962 to £61.8 million in 1967 and to £207.1 million by 1971. In the year ending October 1974, Rank Xerox had a turnover of an incredible £482.3 million.
9   See Chap. 4, n. 33, p. 293.
10   See Daniel J. Boorstin, *The Decline of Radicalism: Reflections on America Today*, Vintage, 1970, p. 10.
11   Anthony Sampson, *Anatomy of Britain Today*, Hodder & Stoughton, 1965, p. 672.
12   This pseudo-personalization could turn up in the USA in the most unexpected places. Toilet seats at hotels and motels were 'Sanitized for your protection' (which often meant little more than that a wrapper printed with those words had been placed over the seat) while you could stand dripping after a shower on 'Your Personal Bathmat'. For years, millions of disposable milk cartons had the words 'Your Personal Milk Container' on their spouts.

All this could at times be a little threatening. One perfume was advertised as being 'as individual as you are' — no doubt a potent appeal in a society often concerned about conformism; then there was the charity appeal that warned 'If you don't do it, it won't get done.'

If you, the consumer, were treated as though you were personally known to the big companies whose products you received, they often pretended that this relationship went two ways. Safeway stores, for instance, as part of their consumer campaign in the early 1970s, encouraged customers to send in any questions or complaints that they might have had. On the address side of their business reply cards was written POSTAGE WILL BE PAID BY MR ROBERT L. JAYNES, Vice President, Division Manager— and then the Safeway address. Did they really think that their customers would imagine Mr Jaynes paying for them to write to him personally about their problems? Maybe so.

Maybe audiences of news programmes really felt that if Frank Phillips or Gerald Priestland or Walter Cronkite were telling them about the world it would, somehow, be a more manageable place. At any rate, this mentality is consistent with the fact that radio and television programmes of all sorts were increasingly likely to be introduced or presented or 'hosted' by familiar personalities, whether or not they happened to know anything very much about the particular subject-matter of this or that particular programme.

Here is one final example of pseudo-personalization—appropriately from the commercial world. If you were in New York and were suffering from insomnia, you could at one time phone a special number and a sympathetic woman would say:

Hallo, there; this is your Lullaby Lady. I'm so sorry you can't sleep. Let me suggest three of my best sleep coaxers. First, a tranquillizing bath at exactly 98 degrees warmth; relax in it for twenty minutes then pat yourself dry gently. Or two, try a lulling sound that is rhythmic, like the whirl of wheels or the groan of a motor, or the muffled ticking of a clock. Or three, try the tranquillizing massage which can be easily learned and applied by husband or wife to each other. I'll be very glad to explain each of these sleep coaxers and many other ideas. Just write to me or, better still, come in and see me: Your Lullaby Lady . . .

and then follows the inevitable commercial for a 'Sleep Center' complete with address—and a final 'Sweet Dreams'.

13   Gordon Davidson, Artistic Director of the Mark Taper Forum, Los Angeles, interviewed on KCET-TV, Los Angeles, 5 Jan. 1973.
14   Peter Brook, *The Empty Space*, Pelican edn, 1972, p. 83.
15   Even the generally sedate London *Times* put advertisements in programmes on sale at concerts of classical music proclaiming that William Mann, their music critic, was among other things, 'Beatles prophet' and 'dance band founder'.
16   George Melly, *Revolt Into Style*, Penguin edn, 1972, p. 10.
17   Charles Hampden-Turner, *Radical Man*, Schenkman, 1970, p. 28.
18   *Life* Magazine, 10 May 1969.
19   The 'permissiveness' or otherwise of child-raising techniques is

notoriously hard to assess and of course varies from one social segment or individual parent to another. There is some consensus, however, that in both the USA and Britain, middle-class parents in the post-war decades seem to have been more permissive with their children and more inclined to think of the family as a sort of participatory democracy than were working-class parents, and that this permissive tendency was more pronounced in the USA (perhaps on account of a proportionately larger middle class) than in the UK. (For a British view of children and child-rearing, see p. 93).

However, certain qualifications must be added. In the first place it has been suggested by some observers that, in the words of Thomas C. Cochran (*Social Change in Industrial Society*, Allen & Unwin, 1972, p. 37), the 'maximum of permissiveness in both home and school was probably reached between 1925 and 1930', a trend arrested by depression and war. And, back in the nineteenth century, John Muirhead, visiting America from Victorian England, was struck by the fact that 'the theory of the equality of man is rampant in the nursery.' (Quoted in S. M. Lipset, *The First New Nation*, Anchor, 1967, p. 137.) Hence my use of the phrase 'a return to' more permissive child-rearing attitudes. Second, that American middle class which was to be in the forefront of the permissiveness of the Spock era may have been *more* authoritarian in its attitudes than the working class during the 1930s and 1940s and even later. W. Lloyd Warner, in a book first published in 1953 and reissued nine years later (*American Life, Dream and Reality*, University of Chicago Press, 1960 edn, p. 124) was still able to assert categorically that 'the lower-lower class . . . is the most permissive with its children.' Third, one should add to the variable of class that of race, particularly in American society. It has often been remarked that black parents—particularly black mothers—tend to be physically closer to their children, to wean them and bowel-train them later, and to put fewer restrictions on them generally than middle-class white parents. Black children, similarly, would tend to be less inhibited than white middle-class children about the expression of their sexuality and their aggressiveness and more anxious for immediate gratification of their desires. The same children could, however, also be beaten, ordered about, and punished in a way that few middle-class white parents would tolerate.

20 David Riesman, *The Lonely Crowd*, Yale University Press, 1950.
21 'Everybody's Doing It' said the advertisements in Britain for Brooke Bond Instant Coffee in the 1970s, an echo of the 'Two Million Housewives Can't Be Wrong' style of detergent advertisement a generation earlier. Player's advertised one of their brands

of cigarette with the slogan: 'People like you are changing to Number 6.' The appeal in these instances was a direct encouragement to people to subordinate their personal tastes to those of others around them. This kind of directed cultural sociability did not worry the British overmuch; perhaps they were confident of their ability to withstand it. But it recurred again and again in American literature as a theme to be feared, and was a favourite target with critical foreign observers. Americans, wrote Salvador de Madariaga in his essay 'Americans are Boys', seek out one another's company for everything. 'Play and prayer, feast and fast, lesson and leisure—all is arranged in common. Even the most individualistic enterprises . . . America is the land of "petting parties".' (Quoted in H. S. Commager (ed.), *America in Perspective*, p. 268).

The most serious concern, however, was not about conformism of behaviour but conformism of thought. In 1952, at the height of the McCarthy era, Justice William O. Douglas wrote that the greatest danger of the period

> is not inflation, nor the national debt, nor atomic warfare. The great, the critical danger is that we will so limit or narrow the range of permissible discussion and . . . thought that we will become victims of the orthodox school . . . The times demand a renaissance in freedom of thought and freedom of expression, a renaissance that will end the orthodoxy that threatens to devitalize us.

(Article in the *New York Times* Magazine Section, 13 Jan. 1952).

A few years later, Arthur M. Schlesinger Jr considered society 'threatened by homogenization' and made a plea for 'the grouch and the grumbler, the sourpuss and the curmudgeon, the non-constructive critic, the voice of dissent and the voice of protest.' (*The Politics of Hope*, Eyre & Spottiswoode, 1964, p. 236.) The essay in which these words appear was first published in 1956.

22 David Riesman, op. cit., p. 373. The fears and attractions of being alone and/or lonely were frequent features of the popular culture of the 1950s and 1960s. The Beatles' lyrics, for instance, were full of lonely characters like Eleanor Rigby or the girl who's 'leaving home after living alone for so many years'—and one of their most famous discs was entitled *Sergeant Pepper's Lonely Hearts Club Band*.

23 Daniel J. Boorstin, *The Decline of Radicalism*, Vintage, 1970 Chaps. I, II.

24 See *Newsweek*, 23 Sept. 1968, with its cover story on 'Bringing Up Baby' subtitled, 'Is Dr Spock to Blame?' For Spock's personal disavowal of any deleterious influence, see, *inter alia*, his article

'Don't Blame Me' in *Look* Magazine, 26 Jan. 1971. A couple of years later, Spock himself was having second thoughts. In January 1974, in the American magazine *Redbook*, he acknowledged that many parents had problems with their children because they were afraid of being firm with them—afraid that, if they *were* firm with them, they might alienate the child and lose its love. Spock traces this problem back to the influence that he and other writers had on American parents. 'Of course,' he wrote, 'we did it with the best of intentions, by giving talks and writing articles on child-rearing with the idea that these would be helpful. We didn't realize, until it was too late, how our know-it-all attitude was undermining the self-assurance of parents.' See the report 'Dr Spock Tells All Parents: I Was Wrong' in *The Times*, 23 Jan. 1974 (and, the following day, Philip Howard's article 'How We Are Getting Over the Shock from Dr Spock').

25 The titles of two best-selling books: William H. Whyte, *The Organization Man*, Simon & Schuster, 1956, and William J. Lederer, *A Nation of Sheep*, Norton, 1961.

26 Opinion polls on people's hopes and fears showed that, in the USA at least, there was less concern by the later 1960s and early 1970s than there used to be about one's personal material prospects, but a great deal more about matters of a social and communal nature: inflation, drugs, pollution, crime, and political stability. See Albert H. Cantril and Charles W. Roll Jr, *Hopes and Fears of the American People*, Potomac Associates Inc., 1971, p. 52. See also, Chap. 1, n. 3, p. 277.

27 The 1970 American census showed that one person in five travelled across a county line each day *en route* to work; about the same proportion of the population moved house every year. The rate of domestic mobility should not, however, be exaggerated. Many people moved from one home to another within the same neighbourhood, and there was a rise during our period in the proportion of dwellings in owner occupation (in England and Wales from 26 per cent in 1947 to just over 51 per cent in 1969; see *Strategic Plan for the South East*, HMSO, 1971, vol. 2 para. 1-51). A sort of compromise between the rival attractions of domestic stability and mobility found its expression in the burgeoning (particularly in the USA) of 'mobile homes'. The Bank of America, accompanying its advertising with all the traditional appeal of 'happy-coupleness' and a love-nest close to nature and the sunsets, even offered loans for your 'Home Sweet (Mobile) Home'. For the most obvious types of mobility, the enormous growth of public and private transportation, see above, p. 168.

Even if people did not actually move home, they were *at* home less and less. According to the US Bureau of the Census, there was a 12 per cent decline in households with one person or more at home between 8.00 am and 3.00 pm between 1960 and 1970 (AP report in *Los Angeles Times*, 19 Feb. 1973).

28 For these reasons, the idea of 'action' gained currency. Ovaltine was the 'modern action drink' while Wella was the hairdressing 'for Men where the Action is'. The BBC's sedate Radio Three introduced a record programme in which its guest—often an academic or writer—was billed as this week's 'Man of Action'.

29 Novelty of experience was a selling point in the British advertisements of two organizations as different from each other as the Post Office ('Be A Postman. No Two Days Are The Same'), and the computer dating company, Dateline ('Are You Sitting Next To The New Man In Your Life?').

30 In Britain, the most successful television news programme for some years was probably ITN's *News At Ten*, a programme whose presentation formula was clearly modelled in a number of ways on the Huntley-Brinkley show on NBC.

31 Nothing fulfilled the exigencies of the TV screen more efficiently than the television commercial. One reason for their short, sharp, quick-fire style was the rapidly mounting cost of air-time; sixty seconds on American network TV by the late 1960s could cost something in the region of $50-60 thousand, about a thousand dollars a second. But even without this financial pressure, the advertisers would surely not have remained behind the general tendency among programme makers to assume that the attention span of listeners and viewers was constantly getting shorter. Indeed commercials usually tended to be ahead of new programme styles, not behind them.

Another respect in which the transitoriness of the television image played its part in modifying other aspects of the culture was in the rise in the popularity of 'telegenic' (i.e. 'action') sports such as football and basketball, and the relative decline in popularity of baseball in the USA and, above all, cricket in Britain—games in which the field was large, the ball small, and opportunities for time-wasting and standing still abundant.

32 The high divorce rate in Britain and the USA in the post-war years is well known. In the USA in the mid-sixties, something like one marriage in four ended in divorce and in some parts of the country the rate was more like one in two. The language of relationships—his 'chick' or 'bird', her 'guy' or 'feller'—was extraordinarily imprecise, and this probably reflected the imprecision and adaptability required if one was to capture accurately the constantly shifting nature of many modern relationships. Rela-

tionships that were essentially transitory could not be adequately encapsulated by a vocabulary whose most precise expressions had evolved out of the more traditional need to describe relationships that were stable and lasting.

33 When British managers and their wives were considering moving house, an important factor—especially for the wives—was the question of making new friends. One wife is quoted by J. M. and R. E. Pahl (*Managers and Their Wives*, Allen Lane The Penguin Press, 1971, p. 54) as saying that she would not mind moving because 'I have learnt to make friends more easily and I look forward to seeing and living in different countries.' The friends and the new countries were all blended into the kaleidoscopic background of an ever-changing existence. Many of the wives in the Pahls' study were nervous about the necessity of making new friends—nervous, too, about the adjustment of personal identity that the attenuation or even the ending of old friendships and the acquisition of new ones might imply or entail (see pp. 151 *et seq.*).

34 For more on the concept of a hierarchy of wants, see Abraham H. Maslow, *Motivation and Personality*, Harper, 1954. Maslow develops a hierarchy of five needs, from the most basic (the fundamentals of physical survival), to safety, belongingness and love, esteem and status, and self actualization.

35 Americans, wrote Tocqueville, 'mistrust systems; they adhere closely to facts, and study facts with their own senses.' (*Democracy in America*, p. 163). 'DO IT!' blared the title of Jerry Rubin's book in the late 1960s; don't sit around and think about it—do it! And chronologically and spiritually half-way between Tocqueville's aristocratic submissions and Jerry Rubin's strident expressions of joyous but frustrated yippiedom was the educational philosophy of John Dewey and others that stressed that the process of learning was more enjoyable and more efficient if tightly integrated with practical experience of the topics about which one was learning.

The lengths to which this outlook could be taken are astonishing. In 1969, a group of pupils at a high school in Portland, Oregon, learned about the Depression of the 1930s by spending five days re-living the style of those austere times. They walked to school, limited their spending money to 25 cents, washed their socks and underwear by hand with old-fashioned brown soap, went without television, and ate a diet of beans, hot dogs, hamburgers, lettuce sandwiches and boiled potatoes. The girls denied themselves the luxuries of hair dryers, lipsticks and plastic curlers. (See report in the *Daily Telegraph*, 10 May 1969.) In February 1973, the students at San Francisco High School went even further. For seventy-two

hours they agreed to eat daily only a cup of spinach, half a cup of
rice and a cup of powdered milk. They were participating in a
school project called 'Starve for Survival' and learning about the
world's food shortage. (*Los Angeles Times,* 10 Feb. 1973.)

36 The influence of existential philosophy upon popular British
or American culture was at most indirect. However, as filtered
through the minds of writers such as R. D. Laing or Norman Mailer
—and through the plays of Genet or Sartre himself—the elements
of existentialism reached a wide public. Interest was also stimulated by the popularity of Simone de Beauvoir's multi-volume auto-
biography. In Mailer's Introduction to *The Presidential Papers,*
Corgi edn, 1965, he wrote that 'No President can save America from
a descent into totalitarianism without shifting the mind of the
American politician to existential styles of political thought' and
his first and third 'Papers' deal, respectively, with what he calls
'Existential Legislation' and John F. Kennedy as 'The Existential
Hero'.

37 The main factor leading to the popular absorption in America
and Britain of the ideas of Freud and his followers was the migra-
tion of intellectuals, many of them Jewish, from central Europe in
the 1930s. Among other things, this movement represented virtually a mass exodus of the entire psychiatric profession. Freud himself, and his influential daughter Anna, went to London, as did
Melanie Klein. To the USA went such figures as Herbert Marcuse,
Karen Horney, Erich Fromm and Wilhelm Reich.

38 'Norma,' asks Henry Bech of his mistress when the opportunity
of smoking marijuana presents itself for the first time, '*why* do you
want to cop out with these drugs?'

'I want to have an *experience.* I've never had a *ba*by, the only
wedding ring I've ever worn is the one you loan me when we go
to St Croix in the winter, I've never been to Pakistan. . . My life is
closing in and I hate it and I thought this way I could open it up a
little.' (John Updike, *Bech: A Book,* Fawcett, 1970, p. 99.)

39 'In America,' said Erik Erikson, 'more than anywhere in world
history, truth is associated with newness, always the new.' (Reported
in the *Los Angeles Times,* 31 May 1973.) In Britain, Christopher
Booker wrote a volume about the 1960s and entitled it *The Neo-
philiacs* (Collins, 1969).

40 In her book *And Keep Your Powder Dry,* Margaret Mead describes the vastness and fragmentation of American society and
the way in which people, meeting for the first time, would make
what she calls 'feverish grabs at a common theme'. (Published in
England as *The American Character.* Pelican edn, 1944, p. 31.)

41 The role of stronger drugs, such as mescaline and LSD, in

opening what Aldous Huxley called the doors of perception, is not easy to pin down. During the later 1960s, some younger people allowed their quest for novel experience to point towards these drugs and I can testify that the results of this sort of experimentation could be spectacular. However, the real significance of LSD and the rest probably lay more in the general influence of writers like Huxley or Timothy Leary or lesser gurus upon their readers and friends than in the direct sense-experience of a fairly small number of takers.

42 Ernest Dichter, *Motivating Human Behavior*, McGraw-Hill, 1971, pp. 113, 114, 194.

43 ibid., p. 151.

44 The growth of the market in male cosmetics was dramatic. In 1966 there were in the USA 268 men's colognes, or twice as many as in 1963. (Jules Beckman, *Advertising and Competition*, New York University Press, 1967, p. 24, footnote.)

45 Ernest Dichter, op. cit., p. 194.

46 Tom Wolfe, 'The Life and Hard Times of a Teenage London Society Girl' in *The Pump House Gang*, Bantam, 1969, p. 187.

47 Not to mention the rapidly widening availability of colour television and personal cameras that would take coloured snap shots.

48 An American TV commercial played on the same fears. A man visited the barber and was given luxuriously satisfying service. Then a confidential voice urged women viewers to 'give him the Schick hot lather machine—because he shouldn't have to go to someone else for a little warmth. . .'.

49 Daniel Yankelovich, Inc., *The Changing Values on Campus*, Washington Square Press, 1972, pp. 173-4.

50 Richard Hofstadter, *Anti-Intellectualism in American Life*, Cape, 1964.

51 See above, pp. 171-2.

Chapter 7   *Towards a culture of fusion* (page 227)

1 The antagonism was often intense and it developed its own set of cliches. 'The kids—they want it right now, the things it took us a lifetime to get' complained a typical representative of traditional American values (*Newsweek*, 6 Oct. 1969). There was much premature mourning—or, depending upon the point of view, celebration—over the alleged passing of traditional values; however, time will probably show that some traditional values, albeit in slightly altered forms, survived the buffeting of the 1960s with

surprising fortitude. It will not, however, be possible to make a definitive judgement on this for many decades to come.

2 Between 1969 and 1970, the difference between my graduate students and my undergraduate students was very large. The undergraduates said they were tired of the whole thing. The graduate students were proud of what they had done, but they were influenced by those who were tired: nothing is more catching than weariness and nothing is more corrupting.

Thus, in the last years, most students have gone back to a calm, pleasant, well-mannered acceptance of life in America as it is. . . .

(Lillian Hellman, Commencement Address at Barnard College, 14 May 1975 [reprinted in *New York Times*, 4 June].)

3 Jeremy Seabrook, *City Close-Up*, Allen Lane The Penguin Press, 1971, p. 162.

4 It was reported that, during the filming of *All The President's Men*, Bob Woodward had some difficulty getting an appointment to see President Ford; Robert Redford, getting to know the White House vicinity for his film role as Bob Woodward, was seen by Susan Ford and ushered immediately to the presidential presence for a long chat.

5 Quoted by Marshall McLuhan on *24 Hours*, BBC-TV, 19 Aug. 1971.

6 See Tom Wolfe and E. W. Johnson (eds), *The New Journalism*, Pan, 1975; in particular Wolfe's excellent introductory essay.

7 Daniel J. Boorstin, *The Image*, Pelican edn, 1963, p. 242.

8 That this was nothing like as easy as some people feared was well known to the advertisers themselves. The most famous instance of a product being extensively advertised but failing to sell was the Edsel motor car, launched amidst a huge flurry of carefully planned publicity by Ford in 1958. Despite the $250 million that Ford invested in the Edsel, people just did not buy it.

9 It has often been noted that much of the finest American work in the arts has been characterized by a freshness, a primitivism, an almost childlike innocence. 'The great works of American fiction', wrote Leslie Fiedler (*Love and Death in the American Novel*, Paladin, 1970, p. 24), 'are notoriously at home in the children's section of the library, their level of sentimentality precisely that of a pre-adolescent.'

10 'Library Sets Up Dial-A-Story for Tots—Adults Jam Lines.' This was the headline (*Los Angeles Times*, 11 Apr. 1973) to a story about the surprising response to an imaginative project by the San Francisco Public Library.

11 For the professionalization of sports in Britain, see also pp. 110-111.

12 John G. Cawelti compared the values and ideas of life in children's books in America in the mid-nineteenth century and the mid-twentieth century. He found that, while the Rollo series by Jacob Abbott, Goodrich's Peter Parley books or the McGuffey readers all emphasized hard moral discipline or self-improvement, contemporary school texts such as the Dick and Jane series were more likely to stress such things as the value of play and of sharing rather than achieving. John G. Cawelti, *Apostles of the Self-Made Man*, University of Chicago Press, 1965, p. 208.

13 Quoted in William Braden, *The Age of Aquarius*, Eyre & Spottiswoode, 1971, p. 167.

14 'Barbie in blue jeans way outsells Barbie in a wedding gown.' —Spencer Boise, Vice President for Corporate Affairs, Mattel Corporation (Quoted in *Los Angeles Times*, 10 Dec. 1972). By the middle seventies, women had begun to be heard with such success that it was possible for no less an institution than the BBC to advertise, in the pages of *The Listener*, for a 'HANDYMAN (male or female)'.

15 For an early description and analysis of 'Uni-sex', see *Newsweek*, 14 Feb. 1966. The article is good on quotable quotes ('Girls are looking like boys who look like girls') and gives an amusing run-down of the various manifestations of 'Uni-sex'—southern Californian nymphettes in heavy boots, men with beige shirts embroidered with turquoise flowers, and the success of 'His-Her' cologne. But when it comes to explanation, *Newsweek* is rather poor and relies on the opinions of 'most psychologists' (e.g., that the matriarchal, overly protective mother has now been replaced by a more competitive 'Momma A Go-Go').

Chapter 8 *The Americanization of British Culture?* (page 257)

1 H. A. L. Fisher, *A History of Europe*, Edward Arnold, 1949, p. v.

2 'I must say it's pretty dreary living in the American age,' complains Jimmy Porter in *Look Back in Anger*, '—unless you're an American of course. Perhaps all our children will be Americans. That's a thought isn't it?'

3 The influence of Britain upon the culture of modern America was probably strongest in the form of the youth culture, Carnaby Street and the Beatles and the rest, in the 1960s. However, among many older and more traditionally-minded Americans there was a touching admiration for almost anything spoken with an English accent (at least an upper-class English accent), while the acquisition of the *Queen Mary* and London Bridge — not to mention

the stone-by-stone transportation of a Wren church from London to Fulton, Missouri—suggests a craving after some of the more sizable monuments to the culture of the British elite.

4 Zbigniew Brzezinski, *The Technetronic Age* (article condensed from *Encounter*, in *Dialogue*, USIA, vol. 2, no. 4, 1969).

5 Kenneth Keniston, *The Uncommitted*, Dell, 1969, p. 211.

6 One of the most obvious exports to embody American social attitudes and values was the movie.

In the fifties American films occupied 70 per cent of the available projection time in the United Kingdom; 85 per cent in the Republic of Ireland; 65 per cent in Italy; 60 per cent in Mexico.

(Michael Wood, *America in the Movies*, Secker & Warburg, 1975, p. 193.)

7 The term is Daniel Bell's. See *The Coming of Post-Industrial Society*, Heinemann, 1974, particularly the Introduction in which Bell discusses the genesis of the idea and the term and refers to the work of others in fields adjacent to his own.

8 The British imitation of the American accent was widespread and often scarcely recognized. The first 'a' in 'transport' and 'transatlantic' was generally given a flat American sound in Britain by the 1970s, while 'statutory' and 'secretary' were increasingly given four syllables instead of three. The speakers on many radio and television commercials and pop record shows would affect a deep American 'r', while 'legislature' showed signs of becoming 'legislay-tcher' and forgetful people started to suffer from 'amneezher'.

9 By 24 November 1974, the British quality weekly the *Sunday Times* was able to have as its principal headline: 'Mrs Thatcher to run against Heath' (though the story told in its first sentence of Mrs Thatcher's decision to 'stand' in the election for the Conservative leadership).

Acknowledgements

I would like to thank the following for kind permission to reprint substantial quotations from copyright sources: Oxford University Press: quotation from Stanley Baldwin printed in Rupert Wilkinson, *The Prefects* (p. 87); Collins Publishers: quotation from Arthur Bryant, *The Years of Endurance* (p. 100); Longman Group Ltd: quotations from Neville Cardus, *Cricket* (pp. 102-3); Williams & Glyn's Bank: quotation from Neville Cardus, *Days in the Sun* (Hart-Davis, 1948) (p. 103); Hodder & Stoughton Ltd: quotation from *Peter Pan* (J. M. Barrie) retold by May Byron (p. 104); Blond & Briggs Ltd: quotation from Simon Raven, *The English Gentleman* (p. 112); Anthony Sheil Associates Ltd: quotation from Theodore H. White, *The Making of the President 1968* (Cape 1969) (pp. 151, 155); *Newsweek*: quotation from Daniel J. Boorstin in issue of 6 July 1970 (p. 159); Simon & Schuster Inc.: quotation from Roderic Gorney, *The Human Agenda* (p. 187); McGraw-Hill Book Co.: quotations from Ernest Dichter, *Motivating Human Behavior* (pp. 214, 219); *New Society*: quotation from letter published in issue of 8 November 1973 (p. 275); The Essex Music Group and Harmony Music Ltd: quotation from Tom Paxton, 'What Did You Learn In School Today?' (p. 278); Mr Woodrow Wyatt: quotation from broadcast discussion with Bertrand Russell (p. 283); The Past and Present Society and E. P. Thompson: quotation from E. P. Thompson, 'Time, Work-Discipline and Industrial Capitalism' (p. 287); Penguin Books Ltd: quotation from Dorothy Whitelock, *The Beginnings of English Society* (p. 289); Alfred A. Knopf Inc.: quotations from H. L. Mencken, ed., *Americana 1926* (p. 295).

In addition, I would like to thank a number of people who were of help to me while this book was in the process of preparation. In particular, the following read some or all of the manuscript in its early stages and made detailed and positive criticisms: Peter Burke, Thomas F. Carney,

Marcus Cunliffe, Diane Franklin, Walter Wells; they will recognize the extent to which their helpful suggestions have, where adopted, improved the book, and they bear no responsibility for its shortcomings. In addition, thanks are due to Carol Gigg who typed the manuscript. And to Janet, of whose many contributions the typing of the Notes was merely the most concrete.

London   DS
Bicentennial Day 4 July 1976

Index of Authors and Sources

NB This is a list of the principal authors, books and journals I have mentioned by name in the text or the notes. It is in no way a comprehensive bibliography.

General Index

NB   Some words and concepts—those, for instance, related to 'America', 'values', 'post-war', 'culture', 'new' etc.—help to form the central argument of this book and appear throughout. I have not included these in the index (except where definitions or special usages or derivations occur).